TAKING AFRICA FOR JESUS

TAKING AFRICA FOR JESUS

By
Joshua Schwisow
and Kevin Swanson

Generations
PASSING ON THE FAITH

Copyright © 2023 by Generations

All rights reserved.
Printed in the United States of America
2nd Edition, 1st Printing, 2023

ISBN: 978-1-7332304-5-2

Scripture taken from the New King James Version®. Copyright © 1982 by Thomas Nelson. Used by permission. All rights reserved.

Cover Design: Justin Turley
Interior Layout Design: Sarah Lee Bryant

Published by:
Generations
19039 Plaza Drive Ste 210
Parker, Colorado 80134
www.generations.org

For more information on this and
other titles from Generations,
visit www.generations.org or call 888-389-9080.

Contents

1. Introduction to Africa ⋯⋯⋯⋯⋯⋯⋯⋯⋯⋯⋯⋯⋯ 9
2. Egypt (Part 1) ⋯⋯⋯⋯⋯⋯⋯⋯⋯⋯⋯⋯⋯⋯⋯⋯ 21
3. Egypt (Part 2) ⋯⋯⋯⋯⋯⋯⋯⋯⋯⋯⋯⋯⋯⋯⋯⋯ 31
4. Egypt (Part 3) ⋯⋯⋯⋯⋯⋯⋯⋯⋯⋯⋯⋯⋯⋯⋯⋯ 39
5. Christianity Spreads to Africa ⋯⋯⋯⋯⋯⋯⋯⋯⋯ 49
6. Church Life in North Africa ⋯⋯⋯⋯⋯⋯⋯⋯⋯⋯ 59
7. The Martyrdom of Perpetua and Felicity ⋯⋯⋯⋯ 69
8. Cyprian of Carthage ⋯⋯⋯⋯⋯⋯⋯⋯⋯⋯⋯⋯⋯⋯ 77
9. Athanasius of Alexandria ⋯⋯⋯⋯⋯⋯⋯⋯⋯⋯⋯ 85
10. Augustine of Hippo ⋯⋯⋯⋯⋯⋯⋯⋯⋯⋯⋯⋯⋯⋯ 97
11. The Rise of Islam ⋯⋯⋯⋯⋯⋯⋯⋯⋯⋯⋯⋯⋯⋯ 109
12. Raymond Lull: Missionary to the Muslims ⋯⋯⋯ 119
13. The African Slave Trade ⋯⋯⋯⋯⋯⋯⋯⋯⋯⋯⋯ 131
14. Exploration and Colonization of Africa ⋯⋯⋯⋯ 141
15. The Moravians in South Africa ⋯⋯⋯⋯⋯⋯⋯⋯ 151
16. Robert Moffat: Missionary to South Africa ⋯⋯⋯ 161
17. The Gospel in Namibia ⋯⋯⋯⋯⋯⋯⋯⋯⋯⋯⋯⋯ 173
18. David Livingstone ⋯⋯⋯⋯⋯⋯⋯⋯⋯⋯⋯⋯⋯⋯ 181
19. Samuel Adjai Crowther: A Slave Boy Rescued ⋯⋯ 193
20. Alexander Mackay: White Man of Work ⋯⋯⋯⋯ 203
21. Mary Slessor: The Lord's Servant in Calabar ⋯⋯ 215
22. Samuel Zwemer: Missionary to Arabia and Egypt ⋯ 227
23. C.T. Studd: Missionary to the Congo ⋯⋯⋯⋯⋯ 237
24. Recent Stories from Africa ⋯⋯⋯⋯⋯⋯⋯⋯⋯⋯ 247

LIST OF IMAGES ⋯⋯⋯⋯⋯⋯⋯⋯⋯⋯⋯⋯⋯⋯⋯⋯ 260

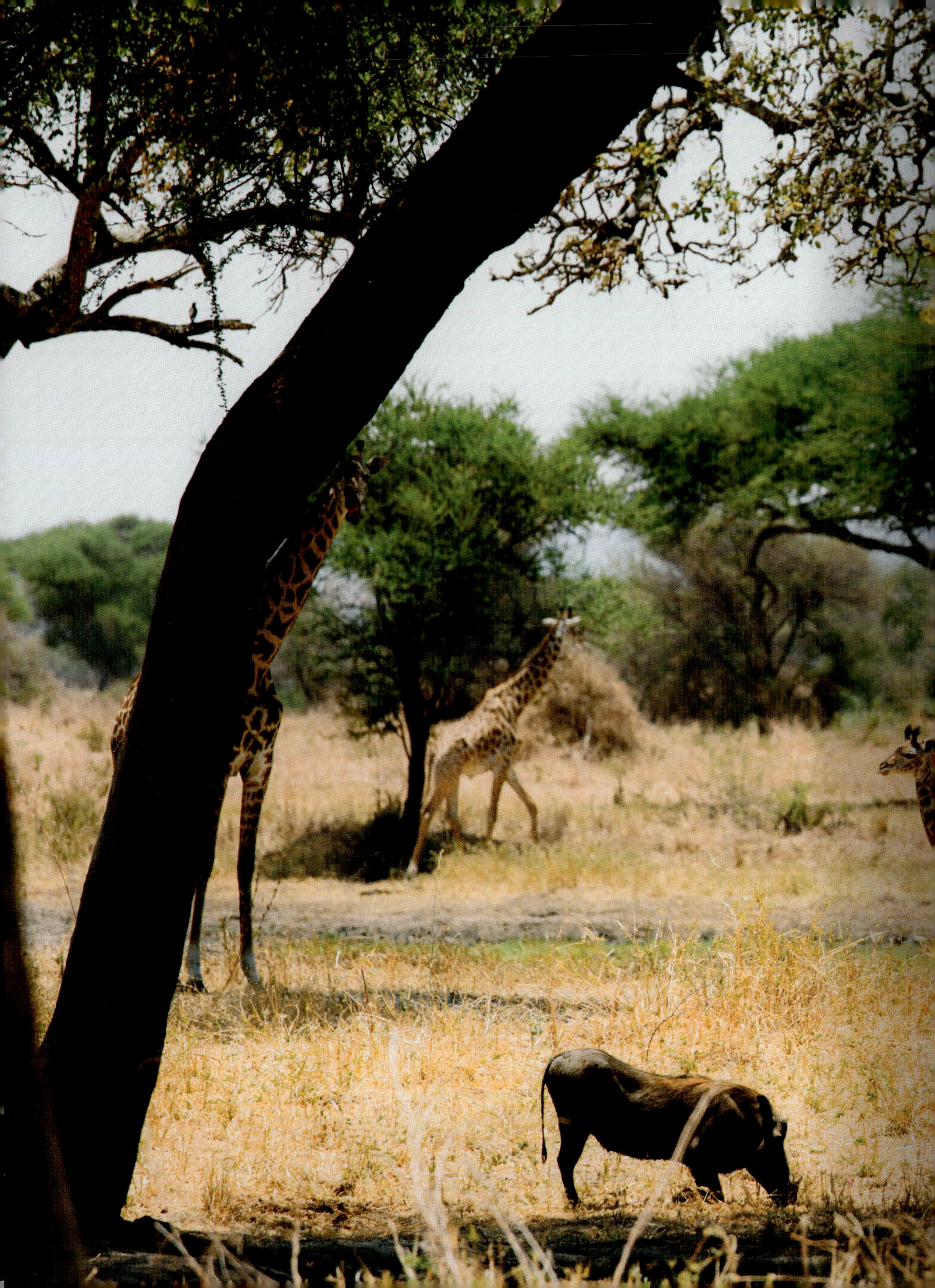

TAKING AFRICA FOR JESUS
Map Index

Chapters 7, 8, 12

Chapter 10

Chapters 2, 3, 4, 5, 9, 22

Chapter 11

Chapters 19, 21

Chapter 23

Chapter 20

Chapter 18

Chapter 16

Chapter 17

Chapters 14, 15

MT. KILIMANJARO

Introduction to Africa

Oh, let the nations be glad and sing for joy! For You shall judge the people righteously, And govern the nations on earth (Psalm 67:4)

In this book, you will learn the history of one of the world's largest continents. This is the landmass we call Africa. This enormous continent is over 11 million square miles. It is the second largest continent in the world. Today, there are over 50 distinct countries in Africa. Each has its own languages, government, and people groups.

Africa has been the theater of many of God's greatest works in history. The gospel of Jesus Christ took root here after Jesus' ascension. Today, Christianity is expanding at a rapid rate throughout the continent. In Africa, Jesus is bringing all His enemies under His footstool (1 Cor. 15:25).

Yet Africa is also a continent filled with many sad stories. The fall into sin brought terrible things into the world. Like other peoples, Africans have suffered in many ways throughout history. These sufferings include deadly plagues, natural disasters, and enslavement. Africa has also been conquered by foreign powers. But God has purpose even in the sad stories of Africa's history. This history is still a part of His ultimate plan for the world.

THE FOUR REGIONS OF AFRICA

And He has made from one blood every nation of men to dwell on all the face of the earth, and has determined their preappointed times and the boundaries of their dwellings, so that they should seek the Lord, in the hope that they might grope for Him and find Him, though He is not far from each one of us. (Acts 17:26-27)

Before you learn Africa's history, let's look at Africa itself. Let's look at the geography,

REGIONS OF AFRICA

North Africa	Mountains, deserts
West Africa	Grasslands
East Africa	Mountains, plateaus
Central and South Africa	Grasslands, rainforests, swamps, deserts

MAP OF AFRICA

climate, and animals of this continent. We will begin by studying Africa's geography.

Africa is divided into four major regions. These four regions are North Africa, West Africa, East Africa, and Central and Southern Africa. Each of these regions have different geographical features and different climates.

North Africa contains many rocky mountains. In the southern portion of North Africa, the enormous Sahara Desert stretches across the continent. The Sahara is the world's largest desert.

West Africa is the most populated re-

MOUNTAINS IN AFRICA

Mount Kilimanjaro	19,341 feet (5,895 meters)	Tanzania
Mount Kenya	17,058 feet (5,199 meters)	Kenya
Mount Stanley	16,762 feet (5,109 meters)	Uganda and the Congo

gion of Africa. It contains much grassland. This makes West Africa a good place for farming.

East Africa contains many mountains. It also contains what are known as plateaus. A plateau is a large raised area of level land.

Central and Southern Africa is mostly flat. This region of Africa also contains many rainforests and swamps. There are also a few deserts in Central and Southern Africa. These deserts are known as the Namib and the Kalahari deserts.

MOUNTAINS IN AFRICA

**Your righteousness is like the great mountains;
Your judgments are a great deep;
O LORD, You preserve man and beast.
(Psalm 36:6)**

Mountains can be found in all four regions of Africa. The tallest mountains are mostly found in East Africa. One of the most impressive of God's creations in Africa is Mount Kilimanjaro. This mountain is the tallest in Africa, standing at 19,341 feet (5,895 meters). It is a volcano that is currently dormant. Kilimanjaro is found in the country of Tanzania. Because of its incredible height, it is very cold at its summit. The average temperature at the top is about 19 °F (-7 °C). Snowfall occurs throughout the year at the summit.

The second tallest mountain in Africa is Mount Kenya. This beautiful mountain stands at 17,058 feet (5,199 meters). It is located in the country of Kenya.

On the western border of Uganda, you will find the third tallest mountain in Africa. Mount Stanley, also known as Mount Ngaliema, is 16,762 feet tall (5,109 meters). In all, Africa contains twelve mountains that are over 10,000 feet tall.

Praise God for these examples of His glory and power!

RIVERS IN AFRICA

**Let the rivers clap their hands;
Let the hills be joyful together before the LORD,
For He is coming to judge the earth.
With righteousness He shall judge the world, and the peoples with equity.
(Psalm 98:8-9)**

The four largest rivers in Africa are the Nile, the Congo, the Zambezi, and the Niger. These four major rivers are very important to the peoples of Africa. They provide water for growing crops. The fish in their waters provide a good source of food. God's merciful hand has provided these great rivers to the peoples of Africa.

The longest of these rivers is the Nile River. At over 4,000 miles in length (6,400 kilometers), the Nile River is the longest river in the world. It is over twice the length of the Mississippi River in the United States. The only real rival to the Nile River is the Amazon River in South America. The Amazon has a greater amount of water, but the Nile is the longest.

For millennia the Nile River has created fertile farmland along its banks. Even in desert-like regions such as Egypt, people were able to survive because of the Nile. Before the creation of man-made dams, the Nile would flood its banks regularly. Farmers would plant their crops to take advantage of these flood cycles. Now, with dams in place, the waters of the Nile are diverted to grow even more crops in desert regions.

The Congo River flows through the rain forests of the Republic of Congo and the Democratic People's Republic of the Congo. (These are two different countries with a similar name.) The Congo is the second longest river in Africa. It is about

THE NILE RIVER

RIVERS IN AFRICA

Nile River	4,000 miles (6,400 kilometers)
Congo River	2,900 miles (4,700 kilometers)
Niger River	2,600 miles (4,180 kilometers)
Zambezi River	2,200 miles (3,540 kilometers)

2,900 miles in length (4,700 kilometers). The Congo is also the world's deepest river. In some parts of the Congo River, the water is as deep as 720 feet (220 meters).

The Niger River is the third longest river in Africa. It is 2,600 miles in length (4,180 kilometers). The Niger River begins in Guinea and empties into the Atlantic Ocean in the Niger Delta.

The fourth longest river in Africa is the Zambezi River. This river travels through six African countries. It is 2,200 miles long (3,540 kilometers). However, only a small portion of this length can be traveled by boat. The Zambezi contains many waterfalls and rapids. This makes boat travel down the river very dangerous or even impossible.

One of the most astounding of God's creations in Africa is Victoria Falls. At one point in its journey, the Zambezi River plunges into a canyon. We call this part of the river Victoria Falls. It is one of the largest waterfalls in the world. The spray and mist from the falling water is so enormous that it can be seen as far as 40 miles away (65 kilometers).

VEGETATION REGIONS IN AFRICA

And God said, "See, I have given you every herb that yields seed which is on the face of all the earth, and every tree whose fruit yields seed; to you it shall be for food." (Genesis 1:29)

The different climates of Africa create varying landscapes. There are three major vegetation regions in Africa. These three are Tropical Rain Forests, Tropical Savannas, and Deserts.

Tropical rain forests are regions where rain falls all year long. There are numerous rain forests in Africa. They are mostly in West and Central Africa. The rain forests in Africa make up about 20% of the continent. This collection of water and greenery supports a lot of wildlife. Animals such as chimpanzees, hippos, and gorillas live in these regions. The forests are so dense here that people have to clear trees to construct their villages.

Tropical savannas are the most common regions in Africa. These regions have tall grass, bushes, and some trees. They do not receive as much rainfall as the rainforests. For this reason, they are sometimes drier. The tropical savannas have two seasons: dry and wet. During the dry season, farming stops. But once the wet season begins, farmers give their attention to planting crops. Common animals here include zebras, lions, elephants, and African buffalo.

Africa contains the largest amount of desert land in the world. The world's largest desert is the Sahara Desert. The Sahara Desert is about the size of the United States or China. Most of the Sahara Desert receives no rainfall at all. The southern edge of the Sahara connects to a savanna region called the "Sahel." This region is very hot and dry, but it does receive a small amount of rainfall each year (about 4 to 8 inches). The Sahara Desert is one of the hottest places in the world. The average temperature is over 100 °F (38 °C). In some cases, the temperature has reached 116 °F (47 °C). The only place in the world that has a hotter temperature on record is Death Valley, California. These are the average air temperatures. But the sand is much, much hotter. Sand in the Sahara Desert can reach 176 °F (72 °C)! If you have ever been to the beach on a hot day, you know that the sand can be so hot it will burn the bottom of your feet. Much of the sand in the Sahara would melt your shoes!

The Namib and Kalahari Deserts are quite large. But they are not nearly as big as the Sahara Desert. They are both located

AFRICAN ELEPHANTS

1. INTRODUCTION TO AFRICA 15

SAHARA DESERT

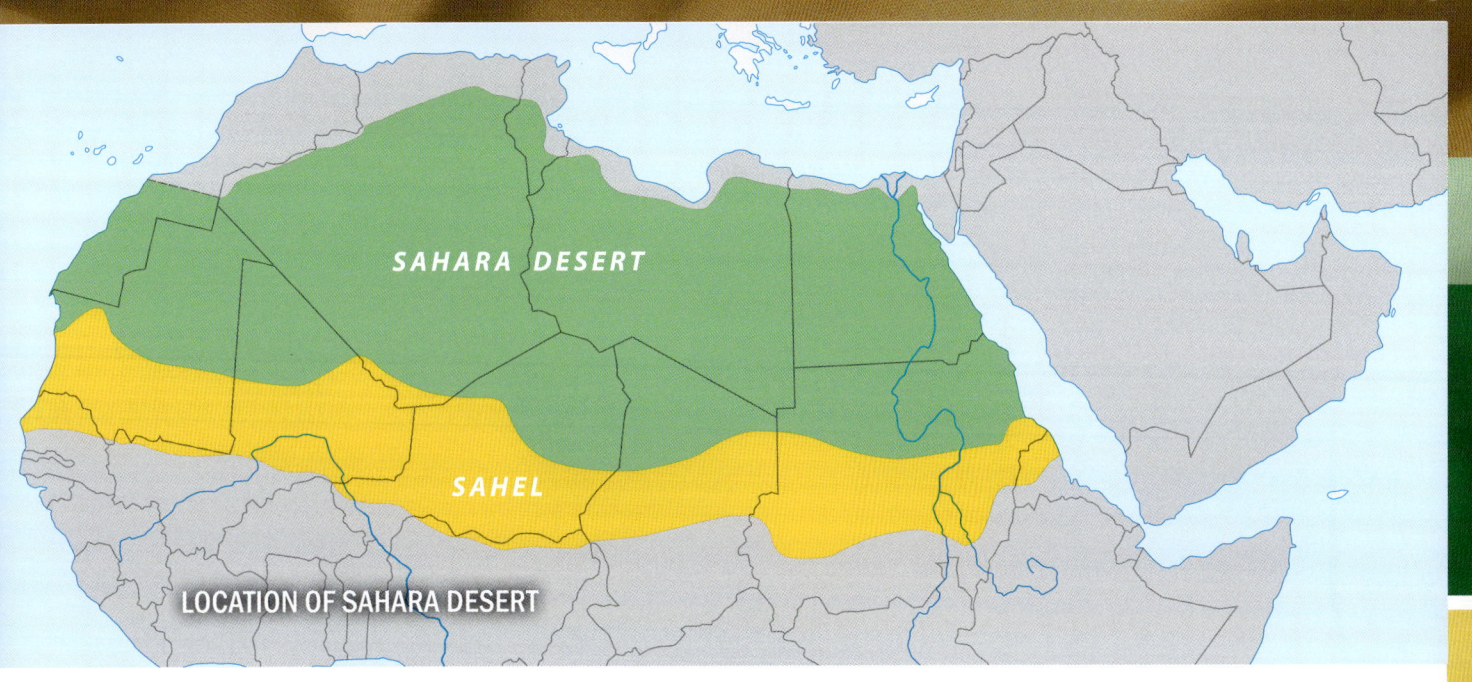

SAHEL

LOCATION OF SAHARA DESERT

in the southern portion of Africa.

THE ECONOMY OF AFRICA

Many African nations began as colonial projects. Foreign empires and nations founded and ruled these areas. For centuries these African countries were dependent on an outside power. But, in recent years, a major move towards independence has occurred in Africa. Now that African countries are independent, they have to stand on

SAHARA DESERT

MUD HUT IN SUDAN

their own. They face numerous economic challenges today. First, many of the countries still rely on foreign aid. This means that many Africans are dependent on other nations. They are not building their own economies. Billions of dollars in foreign aid has not been helpful to Africa. Instead, it has harmed many African nations.

Also, many African nations experience high levels of corruption. Rulers and officials lie and steal to gain money and power for themselves. This corruption affects people at every level of society. Imagine what would happen if you couldn't trust any of the police officers in your own town. What if you knew that a judge in the courtroom would only rule justly if you slipped him a $100 bill before the trial? This is the kind of thing many Africans experience. Clearly, the nations of Africa are still in much need of Jesus' saving work. They need His power to deliver them from the sins of envy, pride, and the love of money.

Many Africans experience higher levels of disease than nations in Europe and America. Malaria is a very common disease. Though it is not always deadly, it does take many lives. HIV/AIDS is also a common disease that kills many at a young age. When disease is common and people die at a younger age, this hampers the growth of an economy.

The majority of Africans live on small plots of lands. They farm their own food and live on anything they can grow. This means that many Africans never become wealthy. They don't develop businesses or large family economies. They are busy just trying to feed and clothe their families. Africa's national structure is also poorly-developed compared to Western nations. Its energy, roads, communication, and transportation are often not very developed. Travel is much slower and more dangerous than in other countries. For example, an American can drive from Washington DC to New York City in about 4 hours (a distance of some 220 miles). But to drive the same distance in Africa can take up to 8 hours.

Sectors of Africa are also experiencing military conflicts. The devastation of war brings much suffering with it. War displaces families from their homes. It destroys towns. It disrupts trade and production. African nations that experience high levels of conflict have struggling economies.

As Christians, we should pray for the peace of Christ to come to these nations. We should also pray that the nations would be blessed with fruitful lands and families as a result of the gospel. Healthy economies can only exist when people follow the ways of the Lord.

RELIGIONS IN AFRICA

For all the gods of the peoples are idols, But the LORD made the heavens. (Psalm 96:5)

The two largest religions in Africa are Christianity and Islam. At this time,

CHRISTIAN CHURCH IN RURAL KENYA

RELIGION IN AFRICA

Christianity	49%
Islam	42%
Tribal Religions	8%
Other/None	1%

Christians outnumber the Muslim population by about 6%. These religions are generally divided by regions. Most Muslims reside in North Africa. The majority of Christians live below the Sahara Desert. (This area is called sub-Saharan Africa). Both Christianity and Islam are growing. This is due mainly to a higher number of births than countries in the West. A large portion of Africa still follows traditional tribal religion. Those who claim "no religion" in Africa are only a tiny fraction of the population (about 1%). In certain African nations, Christians face severe persecution. Some of the most dangerous places to be a disciple of the Lord Jesus include Libya, Sudan, Egypt, Somalia, Nigeria, and Eritrea. Much of this persecution comes from radical Muslim groups.

LEMURS FROM MADAGASCAR

PYRAMID OF GIZA

Egypt (Part 1)

The earliest African records of human history come mainly from Egypt. In the next few chapters, we will examine the history of this ancient culture.

Egyptian records offer us many conflicting lists of rulers and pharaohs. Many historians do not accept biblical revelation. They want to date the history of Egypt back into 3200 BC. Yet the Egyptian records do not give us a clear timeline. It is best for us to look to the chronology of Holy Scripture. We know that we can trust this because it is God's perfect Word.

EARLY EGYPTIAN HISTORY

Around 2300 BC, the pharaohs of Egypt began building pyramids. Djoser was the first pharaoh to begin building these massive structures.

Pyramid-building continued after Djoser's reign. Pharaoh Seneferu, who ruled somewhere around 2282 BC, built his own pyramid. His Bent Pyramid looks a little lopsided. His architects must have changed the design while they were building it. The angle begins at 55° and ends at 43° towards the upper levels.

Pyramid-building developed quickly within a few short generations. When Seneferu's son Cheops took the throne of Egypt, the empire was ready to build the biggest pyramid of all. It was constructed at Giza. The builders used 2.3 million blocks weighing an average of seven tons each. At 450 feet (137 meters) high, Cheops' pyramid was one attempt to make a tower to "reach the heavens." In history, sinful people try again and again to prove that they are as great as God is.

The pyramid at Giza was the largest pyramid of all. It was also the most accurately built pyramid in Egypt's history. It was completed only seventy-five years after pyramid-building began. It probably took 40,000 men to build the Great Pyramid. When it was being built, the population of Egypt was probably somewhere around 2,000,000.

The world population following the flood may have reached about

THE BENT PYRAMID

THE SPHINX

4,000,000 by the year 2258 BC. Therefore it is possible that the Great Pyramid was built somewhere around 2258 BC. This is about 160 years after the Tower of Babel. It is possible that these pharaohs borrowed their ideas for a tower "that would reach to the heavens" from the Tower of Babel.

Noah's son Ham had a son after the Flood named Mizraim. Mizraim would have been born around 2478 BC. It is quite possible that he began to settle what would become the country of Egypt around 2450 BC. The Great Pyramid at Giza would be built about 200 years later.

The oldest piece of writing found in Egypt comes from this same era. In AD 2013, archeologists uncovered an ancient papyrus in a cave near the Red Sea. The papyrus was a logbook or diary kept by an inspector. The inspector was working on shipping huge limestone blocks down the Nile for the Great Pyramid of Giza. The logbook lists payments for food and labor. The author, Merer, wrote about Ankhhaef, who was Pharaoh Cheops' half-brother. Merer wrote that Ankhhael was "chief for all the works of the king."

We can learn several important things from this record. First, ancient man was just as intelligent as modern man. He used writing, accounting, and technology like we do. We should never doubt that Adam and Eve were able to communicate through writing. Second, the oldest known writings date from the 23rd century. We can assume that the worldwide flood occurred shortly before this time. It would have destroyed all earlier written records. That is probably why we find no written records from before this time.

Pharaoh Cheops' sons Djedefre and Khafre followed him. Khafre built the tremendous Sphinx and the Pyramid of Khafra. This was the end of the grandest pyramid-building period in history. This period all took place around Giza and probably ended around 2150 BC. This is about the same time Abram of the Bible was born (Gen. 11:26). In God's providential plan, Egypt began experiencing internal strife and discord. This turmoil would continue for the next 200 years. The Upper Kingdom and Lower Kingdom of Egypt were divided against each other. The priests and the political leaders also fought among themselves. This conflict would hinder further cultural progress.

ABRAM VISITS EGYPT — 2076 BC

During this period of brokenness, the Lord brought His chosen man Abram to Egypt. Abram's influence seemed to strike the fear of God in the heart of Pharaoh during his visit. In Genesis 12, Abram moved into Egypt for a time because of a famine in the land of Canaan. While he was there, Pharaoh Makdea tried to take Abram's wife Sarai. He prepared to add the woman to his harem. But the Lord sent "great plagues" to his house (Gen. 12:17). Pharaoh decided it would be best to send Abram away from Egypt. When he left, Abram received gifts of oxen, donkeys, camels, and servants.

Shortly afterward, Abram met another important figure in the history of the world. This figure was Melchizedek, king of Salem. This man was also a priest, and Abram gave him a tithe. Melchizedek blessed Abram with these words:

> **Blessed be Abram of God Most High,**
> **Possessor of heaven and earth,**
> **And blessed be God Most High,**
> **Who has delivered your enemies into your hand. (Genesis 14:19-20)**

In a world of war, a symbol of peace came from the King of Salem (which means peace). In a world of evil kings, Abram saw a glimmer of hope that a good King would arise. In a world of sin, we need a priest, a perfect Priest. We need a priest who will atone for the sins of the world. A prophet represents God to man by bringing God's message to man. However, man also needs a priest. He needs someone who will stand before God and represent him to God.

Who was this mysterious Melchizedek? Some believe he was an angel. Some believe that he was Shem, because Shem outlived Abraham. The Book of Hebrews speaks of Melchizedek as having no beginning, at least in this world. We do not know where Melchizedek came from or when he died, or if he died. But we do know that he was a type of the Christ who was to come.

Melchizedek was very similar to Jesus in many ways. First, both Melchizedek and Jesus are the King of Salem. Jesus Christ was declared to be the King of the Jews. He is also the King that rules from the New Jerusalem to this day. The Book of Hebrews explains:

But you have come to Mount Zion and to the city of the living God, the heavenly Jerusalem, to an innumerable company of angels, to the general assembly and church of the firstborn who are registered in heaven, to God the Judge of all, to the spirits of just men made perfect, to Jesus the Mediator of the new covenant, and to the blood of sprinkling that speaks better things than that of Abel. (Hebrews 10:22-25)

Secondly, both Melchizedek and Jesus serve in the offices of king and priest. In ancient Israel, the kingly line came from the tribe of Judah. The priestly line came from the tribe of Levi. Therefore it was impossible for anyone to be both a priest and a king.

Thirdly, it was God Himself who made

ABRAHAM MEETS MELCHIZEDEK

both Melchizedek and Jesus priests.

Fourthly, both Melchizedek and Jesus come from a second line of priests. Neither of them came from the line of Levi. Instead, they came from the mysterious line having "no beginning."

Fifthly, both Melchizedek and Jesus had a higher authority than Abram. Abram paid his tithes to Melchizedek. He did this because he submitted to the priest's authority. Levi was Abram's great-grandson. Therefore Levi's priesthood had less honor than the priestly line of Melchizedek.

For this Melchizedek, king of Salem, priest of the Most High God, who met Abraham returning from the slaughter of the kings and blessed him, to whom also Abraham gave a tenth part of all, first being translated "king of righteousness," and then also king of Salem, meaning "king of peace," without father, without mother, without genealogy, having neither beginning of days nor end of life, but made like the Son of God, remains a priest continually. Now consider how great this man was, to whom even the patriarch Abraham gave a tenth of the spoils. And indeed those who are of the sons of Levi, who receive the priesthood, have a commandment to receive tithes from the people according to the law, that is, from their brethren, though they have come from the loins of Abraham; but he whose genealogy is not derived from them received tithes from Abraham and blessed him who had the promises. Now beyond all contradiction the lesser is blessed by the better. Here mortal men receive tithes, but there he receives them, of whom it is witnessed that he lives. Even Levi, who receives tithes, paid tithes through Abraham, so to speak, for he was still in the loins of his father when Melchizedek met him. (Hebrews 7:1-10)

KING TUT'S GOLDEN MASK

WRONG-HEADED CIVILIZATION

**Why do the nations rage,
And the people plot a vain thing?
The kings of the earth set themselves,
And the rulers take counsel together,
Against the Lord and against His Anointed, saying,
"Let us break Their bonds in pieces
And cast away Their cords from us."**

**He who sits in the heavens shall laugh;
The Lord shall hold them in derision.
(Psalm 2:1-4)**

Fallen man continues to build bigger empires and kingdoms in history. He continues to live in rebellion against God. The pyramids themselves are a picture of man's vain egotism and pride. The pyramids were useless buildings. Nobody lived in them. Nobody worked in them. Nobody even stored anything useful in them. They were built on a wrong worldview. The builders foolishly thought that the pharaohs would become gods in the afterlife. Somehow they thought that all the things they buried with the corpses would help the dead in the next life.

Instead of leaving their resources to living people, they wasted them on building worthless pyramids. They buried their treasures with dead bodies. It wasn't long before thieves figured out they could rob the pyramids. Soon the Egyptians began hiding the graves of their pharaohs. When Pharaoh Tutankhamen died in 1325 BC, he was buried in a hidden grave. It would take over three thousand years before Howard Carter discovered the hidden tomb in the Valley of the Kings.

Egypt was the first empire to perfect the art of big government. Egyptian dynasties had very big governments with lots of employees. These employees were usu-

EGYPTIAN ART DEPICTING SLAVES

ally given ridiculous projects. Tasks like pyramid-building required a large number of accountants, taxmen, and census clerks. The vizier (or prime minister) was put in charge of the government. This included the treasury and the bureaucracy. Egyptians typically used grain, yeast, cattle, or beer as money.

Slavery was common in Egypt. For example, it took 800 slave rowers in 27 boats to transport large obelisks down the Nile. During his reign, Rameses III sent 113,000 slaves to work in the temples. Slaves were killed and buried with the pharaohs in their tombs.

The pharaoh was treated like a god. Twenty people were in charge of his hair, makeup, and dress. One person was assigned to carry his sandals. Another person was called "the overseer of the cosmetic box." With such luxury, the pharaohs usually became self-centered and pleasure-loving. Incest was common with these rulers. One vizier described his pharaoh like this: "What is the king of Upper and Lower Egypt? He is a god by whose dealings one lives, the father and mother of all men, alone by himself without an equal."

Egyptians studied medicine very diligently. Their doctors specialized in various medical fields such as childbirth or eye problems. A 1600 BC medical papyri lists 48 forms of surgery that Egyptian doctors used. They treated skull fractures, spinal injuries, and other serious problems. The first medical manual comes from ancient Egypt (the Kahun Papyrus, about 1825 BC). Not surprisingly, this early medical science includes ways to prevent pregnancy. Sinful people are usually quick to find ways to destroy life, even unborn life.

The Lord God warned the Israelites not to practice these sins. He declared:

> When you come into the land which the LORD your God is giving you, you shall not learn to follow the abominations of those nations. There shall not be found among you anyone who makes his son or his daughter pass through the fire, or one who practices witchcraft, or a soothsayer, or one who interprets omens, or a sorcerer, or one who conjures spells, or a medium, or a spiritist, or one who calls up the dead. For all who do these things are an abomination to the LORD, and because of these abominations the LORD your God drives them out from before you. You shall be blameless before the LORD your God. For these nations which you will dispossess listened to soothsayers and diviners; but as for you, the LORD your God has not appointed such for you. (Deuteronomy 18:9-14)

These abominable activities were common among the Egyptians. These people were especially enslaved to the devil through the use of witchcraft. They scrawled magic spells in hieroglyphics on the walls of their pharaohs' tombs. In the 16th century BC, they assembled a "Book of the Dead." It included 192 spells. This magic was supposed to help the dead control their future in the afterlife. It was also supposed to manipulate the gods.

RITUAL ILLUSTRATION FROM *THE BOOK OF DEAD*

The Egyptians believed that if the dead knew the mystical names of certain gods or demons, they would have control over them. Sinful mankind is often still attracted to these mystery religions from Egypt. However, Christians understand that Egyptian religions were perverse, deceptive, and enslaving. These beliefs were a way that the devil deceived the nations. By them he distracted people from knowing the true and living God. This was another way to "suppress the truth" of God in unrighteousness (Rom. 1:19).

Man is always eagerly searching for super-human powers, a godlike position, and secret knowledge. This is why he is interested in demonism, spiritism, occultism, and secret societies. Demonic power is especially exciting for people in rebellion against the true and living God. They are captivated by it. They honor the witchdoctors who cast spells or perform wonders.

The magicians of Egypt who battled with Moses were well aware of what was at stake. Their very position was threatened by the true and living God. The all-sovereign Lord allowed them to have a little power. Moses' serpent consumed theirs. Then they duplicated two of the plagues. But the magicians had to admit defeat in the end. The demonic powers of Egypt were useless against Almighty God, the Creator of heaven and earth.

Now the magicians so worked with their enchantments to bring forth lice, but they could not. So there were lice on man and beast. Then the magicians said to Pharaoh, "This is the finger of God." But Pharaoh's heart grew hard, and he did not heed them, just as the LORD had said. (Exodus 8:18-19)

EGYPTIAN RELIGION

Two things marked the basic worldview of the Egyptians. These two things are a picture of the way sinful man still thinks. First, they believed in evolution. Secondly, they did not believe in a God who ruled over all. Nor did they believe that God was entirely separate by nature from His creation.

Egyptian religious texts quote the god Neb-er-tcher. He declares: "I evolved the evolving of evolutions. I evolved myself under the form of the evolutions of the god Keeper, which were evolved at the beginning of all time . . . I developed myself out of the primeval matter. My name is Osiris, the germ of primeval matter."

The Egyptians believed that men and gods were made of the same nature. They thought that the gods were just a little further up the pyramid of being. Since the priests were considered to be of the same nature as the gods, they thought they could manipulate the gods. The miracles that Moses brought about came by the command of God. But the miracles that the demons performed for the Egyptians came by the command of the priests. The *Book of the Dead* was simply a collection of magic spells. Man thought he could use these spells to manipulate the gods. This, of course, is the type of god that sinful man prefers. He doesn't want to think that he is subject to an all-powerful, sovereign God, especially when he finds that he has sinned against this God. Man's pride will not let him submit to the concept of a God who is truly God and who is above all and sovereign over all.

The Book of the Dead was intended to provide a "way" in the afterlife. Just in case someone might forget what to say to the gods (or "God"), this manual was supposed to offer adequate preparation. Chapter 125 of *The Book of the Dead* reveals a self-justification and a fatal lie:

- I have not committed evil against men.
- I have not mistreated cattle.
- I have not committed sin in the place of truth.
- I have not seen evil.
- I have not killed.
- I have not caused anyone suffering.

Sadly, such vain and lying testimonies will not help anyone who stands before the great Judge of the earth on judgment day. All have sinned and come short of the glory of God. But the good news is that the gift of God is eternal life through Jesus Christ our Lord (Rom. 6:23). ∎

THE PYRAMIDS OF GIZA

Egypt (Part 2)

In this chapter, we continue our survey of Egypt's history. Part of the problem we find when trying to figure out Egyptian chronology is that sometimes multiple pharaohs ruled at the same time. Fathers and sons would rule at the same time. Some pharaohs also ruled in the northern kingdom (near modern-day Cairo) at the same time that others ruled in the south near Thebes. The timeline of Egyptian historical records is so confusing that it is hardly worth using.

Around 1990 BC, a military leader named Amenemhet tried to form Egypt into an empire. He was not a pharaoh himself, but he wanted to create a strong power state. Amenemhet went to war with the Nubians. These peoples had a flourishing culture further up the Nile River (in modern-day Ethiopia). After fighting many offensive battles, the Egyptians finally won. They took control of the Nubian land and changed its name to "Cush." These peoples served Egypt for the next 700 years.

JOSEPH SOLD INTO SLAVERY

THE HYKSOS

When empires become immoral and pleasure-loving, they become easy targets for their enemies. There are always greedy, warlike tribes who are happy to steal the riches of wealthy empires. Inner corruptions turn an empire into an easy target. These empires can be defeated by military victories and can also be plundered by a slow immigration of poorer tribes and neighboring countries into their territory.

After Amenemhet died, Egypt still enjoyed national prosperity for a while. However, the empire started to weaken when internal fighting began. Soon a tribe of nomad warriors called the Hyksos became a problem for Egypt. At first, this tribe from the northern lands of Canaan settled into a city on the Nile Delta. They had developed better bow-and-arrow technology than the Egyptians. They also used horse-drawn chariots. With these superior skills, they quickly conquered the Egyptians. The Hyksos ruled from about 1700 to 1600 BC.

JOSEPH BECOMES VIZIER OF EGYPT

BIRTH OF JOSEPH — 1911 BC

Egypt's troubles were a picture of every kingdom and tribe in the world. The world needed a solution for death, and it could not find it in the pyramids. The world needed deliverance from famine, slavery, and war. But the pharaohs could not bring this deliverance. God had another plan to deliver the world, but His plan did not rely on the pharaohs. Instead He was working through the Seed of Abraham. While Egypt was fighting for more power, a child was born to Abraham's grandson. The child's name was Joseph.

When Joseph was born, Egypt was a proud empire. It controlled Nubia to the south and both Upper and Lower Egypt as well. Joseph was Abraham's great-grandson, born to Jacob, the son of Isaac. Joseph was Jacob's favorite son, but out of hatred and jealousy his brothers sold him into slavery in Egypt. As God's providential plan played out, Joseph was made vizier (or prime minister) over the land of Egypt.

Then Pharaoh said to Joseph, "Inasmuch as God has shown you all this, there is no one as discerning and wise as you. You shall be over my house, and all my people shall be ruled according to your word; only in regard to the throne will I be greater than you." And Pharaoh said to Joseph, "See, I have set you over all the land of Egypt." Then Pharaoh took his signet ring off his hand and put it on Joseph's hand; and he clothed him in garments of fine linen and put a gold chain around his neck. And he had him ride in the second chariot which he had; and they cried out before him, "Bow the knee!" So he set him over all the land of Egypt. Pharaoh also said to Joseph, "I am Pharaoh, and without your consent no man may lift his hand or foot in all the land of Egypt." And Pharaoh called Joseph's name Zaphnath-Paaneah. And he gave him as a wife Asenath, the daughter of Poti-Pherah priest of On. So Joseph went out over all the land of Egypt. (Genesis 41:39-44)

During the 12th dynasty, Pharaoh Sesostris appointed a vizier over Egypt. The vizier's name was Mentuhotep. History says that his words were "like the declaration of the king's power." And we read from ancient records that this Mentuhotep "appears as the alter ego of the king. When he arrived, the great personages bowed down before him at the outer door of the royal palace." These words are very similar to the account we have in Genesis (Gen. 41:43). This vizier could very well have been Joseph.

Joseph was appointed to manage the food supply of Egypt. He gathered food during the seven years of good harvest. During the seven years of famine that followed, he fed the people of Egypt. Ancient records show that a severe famine occurred during the reign of the Pharaoh Senusret.

The famine that the Lord ordained in the land of Egypt also extended into Canaan where Jacob and his sons lived, so the family was forced to travel to Egypt for food. When Joseph's brothers arrived in Egypt, they did not recognize Joseph until he tested them and then revealed himself to them.

This story teaches us a clear message. Man needs a deliverer. He needs someone who will deliver him from the threat of death and death itself. God promised Adam and Eve that the Seed of the woman would crush the evil serpent. He would destroy the "bad guy" or the source of evil. But man also needed to be saved from the consequences of sin and the curse of death. In the history of Joseph and his brothers, God created an object lesson for us. The parallels between Joseph and Jesus, our true Savior, are amazing.

- They were both beloved of their fathers (Gen. 37:3a; Matt. 3:17b).
- They were both envied and hated without a cause (Gen. 37:4; Mark 15:10; John 15:25b).
- They both prophesied of a day in which they would rule (Gen. 37:7; Matt. 26:64b).
- They were both sent by the father to seek out their brothers' condition (Gen. 37:14a; Luke 20:13b).
- They were both rejected and condemned to die (Gen. 37:18b; Luke 23:21).
- They were both stripped of their clothing (Gen. 37:23b; Matt. 27:28a).
- They were both thrown into a pit, alone and forsaken (Gen. 37:24a; Matt. 12:40b).
- They were both sold for silver into the hands of Gentiles, Joseph for 20 pieces of silver, and Jesus for 30 (Gen. 37:28b; Matt. 26:15b).
- They were both raised out of the pit (Gen. 37:28a; 1 Cor. 15:4b).
- They both became slaves (Gen. 39:1-2; Luke 22:27b; Phil. 2:7b).
- They both prospered in what they did (Gen. 39:3b; Isa. 53:10b).
- They both resisted temptation (Gen. 39:7-12; Heb. 7:26; 4:15b).
- They were both falsely accused (Gen. 39:17-18; Matt. 26:60-61).
- They were both numbered with prisoners or transgressors (Gen. 39:20a; Luke 23:33).
- They were both promised deliverance after three days (Gen. 40:13; Luke 23:43b).
- They both proved to be good counselors (Gen. 41:39; Isa. 9:6b).
- They were both promoted to honor and glory and given a new name (Gen. 41:41; Phil. 2:9).
- They both had people bow to them (Gen. 41:43b; Phil. 2:10a).
- They both provided bread for those in need (Gen. 41:57a; John 6:35a).
- Their brothers did not recognize either of them (Gen. 42:8; 2 Cor. 3:14a; John 14:9a).
- Both of them were unjustly dealt with, according to God's purpose.
- In both cases, the greater good was to

bring about a great salvation (Acts 2:23; Gen. 50:19-20).
- The story ends in both cases with an announcement of peace and reconciliation (Gen. 45:3-8; John 20:9-10).

Most importantly, Joseph provides a picture of a great salvation that God is bringing about for His people. It was God who sent Joseph into Egypt. It was God who sent a famine that devastated the people in Egypt and in the surrounding area for seven straight years. It was God who sent the brothers to Egypt. It was God who kept the people of Israel in Egypt for many generations. All this was done because God desired to demonstrate a great salvation from death in Joseph. He would bring another great salvation through Moses four hundred years later.

Then Joseph said to his brothers, "I am Joseph; does my father still live?" But his brothers could not answer him, for they were dismayed in his presence. And Joseph said to his brothers, "Please come near to me." So they came near. Then he said: "I am Joseph your brother, whom you sold into Egypt. But now, do not therefore be grieved or angry with yourselves because you sold me here; for God sent me before you to preserve life. For these two years the famine has been in the land, and there are still five years in which there will be neither plowing nor harvesting. And God sent me before you to preserve a posterity for you in the earth, and to save your lives by a great deliverance. So now it was not you who sent me here, but God; and He has made me a father to Pharaoh, and lord of all his house, and a ruler throughout all the land of Egypt." (Genesis 45:3-8)

Joseph became a savior for his brothers. He would save the whole family from starvation and death. All of this points to the coming Messiah. This Messiah would best be known by His birth name "Jesus." Jesus is translated "Savior" or "Deliverer."

"You shall call His name Jesus, for He shall save His people from their sins." (Matthew 1:21)

All of us are born spiritually famished. We are in need of salvation from spiritual starvation and death. We are by nature in bondage to sin, death, and the devil. We are in need of salvation from the bondage of these tyrants. God gave us a picture of this in the spectacular deliverance that would come at the Red Sea. He would fulfill this picture in Jesus Christ by His death and resurrection.

THE BIRTH OF MOSES — 1520 BC

After another national decline in Egypt, Thutmose I started rebuilding the empire between 1493 and 1506 BC. This pharaoh chased the Hyksos out of the country and up into Canaan. Then he gained control of the southern portions of Canaan. He recaptured Nubia and hung the Cushite king's body over the bow of his ship. However, under his grandson Thutmose III, Egypt reached the height of its power (reign: 1475-1425 BC). He gained control over Canaan, Syria, and parts of Cush. God was setting the stage for the greatest deliverance in human history. In this

MOSES RESCUED

deliverance, the Egyptian empire would be defeated at the hands of an Almighty God.

During this time the children of Israel became slaves in Egypt. They had lived happily in the land of Goshen for many generations (between 1840 and 1440 BC). The seventy that had come down into Egypt had turned into about 2,000,000 persons.

Pharaoh now made life very difficult for the Israelites. He was concerned that these people were stronger and mightier than he was (Ex. 1:9). He was also afraid that they would "join our enemies and fight against us" (Ex. 1:10). He set taskmasters over them to "afflict them." Then, he instructed the Hebrew midwives to kill the boy babies born to the Hebrew mothers (Ex. 1:16). Shiphrah and Puah, the midwives, refused to obey the king because they feared God.

The Israelites were assigned to build bricks of mud and straw. By the reign of Sesostris III (around 1800 BC), the Egyptians had stopped using stones for their buildings. Many cities were built out of bricks made up of mud and straw.

The Israelites may have lived in the village of Kahun. This village consisted of a large Semitic slave population. An ancient papyrus discovered in 1933 listed 100 domestic servants. It included at least 48 names of Semitic or Jewish origin. These names include Shiphrah (the Hebrew midwife), Issachar, and Ashar. Also, a large number of infants have been discovered in cemeteries in Kahun and Tell ed-Daba. Wooden boxes hidden under homes in Kahun contained many babies. Sometimes the babies were "buried two or three to a box, and aged only a few months at death." Archeologists also found that 65% of the dead at the cemetery in ed-Daba were infants.

SAVING THE BABIES

By faith Moses, when he was born, was hidden three months by his parents, because they saw he was a beautiful child; and they were not afraid of the king's command. (Hebrews 11:23)

When God cursed the serpent in the garden, He said there would be enmity between the seed of the serpent and the seed of the woman. The devil would always remember that a baby born of the woman would eventually crush his head. For this reason he did not want these babies to survive. Thus the devil loves the terrible crime of abortion and infanticide (the murder of children). He tried to kill all the male babies in Egypt. He thought he could prevent the Messiah's line and save himself. Of course, it is always foolish to battle against God's purposes. But wicked rulers like the Egyptian pharaoh always support the devil and his ways.

Women of faith, like Moses's mother, are adamantly pro-life. They will always do their utmost to save the lives of their babies. So, by faith, Moses' mother hid her little baby in an ark she had made and floated him in the Nile River among the bulrushes for three months. His sister Miriam watched out for him until one day when the little baby was discovered by Pharaoh's daughter.

This probably occurred around the time of the reign of Amenemhet III. This king had only two daughters. According to the first century historian Josephus, the daughter who found Moses was herself childless. Josephus quotes the woman: "As I have received him [Moses] from the bounty of the river, in a wonderful manner, I thought proper to adopt him for my son and the heir of thy kingdom." It turns out that Amenemhet III's daughter Sobekneferu was childless for a brief time and took the throne when her father died. This is possible since Moses was exiled after he killed the Egyptian for beating an Israelite slave.

While Moses wandered as a shepherd and raised his two sons in the wilderness, Egypt reached the zenith of its power under Thutmose III.

STATUE OF PHARAOH THUTMOSE III

Egypt (Part 3)

And God spoke to Moses and said to him: "I am the LORD. I appeared to Abraham, to Isaac, and to Jacob, as God Almighty, but by My name LORD I was not known to them. I have also established My covenant with them, to give them the land of Canaan, the land of their pilgrimage, in which they were strangers. And I have also heard the groaning of the children of Israel whom the Egyptians keep in bondage, and I have remembered My covenant. Therefore say to the children of Israel: 'I am the LORD; I will bring you out from under the burdens of the Egyptians, I will rescue you from their bondage, and I will redeem you with an outstretched arm and with great judgments.'" (Exodus 6:2-6)

Moses left Egypt for 40 years and escaped to the land of Midian, where he married and had two sons. While tending his sheep, Moses came upon a burning bush. There he encountered the Lord God of his fathers Abraham, Isaac, and Jacob. God revealed His Name "Yahweh" to Moses and explained His Name as "I am who I am." God always has existed and He always will exist. He is the Source of all life and all existence.

The Lord also told Moses His intention to deliver His people from Egyptian slavery. He explained His commitment to fulfill the covenant promise He made to Abraham. Then He commissioned Moses to lead the people of Israel out of Egypt. At first, Moses was afraid to take up the task. But his faith grew into the challenge in the days and weeks that followed.

It is clear that God had a higher and more important purpose for Israel and Egypt. His purpose was to provide a powerful object lesson that will never be forgotten as long as this world continues. Man needs redemption. By nature, every person born into this world is a slave to sin. Because slaves cannot purchase their own freedom, they must be redeemed by someone else. Thus, God allowed Israel to become enslaved in Egypt so that He could purchase their freedom.

The price to redeem the Israelites was extremely high—the judgments of God upon Egypt (Ex. 6:6). Ultimately, God paid for their freedom by taking the lives of every firstborn son in Egypt—100,000 dead sons. This was only an illustration of the real redemption that was yet to come. The price of redeeming God's people from the slavery of sin comes only at the cost of the life of God's firstborn. This firstborn is His only begotten Son—the Lord Jesus Christ. It was a high price to pay.

For the following 1,400 years, the Israelites would have to redeem the firstborn

THE PLAGUES OF EGYPT

Plague 1	Water to blood	Hapi — The god of the Nile
Plague 2	Frogs	Heket — The goddess with the head of a frog
Plague 3	Dust of the earth turns into gnats	Geb — The god of the earth
Plague 4	Flies	Khepri — The god of insects
Plague 5	Livestock die	Hathor — The goddess with the head of a cow
Plague 6	Boils and sores	Sekhmet — The god of disease
Plague 7	Hail and Firestorms	Nut — The goddess of the sky
Plague 8	Locust	Seth — The god of crops
Plague 9	Darkness	Ra — The god of the sun
Plague 10	Death of the firstborn	Pharaoh — The god of the state, man

of their children, their sheep, and goats (Ex. 13:11-14). They would have to pay the temple a certain fixed price to redeem their firstborn. This served as a constant reminder that the firstborn Son would one day have to redeem God's people with His own life.

And it shall be, when the LORD brings you into the land of the Canaanites, as He swore to you and your fathers, and gives it to you, that you shall set apart to the LORD all that open the womb, that is, every firstborn that comes from an animal which you have; the males shall be the LORD's. But every firstborn of a donkey you shall redeem with a lamb; and if you will not redeem it, then you shall break its neck. And all the firstborn of man among your sons you shall redeem. So it shall be, when your son asks you in time to come, saying, 'What is this?' that you shall say to him, 'By strength of hand the LORD brought us out of Egypt, out of the house of bondage.'" (Exodus 13:11-14)

THE PASSOVER LAMB

Knowing that you were not redeemed with corruptible things, like silver or gold, from your aimless conduct received by tradition from your fathers, but with the precious blood of Christ, as of a Lamb without blemish and without spot. (1 Peter 1:18-19)

4. EGYPT (PART 3) — 41

Ten plagues were unleashed on the land of Egypt. The last plague would be the worst: the slaughter of the firstborn sons. Each of the plagues targeted one of the key gods worshiped by the Egyptians.

Throughout the ordeal, the Egyptian Pharaoh refused to let the people of Israel go. Over and over again, we read that the king hardened his heart and that God hardened his heart. Ten times, Pharaoh's heart is declared hardened.

And the LORD said to Moses, "When you go back to Egypt, see that you do all those wonders before Pharaoh which I have put in your hand. But I will harden his heart, so that he will not let the people go." (Exodus 4:21)

Several times when dealing with Moses, Pharaoh softened and confessed, "I have sinned against the LORD your God and against you" (Ex. 10:16). But then Pharaoh hardened his heart again.

The Lord preserved the Israelites from this mass killing by instituting the Passover service. A lamb was chosen on a Sunday and slaughtered on the following Thursday. The blood was placed on the lintel of the door and on the two side posts. When the avenging angel came by the Israelite houses, he would see the blood and pass over.

INSTITUTION OF THE PASSOVER

ISRAEL LEAVES EGYPT

This saved the firstborn of Israel from the slaughter. Then the children of Israel roasted and ate the Passover Lamb.

This Passover was later fulfilled in the Lord Jesus Christ. He fit the criteria laid out for the Lamb. The instructions were clear: the Lamb was to be without blemish (Ex. 12:5). None of the bones of the Lamb were to be broken (Ex. 12:46). The Lamb was to be selected four days before it was slaughtered. It was to be roasted with fire, and it was to be killed on an annual basis in Jerusalem. After 1,400 years of the Passover institution, Christ became the Passover Lamb for us. This is taught in 1 Corinthians 5:7. He was a Lamb, holy, harmless, and undefiled. He was selected to be killed upon His entry into Jerusalem four days earlier. Not one of His bones was broken. He was set out in the sun on the cross, pierced by a sword and left to bake in the sun. And He was sacrificed in Jerusalem.

This living, historical illustration ordained by God was intended to demonstrate a mighty redemption from slavery.

SALVATION FROM EGYPT

**To Him who divided the Red Sea in two,
For His mercy endures forever;
And made Israel pass through the midst of it,
For His mercy endures forever;
But overthrew Pharaoh and his army
in the Red Sea,
For His mercy endures forever . . .
(Psalm 136:13-15)**

The miraculous deliverance from Egypt is bigger than any other illustration found in all human history. It was the greatest event in Old Testament history. It was an amazing salvation. It is the greatest visual picture of God's salvation.

After allowing the people of Israel to depart, Pharaoh decided to pursue them. As God directed, Pharaoh's heart was hardened over and over again throughout the ten plagues. After Thutmose and Amenemhet's conquests, Egypt was at the height of its power. By then, they had developed horse-drawn chariots like the Hyksos who once dominated them. The Israelites had no weapons. They had no means of defending themselves, for they were slaves for generations. The Red Sea lay in front of them. A mountain stood on the left and another on the right. There was no means of escape. The Israelites were helpless and had been arguing with Moses from the beginning. This was the spectacular, monumental scene God ordained to show His grand redemption in picture form. We read from Exodus 14:

> And when Pharaoh drew near, the children of Israel lifted their eyes, and behold, the Egyptians marched after them. So they were very afraid, and the children of Israel cried out to the LORD. Then they said to Moses, "Because there were no graves in Egypt, have you taken us away to die in the wilderness? Why have you so dealt with us, to bring us up out of Egypt? Is this not the word that we told you in Egypt, saying, 'Let us alone that we may serve the Egyptians'? For it would have been better for us to serve the Egyptians than that we should die in the wilderness." And Moses said to the people, "Do not be afraid. Stand still, and see the salvation of the LORD, which He will accomplish for you today. For the Egyptians whom you see today, you shall see again no more forever. The LORD will fight for you, and you shall hold your peace." (Exodus 14:10-14)

ISRAEL AT THE RED SEA

Moses raised his rod, and the seas parted. Two million people straggling out over 4-5 miles crossed over the sea on dry land. God raised a wall of water on the right and left as His people escaped through the Red Sea. When all were safely on the other side, the waters returned and destroyed the Egyptian army.

This is an amazing object lesson that helps us understand the power and awesomeness of God's salvation. We cannot save ourselves. We are quite helpless against the enemies of sin, death, and the devil. All we can do is stand still and see the salvation of the Lord. This Old Testament event illustrates the salvation that God gives us through Jesus Christ by His death and resurrection. In this picture, we catch a glimpse of the power and incomparable glory of this salvation.

There is also a violence in this salvation. Our redemption comes by the violent destruction of the enemy. The Lord Jesus crushed principalities and powers and set His people free from the bondage of sin and death. He also set them free from Satan—the greatest tyrant of all. Our Christ was then raised from death by the power of God. Death could not have dominion over Him. We can see a picture of Jesus our Savior holding back the waters of the Red Sea as His people escape—and then letting the waters break upon the armies of the evil one. It is a complete defeat of the enemy and a complete deliverance for His people.

Such a salvation calls for song and dancing. This is how Moses and Miriam responded in Exodus 15.

> **I will sing to the LORD, for He has triumphed gloriously! The horse and its rider He has thrown into the sea! The Lord is my strength and song, and He has become my salvation; He is my God, and I will praise Him; my father's God, and I will exalt Him. The LORD is a man of war; The LORD is His name. Pharaoh's chariots and his army He has cast into the sea; His chosen captains also are drowned in the Red Sea. (Exodus 15:1-4)**

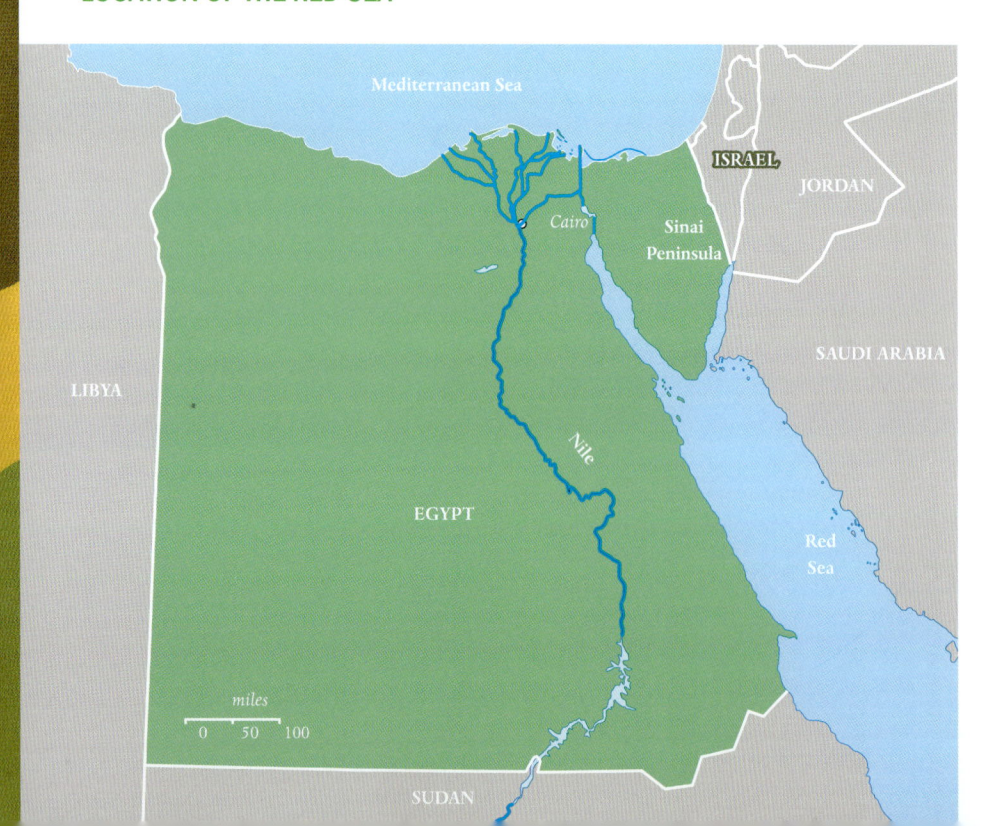

LOCATION OF THE RED SEA

THE DEVASTATION OF EGYPT

History is filled with

LOCATION OF EGYPT WITHIN AFRICA

dramatic and clear examples of God's sovereign power on earth. He judges nations, bringing the proud low and raising up the humble. While kings may believe they are carrying out their own schemes, God is fulfilling His own plan. Indeed, our sovereign God raised Egypt to the height of its power. He raised this Pharaoh to power so that He could show His own power and declare His glory throughout the world.

> **Then the LORD said to Moses, "Rise early in the morning and stand before Pharaoh, and say to him, 'Thus says the LORD God of the Hebrews: "Let My people go, that they may serve Me, or at this time I will send all My plagues to your very heart, and on your servants and on your people, that you may know that there is none like Me in all the earth. . . . But indeed for this purpose I have raised you up, that I may show My power in you, and that My name may be declared in all the earth." ' " (Exodus 9:13-14, 16)**

Archeologists have learned that during the reign of Neferhotep I a sudden departure occurred from the slave-inhabited cities of Tel ed-Daba and Kahun. It appears that these peoples left their tools and possessions in their hasty departure. Mass shallow graves full of many bodies appear at this same time. This would indicate that a terrible plague killed a great many people all at one time. Despite the fact that Neferhotep's pyramid has been identified, his mummy was never found. This is probably because he drowned in the Red Sea. Also, there is no record of his son reigning. Instead, his brother took his place on the throne of Egypt.

In Egyptian records, the first reference to Yahweh, the true and living God, appears soon after the Exodus of 1400 BC. Amenhotep III (who ruled 1391-

46 TAKING AFRICA FOR JESUS

MAP OF ANCIENT EGYPT

1353 BC) speaks of Canaan as "the land of the nomads of Yahweh." Evidently, by the 1360s the Israelites were known to be traveling like nomads through the wildernesses of Canaan. This fits perfectly into the biblical narrative.

Shortly after the Exodus, the Egyptians must have feared God for a brief time. The Pharaoh, Amenhotep IV, suddenly stopped worshiping Amun, the sun god. He also turned away from polytheism. This happened about fifty years after the Exodus. Although the Egyptians were at first horrified by this, the king persisted. He closed down the temples and changed his own name to "worshiper of Aten." He chose the name "Aten" to represent the only true "God" from his point of view. When Amenhotep died, the Egyptians quickly returned to polytheism. They erased all mention of the monotheistic pharaoh from their monuments. They also abandoned the city he had built during his reign.

Over the next thousand years, a few pagan kings repented for a short time. The king of Nineveh and the king of Babylon are examples of this. However, this repentance brought no lasting change until Jesus came.

After its humiliating defeat at the Red Sea, Egypt never returned to its position of glory and power. The nation was destroyed. The Egyptians were easy pickings for the Assyrian armies around 650 BC. Not long afterwards, the Persians ruled over Egypt. Then, in 330 BC, Alexander the Great took Egypt in his conquests. This once-proud nation was ruled by the Greeks for 300 years. The pharaohs afterward acted as puppet governors of Egypt until the time of Julius Caesar.

God destroyed Egypt and led His people to freedom. But Israel continued to live in unbelief. They turned back to Egypt for protection from the Babylonians (Jer. 42-44). Even though God warned them not to go to Egypt for help, the Israelites went anyway. Again and again they showed that they rejected God and His amazing salvation at the Red Sea.

Finally, the Lord spoke through His prophet Jeremiah. He said that Egypt would be destroyed by Nebuchadnezzar in Jeremiah 46:

The word that the LORD spoke to Jeremiah the prophet, how Nebuchadnezzar king of Babylon would come and strike the land of Egypt. . . . "The daughter of Egypt shall be ashamed; she shall be delivered into the hand of the people of the North." The LORD of hosts, the God of Israel, says, "Behold I will bring punishment on Amon of No [the sun god] and Pharaoh and Egypt, with their gods and their kings—Pharaoh and those who trust in him. And I will deliver them into the hand of those who seek their lives, into the hand of Nebuchadnezzar king of Babylon and the hand of his servants." (Jeremiah 46:13, 24-26)

This prophecy was spoken around 585 BC, and its fulfillment followed soon afterwards. ■

RUINS OF THE TEMPLE OF ZEUS IN CYRENE

Christianity Spreads to Africa

> **But you shall receive power when the Holy Spirit has come upon you; and you shall be witnesses to Me in Jerusalem, and in all Judea and Samaria, and to the end of the earth. (Acts 1:8)**

Forty days after His resurrection, Jesus Christ ascended into heaven. Jesus told his disciples to wait in Jerusalem until the Holy Spirit clothed them with power. The Holy Spirit descended on the apostles on the Day of Pentecost (Acts 2). This outpouring of the Spirit equipped the apostles to bear witness to the gospel throughout the world. The gospel spread very quickly far and wide. The Apostle Peter labored among the Jews. Meanwhile, the Apostle Paul preached among the Gentiles in the Roman World.

The Book of Acts records the missionary labors of Peter and Paul. We also have other helpful historical records from the early church. These writings record that other apostles took the gospel to faraway lands. In fact, the Apostle Thomas may have taken the gospel as far the land of India!

How did the Christian faith take root in Africa?

The Christian historian Eusebius tells us that Mark was the first to take the gospel to Africa. Mark was a disciple of the Apostle Peter. He was also the author of the Gospel of Mark. Eusebius tells us that Mark preached the gospel in Egypt and established churches there. Mark might also have gone further west in North Africa. He may have preached in such places as Libya and Algeria. Early records of Christianity are also found in Ethiopia and Nubia (modern-day Sudan).

The New Testament mentions a few Africans by name. It is possible that some of these Africans took the faith of Jesus Christ back to their native lands.

When Jesus was crucified, we learn that a man of Cyrene (modern-day Libya) was forced to carry His cross to Golgotha.

EGYPT AND LIBYA

THE DAY OF PENTECOST

> **Now as they came out, they found a man of Cyrene, Simon by name. Him they compelled to bear His cross. (Matthew 27:32)**

The Gospel of Mark says more about Simon.

> **Then they compelled a certain man, Simon a Cyrenian, the father of Alexander and Rufus, as he was coming out of the country and passing by, to bear His cross. (Mark 15:21)**

Mark or his readers may have known Alexander and Rufus personally. Perhaps this is why Mark mentioned them. It might be that Simon or his sons were responsible for spreading the Christian faith in Cyrene.

We also know that the faith was spread in the region of Ethiopia. Perhaps the eunuch from that country spread the gospel in the royal court. The story of this man is told in Acts chapter 8.

> **Now an angel of the Lord spoke to Philip, saying, "Arise and go toward the south along the road which goes down from Jerusalem to Gaza." This is desert. So he arose and went. And behold, a man of Ethiopia, a eunuch of great authority under Candace the queen of the Ethiopians, who had charge of all her treasury, and had come to Jerusalem to**

5. CHRISTIANITY SPREADS TO AFRICA

worship, was returning. And sitting in his chariot, he was reading Isaiah the prophet. (Acts 8:26-28)

The people of Cyrene are also mentioned in the Book of Acts. They are spoken of as Christians. This means that the Christian faith may have reached North Africa in the 1st or 2nd century AD. In Acts 11 we read:

Now those who were scattered after the persecution that arose over Stephen traveled as far as Phoenicia, Cyprus, and Antioch, preaching the word to no one but the Jews only. But some of them were men from Cyprus and Cyrene, who, when they had come to Antioch, spoke to the Hellenists, preaching the Lord Jesus. And the hand of the Lord was with them, and a great number believed and turned to the Lord. (Acts 11:19-21)

Much of the early history of Christianity in Africa took place in Egypt. It was in this land that Christ's church took root. Many settlements lay along the Nile in Egypt. The most important of these was Alexandria. It was located on the coast of the Mediterranean.

CHURCH LEADERS IN EARLY NORTH AFRICA

And He Himself gave some to be apostles, some prophets, some evangelists, and some pastors and teachers, for the equipping of the saints for the work of ministry, for the edifying of the body of Christ, . . . (Ephesians 4:11-12)

LOCATION OF CYRENE IN MODERN LIBYA

The early church in North Africa was led by a number of influential men. Let's learn more about them now.

Clement of Alexandria (c. 150-215)

Clement of Alexandria was probably born in the city of Athens, Greece. Athens was a city long famous for its philosophers. Clement's parents were pagan. But young Clement converted to the faith some time during his youth. After his conversion, he began traveling, seeking teachers to disciple him in his newfound faith. It was in Alexandria, Egypt where he found a teacher. The name of his teacher was Pantenus. Clement eventually became the main Christian teacher in Alexandria.

CLEMENT OF ALEXANDRIA

During Clement's life, Alexandria was a very important city. It was the second largest city in the Roman Empire. It had one of the largest and most important libraries of the ancient world. The city was also a major trade center in the Mediterranean. Many various materials and supplies passed through its port.

It was in this large city that Clement taught God's people. He also tried to persuade non-Christians of the truth of Christianity. Many of the citizens thought Christianity didn't make sense. Clement argued that Christianity was not absurd. Instead, he wanted to show people that the Christian faith is true. To do this, Clement often quoted the Greek philosophers. He wanted to show that the Christian faith was similar to the teaching of the Greeks. Sadly, Clement did not always base his teachings on the Bible. But God still used this man in the early church in Egypt.

Tertullian of Carthage (c. 155-240)

Now let's look at the life of another influential African church leader. His name was Tertullian. Tertullian was born in the coastal town of Carthage. He spent his entire life in this town. He converted to the Christian faith around age 30. After his conversion, he began to write books defending Christianity. He wrote against the pagans and their denial of the faith. He also wrote against heretics who twisted the teaching of God's Word. Tertullian was one of the first early church leaders to write in Latin. Unlike Clement of Alexandria, Tertullian did not quote the Greek philosophers. He didn't use any non-Christian books to prove his doctrine. He was a vigorous defender of the truth.

However, Tertullian himself was not perfect. He fell into false doctrine as well. In AD 207, he joined a schismatic movement known as the Montanists. (A schismatic is someone who teaches false doctrine and splits or divides the church.) Montanism is named after its founder Montanus. This man converted to Christianity in 155. After his conversion, Montanus began to prophesy. He declared that he was possessed by the Holy Spirit. Two women named Priscilla and Maximilla joined him and began prophesying as well. They believed that their movement was the beginning of a new age. They thought this new age would be marked by a more strictly moral life. This appealed to Tertullian.

The rest of the church opposed Montanism. We do not know why Tertullian joined this group. He may have been drawn to Montanism because of its rigorous moral teachings. Yet, even after Tertullian became a Montanist, he continued writing against heretics. He wrote some valuable works during this time. In one of these books he taught on the Trinity. It was Tertullian who first coined the word "Trinity." We use the word "Trinity" to describe that God is one God in three Persons.

Origen of Alexandria (c. 184-253)

Now let's come back to Alexandria to study Origen of Alexandria. Origen was mentored by Clement. He was born to Christian parents in the city of Alexandria. Under the persecution of Septimius Severus (c. 202), Origen's father was martyred. Origen was eager to follow in the footsteps of his father. He tried to offer himself for martyrdom. But his mother, who was afraid that her son would be killed, hid his clothes so that he could not go out and follow in his father's footsteps.

During Origen's teens, Demetrius was the bishop of Alexandria. He gave Origen the task of training new disciples for baptism. This was a very important responsibility. Soon Origen was well known for his teaching abilities. He founded his

KING EZANA'S STELE IN ETHIOPIA

own academy in Alexandria to train others. During the persecution of Decius (250-251), he had the opportunity to show the strength of his faith. Though he was not martyred, he was tortured, almost to the point of death. Shortly after being released, he died of his wounds in the city of Tyre. He was seventy years old.

CHRISTIANITY IN ETHIOPIA

Next, we turn to one of the most fascinating stories of Christianity in Africa. It is a story illustrating how our God works in mysterious ways.

Sometime in the 1st century, a new kingdom emerged. It was located in the highlands of Ethiopia. The kingdom's name was Axum. This ancient kingdom sat on the northern edge of Ethiopia. It would one day become the dominant kingdom in the region. By the 4th century, it was one of the most powerful kingdoms of Africa. The city was full of stone monuments such as palaces, temples, and obelisks. Axum's wealth grew as the kingdom traded with the Greeks.

In the early fourth century, the king of Axum was Ella Amida. He wanted his successor Ezana to gain new learning. This proved to be a perfect opportunity for Christian missionaries. During this time, two Christian young men went on a journey with other tourists. Their names were Frumentius and Aedesius. Perhaps they were heading to India. Along the way, the group stopped along the Axumite coast. Their sightseeing was quickly cut short when the Axum locals captured the tour group. They put the group to death, sparing only two among them. These two were Frumentius and Aedesius. By God's providence, their lives were preserved.

The Lord gave the young men favor with King Ella Amida. For a time, they served in the royal court. But soon the king died. After his death, his widow turned to the young men for help. Like Joseph in ancient Egypt, these two young men arose to become rulers of the realm. They governed in place of the king's son Ezana, who was still very young. Once Ezana grew up, he took the throne of the kingdom. King Ezana then gave Frumentius and Aedesius freedom to return home. However, Frumentius wanted to reach the Axumites for Christ. He returned to Alexandria and sought counsel from Athanasius. (Athanasius was a pastor in Alexandria. You will learn more about his life in a later chapter.)

When Athanasius learned about Axum, he at once agreed that Frumentius should return to the city. Frumentius was therefore sent back to Axum as a missionary. Through his diligent labors, Ezana converted to Christianity. This Axumite king left behind testimonies to his faith in Jesus Christ. An ancient stone slab found in the ruins of Axum is an example of this. It has references to the "Lord of all" and the "Lord of Heaven." In another ancient inscription, King Ezana testified: "I believe in your son Jesus Christ who has saved me."

Coinage from the kingdom also bears the symbol of the cross.

For a long time, the Christian faith stayed in the kingdom of Axum. It did not penetrate the surrounding lands of Ethiopia. But, in the fifth century, monks from Syria entered Ethiopia. Perhaps they were fleeing persecution. Because of their coming, the faith spread throughout the region. Since they were monks, they brought their monastic traditions with them. This changed the character of the faith in Ethiopia. Monasteries now became dominant over churches.

In the 7th century, North Africa was invaded by Muslims. Most North African kingdoms became Muslim. These conversions from Christianity to Islam took some time. However, after a few centuries, the land changed dramatically. Now there were more Muslims than Christians in these lands. But the land of Ethiopia was different. Christianity in Ethiopia continued for another thousand years. It remained strong, even with little outside influence.

BASIC FACTS ABOUT THE FEDERAL DEMOCRATIC REPUBLIC OF ETHIOPIA

Total Population	108,000,000
Total Area	427,000 square miles
Capital	Addis Ababa
Official Languages	Amharic, English
Primary Religions	Christianity, Islam

ANCIENT ETHIOPIAN CHURCH HEWN OUT OF THE ROCK

PRAYER POINTS: ETHIOPIA

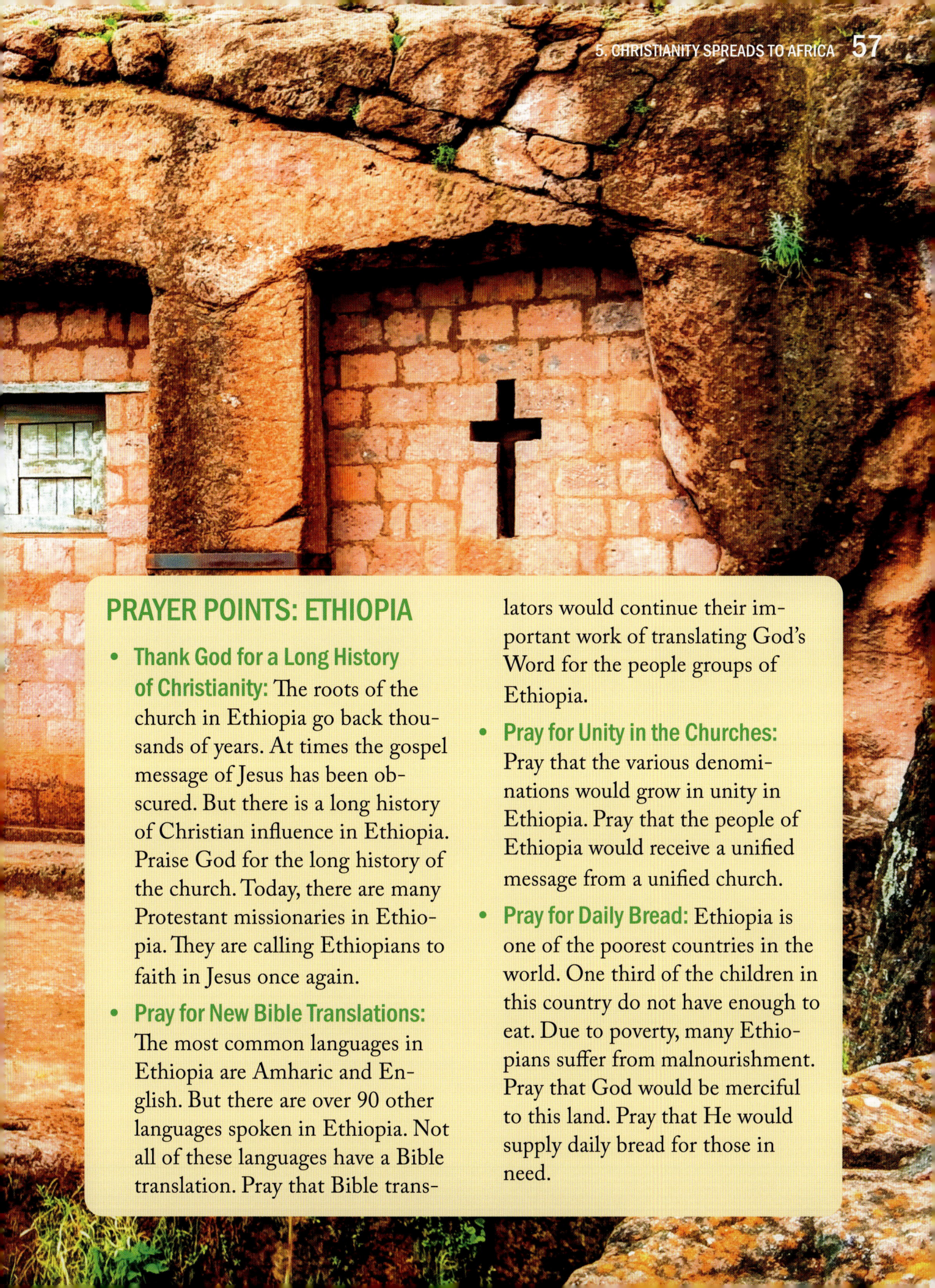

- **Thank God for a Long History of Christianity:** The roots of the church in Ethiopia go back thousands of years. At times the gospel message of Jesus has been obscured. But there is a long history of Christian influence in Ethiopia. Praise God for the long history of the church. Today, there are many Protestant missionaries in Ethiopia. They are calling Ethiopians to faith in Jesus once again.

- **Pray for New Bible Translations:** The most common languages in Ethiopia are Amharic and English. But there are over 90 other languages spoken in Ethiopia. Not all of these languages have a Bible translation. Pray that Bible translators would continue their important work of translating God's Word for the people groups of Ethiopia.

- **Pray for Unity in the Churches:** Pray that the various denominations would grow in unity in Ethiopia. Pray that the people of Ethiopia would receive a unified message from a unified church.

- **Pray for Daily Bread:** Ethiopia is one of the poorest countries in the world. One third of the children in this country do not have enough to eat. Due to poverty, many Ethiopians suffer from malnourishment. Pray that God would be merciful to this land. Pray that He would supply daily bread for those in need.

RUINS OF A CHURCH IN HIPPO

Church Life in North Africa

And they continued steadfastly in the apostles' doctrine and fellowship, in the breaking of bread, and in prayers. (Acts 2:42)

What was it like to go to church in North Africa during the early centuries of the church? When you went to the assembly of God's people, what sort of sermons did you hear? What was the celebration of the Lord's Supper like? How did the people pray? When God's people suffered persecution, did this change how the church gathered for worship and fellowship?

In this chapter, you will learn about how the early Christians of North Africa worshipped and lived the Christian life. Since it was such a long time ago, there are many things we don't know. Most of what we know about these early Christians comes through written sermons and records. The writings of a few early church leaders help us better understand how things were. In this chapter, we will learn about the church from the writings of Tertullian, Cyprian, and Augustine.

GATHERINGS FOR WORSHIP

And let us consider one another in order to stir up love and good works, not forsaking the assembling of ourselves together, as is the manner of some, but exhorting one another, and so much the more as you see the Day approaching. (Hebrews 10:24-25)

Tertullian lived from about AD 155 to 240. His writings help us understand what the church was like in the

MAP OF NORTH AFRICA

59

TAKING AFRICA FOR JESUS

AUGUSTINE OF HIPPO

late 2nd century AD. According to Tertullian, the assembly usually met for worship more than once a week. In some cases, the celebration of the Lord's Supper may have happened every day. Christians in Tertullian's time also participated in a fellowship meal on certain evenings. This was called the "agape meal" or "love feast." This communal meal was probably not a celebration of the Lord's Supper. Instead it was a time for fellowship. Christians would also invite the poor to share in the meal. Through this "love feast," the early Christians showed charity to those who were hungry. Praise in song and prayer also happened at these meals. The meal

BAPTISMAL FROM ANCIENT CHURCH IN ALGERIA

would begin with a public prayer. After eating, those at the feast spent time reading the Scriptures aloud or singing.

Cyprian of Carthage lived from about AD 200 to 258. During his time, the morning assembly for worship became the standard. All Christians in Carthage were expected to attend the worship service.

Augustine lived from AD 354 to 430. His writings give us the most detail about what the worship services were like in the 4th and 5th centuries. These services included readings from Scripture, preaching, and public prayer. They also included offerings, the Lord's Supper, and baptism.

Augustine served as pastor in the church at Hippo. Hippo was a city located in North Africa. In Hippo, men and women worshippers would separate as they entered the church. They would stand on opposite sides of the church during worship. It was normal for Christians to stand for the entire service. There were no pews or chairs to sit on. If someone needed to rest, they would need to leave the service and go outside.

Once the people gathered together, the pastor would greet them by saying "The Lord be with you." The worshippers then responded by saying "And with your spirit." A reader would then step into the lectern and begin reading Scripture aloud. After the readings of Scripture, the pastor (or bishop) would then preach a sermon. During the sermon, the pastor would quote many biblical passages to support his teaching. When the sermon was finished, attendees who were not baptized were dismissed from the service. The celebration of the Lord's Supper was only for baptized believers. Once the non-baptized left, a series of prayers would be offered. Then the offering of gifts was taken up. These offerings would be used for the church or for the poor of the community.

After the offering was taken, the Lord's Supper was distributed. The early Christians of North Africa usually called the Lord's Supper the Eucharist. This word simply means "thanksgiving." In 1 Corinthians 10:16, Paul calls the "cup" the "cup of blessing" or the "cup of thanksgiving." This is where the word eucharist comes from. After communion, a prayer of thanksgiving was said. The people then left the church building.

PREACHING OF THE WORD

I charge you therefore before God and the Lord Jesus Christ, who will judge the living and the dead at His appearing and His kingdom: Preach the word! Be ready in season and out of season. Convince, rebuke, exhort, with all longsuffering and teaching. (2 Timothy 4:1-2)

One of the most important parts of the worship gatherings was the celebration of the Lord's Supper. Christians in North Africa believed this was a central part of worship. The Supper was celebrated at every worship service. Preaching God's

Word was also an essential part of early Christian worship. Tertullian wrote that the public reading of Scripture happened during worship. This included readings from the Old Testament and the New Testament. Tertullian argued it was essential for people to hear the Word of God read aloud in worship. It is important to remember that many Christians did not own their own Bible. Some of them only had access to a portion of God's Word. This made the public reading of God's Word even more precious to them!

**The law of the Lord is perfect,
converting the soul;
The testimony of the Lord is sure,
making wise the simple. (Psalm 19:7)**

Cyprian tells us that accounts of the early martyrs were sometimes read in the church. This probably would have included writings such as the *Acts of the Scillitan Martyrs* and the *Passion of Perpetua and Felicitas*. Readers of Scripture stood and read with a loud voice. There were no microphones available in that day. Therefore readers and preachers had to speak loudly to be heard by everyone.

We still have many of Augustine's sermons to the Christians in Hippo. From these we can learn much about how the Scriptures were preached. The bishop or pastor sat on an elevated chair behind the pulpit and projected his voice to the congregation. Most sermons lasted about 45 minutes to an hour. Augustine normally preached on Saturday, Sunday, and many regular feast days. These feast days were organized around the life of Christ. Augustine often preached through an entire biblical book. When he did, he would often preach every single day of the week. This must have involved a lot of preparation and study!

On Saturdays, Augustine would often preach longer sermons. The smaller congregation that attended on Saturdays was more interested in long expositions of Scripture. The larger Sunday congregation would receive a shorter sermon. On feast days, such as Christmas, Augustine had other problems to worry about. Some people would become impatient with the length of the sermon. They wanted to get off to celebrate holiday festivities. On one occasion, Augustine preached for three hours straight on New Year's Day. This may be the longest sermon he ever preached. He may have done this to keep the congregation away from the non-Christian celebrations taking place that day. These celebrations often involved ungodly practices.

Augustine normally prepared his sermons carefully before preaching. But sometimes he was more flexible. On one particular day of worship, the reader read the wrong psalm. This was not the psalm Augustine planned to preach on. But Augustine took the error to be God telling him to preach on this passage instead. So, without any preparation, Augustine preached on the psalm that was read instead of the planned sermon.

PRAYER IN THE CHRISTIAN LIFE

Continue earnestly in prayer, being vigilant in it with thanksgiving. (Colossians 4:2)

In the early North African church, prayer was an essential part of the Christian life. Early church writings record the prayer habits of the church. Prayer took place in private as well as in the public church body. Tertullian wrote that the Lord's Prayer provided the basic pattern for prayer. Tertullian also recommended that Christians pray on their knees when in private. In public worship, Christians usually prayed standing with their arms extended to heaven. This follows the pattern described by Paul in 1 Timothy 2:8.

I desire therefore that the men pray everywhere, lifting up holy hands, without wrath and doubting. (1 Timothy 2:8)

Tertullian also warned Christians not to follow pagan practices of prayer. Christians do not need to make long prayers to impress God. They do not need elaborate rituals to make God hear them. As the Scriptures teach, God already knows what we need (Matt. 6:8). Tertullian also urged his fellow believers to pray for all people, even enemies. He explained that prayer should focus on spiritual matters first and foremost. But it is also appropriate to pray for physical needs. The Lord's Prayer says to pray for "our daily bread."

Like Tertullian, Cyprian also wrote a book on the Lord's Prayer. Cyprian taught that prayers should be made at least in the morning and evening, but also once more in the afternoon. Of course, Christians were not limited to these set times of prayer. But these set times were considered the basic practice. Cyprian also taught that prayer and fasting should often be practiced together. Fasting would help to set a person free from the distractions of this life and to focus on the Lord. Since the church was facing persecutions during Cyprian's day, he encouraged Christians to pray for strength to stand firm. He exhorted other Christians to pray for those who denied Christ during the persecutions. He told Christians to pray that these people would be restored to the church.

Augustine wrote a book on the Sermon on the Mount (from Matt. 5-7). In this book, Augustine covers our Lord Jesus' teaching on prayer. Augustine tells us that the North African Christians recited the Lord's Prayer each day. He also taught that heart motivation is the most important part of prayer. Augustine encouraged continual prayer. He encouraged his congregation to regularly recite and memorize the Psalms. The Psalms teach us how to pray. When praying for enemies, Christians should not pray for vengeance against them. Instead, Christians should

ROMAN VILLA IN CARTHAGE

pray for their conversion. Augustine also explained that Christians should confess their sins daily and ask God for forgiveness. We find this in the words of the Lord's Prayer: "forgive us our debts."

The writings of these leaders also help us understand some of the common rituals of prayer. Tertullian, Cyprian, and Augustine all mention that Christians would often make the "sign of the cross" on their forehead. This practice is not taught in Scripture. But it did become a common practice. In Hippo, the congregation would often face east when praying. This was a symbolic act. They would "turn to the Lord" in prayer. However, Augustine realized that this was just a symbol. The Lord is everywhere, not just in the east. For the Christians of North Africa, the Lord's Prayer was the most important guide for prayer.

THE DISCIPLINE OF FASTING

Moreover, when you fast, do not be like the hypocrites, with a sad countenance. For they disfigure their faces that they may appear to men to be fasting. Assuredly, I say to you, they have their reward. But you, when you fast, anoint your head and wash your face, so that you do not appear to men to be fasting, but to your Father who is in the secret place; and your Father who sees in secret will reward you openly. (Matthew 6:16-18)

Fasting was common in the early church in North Africa. It was frequently practiced. In Tertullian's writings, we learn that candidates for baptism often fasted in preparation for the day of their baptism. But Christians were free to choose their own times of fasting as well. In many cases, Christians fasted for all or part of the day on Wednesday and Friday. But they would not fast on Sunday, since it was the day of celebrating Christ's resurrection. Sometimes the leaders of the church called for a community fast. They did this when they were seeking the Lord's will in prayer. This follows the pattern of the Christians in Acts who prayed and fasted together.

As they ministered to the Lord and fasted, the Holy Spirit said, "Now separate to Me Barnabas and Saul for the work to which I have called them." Then, having fasted and prayed, and laid hands on them, they sent them away. (Acts 13:2-3)

During the persecutions of Emperor Decius, fasting became even more necessary. Christians faced the loss of property, public position, and sometimes their own lives. They needed the strength of the Lord. The Christians prayed and fasted, asking the Lord for divine strength to resist the world.

By the early 5th century, Wednesday and Friday were normal fasting days. In some parts of Africa, fasting also took place on Saturday. Augustine believed that fasting would help wean Christians from love of the world. It would help them grow in their love for spiritual things. North African Christians believed that the suffering of fasting would help prepare them for suffering in persecution. It is important to remember that the Bible does not command any particular time for fasting. Fasting should be practiced freely. Christians should not be forced to fast on specific days. But the North African Christians remind us that this is still an important Christian discipline.

GIVING TO THE POOR

Therefore, as we have opportunity, let us do good to all, especially to those who are of the household of faith. (Galatians 6:10)

A common Christian practice in the early North African church was giving to those in need. This has always been an essential part of Christian living. As John writes, if the love of God abides in us, then we will give to our brother in need (1 John 3:17). We must love in deed and truth, not just in word (1 John 3:18). Christians showed that they valued Christ above worldly things when they gave away their possessions to care for those in need.

According to Tertullian, the church had a common fund from which care could be given to those in need. This included widows, orphans, the elderly, the poor, and the persecuted. The church would host a regular meal that wasn't just for fellowship. This community meal would also feed the poor in the church. Ministers in the church were also supported out of the common fund. During the persecution under Emperor Decius, Cyprian used the church funds to support Christians in prison. The edict of the Emperor threatened to seize property from those who did not sacrifice to pagan gods. Christians could not participate in the sacrifices. Because of this, many of them lost their property and needed help. Others feared losing their property and therefore offered the ungodly sacrifices. When some of those who had fallen were later restored, they were required to give to the poor. The African Christians believed that this demonstrated their repentance. This showed that they loved Christ more than worldly goods.

In Augustine's time, the church did not face the same persecutions. This is because the church was now established throughout the empire. The persecutions had mostly ended. This meant that the church contained a mixture of both rich and poor. This made the many warnings about riches in the Bible very important for the church in Hippo. Augustine preached on these passages and warned wealthy Christians to avoid pride and selfishness. He did not teach that riches were sinful. But he did warn that riches could lead to sin. The love of money is the root of all kinds of evil (1 Tim. 6:10). Augustine exhorted those who were wealthy to share with the poor. Yet, at the same time, he taught that all Christians had a responsibility to share with others. Everyone should help care for the poor. Augustine also preached that the tithe (10% of one's income) was the minimum that Christians should give.

As bishop in Hippo, Augustine managed many church properties. Some of the money collected through the church's giving was used to build new church buildings and support the ministry. But the church in Hippo was careful to set aside money to give to those in need. This was the first priority in the church's charitable giving.

6. CHURCH LIFE IN NORTH AFRICA

AIT BENHADDOU, MOROCCO

CARTHAGE

The Martyrdom of Perpetua and Felicity

This chapter is a retelling of Perpetua and Felicity's martyrdom in the early AD 200s. The account is adapted from the ancient church document known as The Passion of Perpetua and Felicity.

**Precious in the sight of the Lord
Is the death of His saints. (Psalm 116:15)**

In AD 203 in the seaside town of Carthage lived a young woman. Her name was Vibia Perpetua. She was twenty-two years of age, the daughter of a nobleman. Recently, Vibia Perpetua had embraced the Christian faith. This was much to the consternation of her father. He urged Perpetua to deny her faith and turn back to the old ways of their pagan religion.

"Father," said Perpetua. "Do you see this pitcher lying here?"

Her father answered, "I see it."

She said to him, "Can you call it a broom or a blanket? Can you call it any other name than a pitcher?"

He answered, "No, for that is what it is."

Perpetua smiled. "So I can only call myself what I am. I am a Christian. I cannot call myself anything else."

Days later, Perpetua and other new disciples were baptized in the name of the Father, the Son, and the Holy Spirit. Through baptism, they showed that they had become followers of Jesus Christ.

A few days later, the young disciples were arrested and taken to prison. Their names were Revocatus, Felicity, Saturninus, Secundulus, and the young woman Vibia Perpetua. At this time, Perpetua was nursing her young infant son. For a time, the little boy also lived in prison with his mother.

After the recently baptized disciples were imprisoned, two deacons from the church, Tertius and Pomponius, visited them in prison. The two men encouraged the prisoners to stand fast for Christ despite the hardships they were now enduring.

Tertius and Pomponius were fulfilling the command of God's Word:

Remember the prisoners as if chained with them—those who are mistreated—since you yourselves are in the body also. (Hebrews 13:3)

Perpetua's mother and brother also visited her. They were sorrowful for Perpetua's plight and for her poor baby boy. Perpetua's brother spoke to her, saying, "You may ask the Lord for a vision to see whether this imprisonment will end in your suffering and death or in your being set free."

Perpetua replied, "Tomorrow, I will tell you." Then she prayed, asking the Lord to reveal whether she would suffer for the name of Christ or whether she would be set free from prison. This was the vision that Perpetua told her brother:

> I saw a ladder of bronze. It was very tall, reaching up to heaven. And it was narrow, so that not more than one person could go up at one time. And in the sides of the ladder were all kinds of things made of iron. There were swords there, spears, hooks, and knives. If any went up and was not careful or did not look up, he would be torn and his flesh would cling to the iron. And there was right at the ladder's foot a serpent which lay in wait for those who wanted to go up. And it frightened them so that they were afraid to go up. Now Saturninus went up first.
>
> And he came to the ladder's head, and he turned and said: "Perpetua, I'm waiting for you. But be careful that the serpent does not bite you."
>
> And I said, "It shall not hurt me, in the name of Jesus Christ." And from beneath the ladder, as though it feared me, the serpent softly put forth its head. And as though I tread on the first step, I tread on its head. And I went up. Then I saw a very great space of garden, and in the midst a man sitting, white-headed, in shepherd's clothing, tall, milking his sheep. And standing around in white were many thousands.
>
> And he raised his head and saw me and said to me: "Welcome, child." And he called to me, and from the curd he had from the milk he gave me a morsel. And I took it in my hands and ate it up. And all that stood around said, "Amen." And at the sound of that word, I awoke.

After Perpetua told her brother the vision, both Perpetua and her brother knew what it meant. She was to give her life for Christ. And through her witness for Christ, she would tread the serpent Satan under her feet.

As God's Word says:

The God of peace will crush Satan under your feet shortly. (Romans 16:20)

A few days later, Perpetua's father visited her in prison. He again pled with her to renounce her faith for the sake of her father and her family. If Perpetua would deny Jesus Christ, she would be set free.

Her father said, "Have pity, my daughter, on my grey hairs. Have pity on your father! If I am worthy to be called your father, do not shame me in this way. Think about your brothers. Think about your mother and your aunt. Think about your son. Give up this decision to follow Christ!" This was her father's plea. Then he kissed her hands and bowed at her feet, weeping.

ROMAN AMPHITHEATER IN CARTHAGE

Perpetua said, "Father, whatever God is pleased to do will happen when I am before the tribunal. We do not determine our own path, but all things happen by God's will."

Seeing that Perpetua would not renounce her faith, her father left, full of sorrow.

On another day, the group of Christians were taken to the tribunal. The tribunal was the Roman court of justice. There Perpetua saw that her father had also come with her infant son, who was now in her father's care. Her father urged her, "Perform the sacrifice, and have mercy on your child."

The sacrifice mentioned here was a sacrifice made to the Roman Emperor. Christians like Perpetua believed to perform such a sacrifice was idolatrous.

Hilarian, the procurator of the tribunal, joined his voice with her father's, saying, "Spare your father's grey hairs. Spare your infant boy! Make sacrifice for the emperor's prosperity."

Perpetua answered plainly, "I am a Christian." Perpetua was resolute in her commitment. She would not deny her Lord who had redeemed her.

Hilarian then passed sentence upon the imprisoned disciples. The sentence: death by mauling of beasts. They would be executed in the arena during the Roman games which were being held in celebration of Emperor Septimius Severus' birthday.

Perpetua missed her infant son. She asked Pomponius the deacon to go and

PERPETUA AND HER FATHER

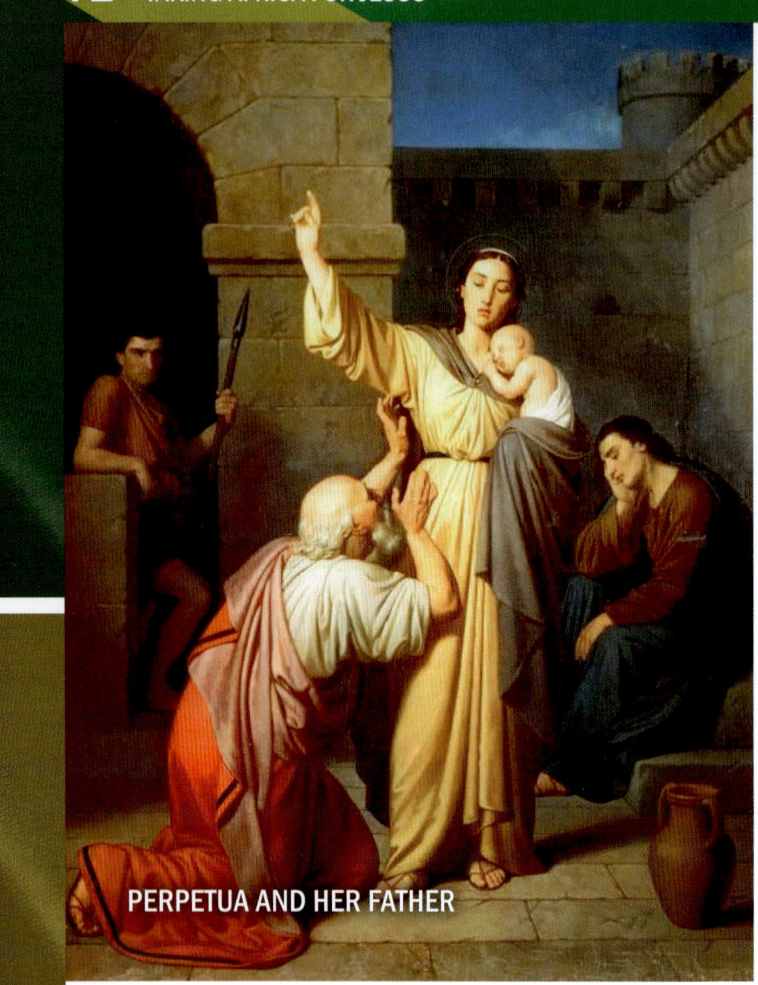

fetch her child from her father. But Perpetua's father would not agree to this. He would not allow the infant to be with Perpetua.

A few days before the games began, Perpetua's father again came to the prison to continue his pleas. He was exhausted from weariness and grief. He began to pluck out his beard, and he fell on his face and cursed his life. He tried every possible way to get Perpetua to renounce Christ for the sake of her life and family. But Perpetua refused to deny her Lord.

Along with Perpetua, another young woman named Felicity was facing death for her commitment to worship and serve Jesus Christ. Unlike Perpetua, Felicity was not a noblewoman. She was a slave. She was not important in the world's eyes. But she was one of God's children just like Perpetua. The Apostle Paul reminds us that many of Christ's followers will be people who are not important in the world's eyes.

> **For you see your calling, brethren, that not many wise according to the flesh, not many mighty, not many noble, are called. But God has chosen the foolish things of the world to put to shame the wise, and God has chosen the weak things of the world to put to shame the things which are mighty. (1 Corinthians 1:26-27)**

As the games drew near, Felicity was around eight months pregnant. She wanted to give birth to her child before entering the arena to face the beasts. She didn't want her child to die when she died. Her fellow Christians prayed together and asked the Lord to let the baby be born before the day of the games came. Three days before the games, Felicity went into labor and was in great pain. One of the prison guards called out to her, "You that are complaining of pain now, what will you do when you are thrown to the beasts, which you were sentenced to when you would not make the sacrifice to the emperor?"

Felicity replied, "I myself am now suffering. But another shall be in me who shall suffer for me, because I am to suffer for Him." Felicity spoke of her Lord Jesus Christ.

7. THE MARTYRDOM OF PERPETUA AND FELICITY

By God's mercy, she safely delivered a baby daughter. Felicity's sister took the child and cared for her.

It was the custom of the Romans to allow condemned prisoners one last meal together. The imprisoned chose to celebrate together the Christian "love feast" like they used to do before their imprisonment.

The day of the games dawned. The Romans saw it as a day of defeat for the condemned Christians. But Perpetua, Felicity, and their fellow Christians knew it would be a day of victory for them. They walked from the prison into the amphitheater with the peace of Christ upon them. The Christians were cheerful with looks of happiness on their faces. They knew they were at the doorstep of heaven.

The Romans then ordered the condemned Christian men to put on the robes of the priests of the false god Saturn. The women were required to wear the dress of the priestesses of Ceres. But Perpetua refused. She said, "I have been sentenced to death because I want to worship Christ. We have devoted our lives to this cause. And we will not do such a thing that you have asked."

The tribune decided to let the matter go and to leave them dressed as they were. Then Perpetua began to sing as if she was already stomping on the head of the serpent. When Hilarian the procurator appeared, Revocatus and Saturninus spoke to him, saying, "You have judged us. But God will judge you."

The audience became angry when these words were spoken, and they urged that the men should be scourged. Revocatus and Saturninus took the blows of scourging, thankful that they were counted worthy to suffer for the name of Jesus Christ.

Then the beasts were released to have their way with the Christians. Revocatus was attacked by a leopard and then a bear. Saturninus was assaulted by a bear.

For the women, a savage cow was prepared who would attack them. Perpetua was first thrown before the cow and fell to the ground. Her hair and clothes were disheveled. But lest the crowd think that she was grieving in sorrow, Perpetua stood up and pinned up her hair. Next, Felicity was thrown down. Perpetua went to Felicity and took her by the hand and helped her up.

Rusticus, another Christian disci-

MOSIAC OF PERPETUA

PRAYER POINTS: TUNISIA

- **Religious Freedom:** The government of Tunisia forbids Christian churches from owning their own property. Churches are not allowed to have bank accounts. Pray that the Lord would provide freedom to the Tunisian Christians. Even though they are oppressed, pray that the Lord would enable these Christians to remain faithful.

- **Missionaries:** Pray that the Lord would send more missionaries into this land. There were once many Christians in the region of Carthage, in modern-day Tunisia. But after the Muslims took over much of North Africa, the church largely disappeared. Today, most Tunisians have still not heard the gospel of Jesus Christ. Pray that Christians from around the world would come to preach the gospel in Tunisia.

ple, was watching all this occur. Perpetua called out to him and said, "Stand fast in the faith, and love one another, and do not be saddened by our suffering."

After the Christians had been mauled by the beasts, the order was given to pierce them with a sword to end their lives. Then Perpetua, Felicity, and their fellow Christians were put to death with the sword.

These were the valiant martyrs of Carthage in the year AD 203. They gave their lives for Christ because they knew that He is worthy of all praise, honor, and service. This is the testimony of Perpetua and Felicity. This was their witness for Jesus Christ. No matter who stands against us, may we also say with Perpetua, "I am a Christian."

BASIC FACTS ABOUT TUNISIA

The ancient city of Carthage was located in what is now modern-day Tunisia.

Total Population:	11,400,000
Total Area:	63,100 square miles
Capital:	Tunis
Official Languages:	Arabic, Berber, French
Primary Religion:	Islam

7. THE MARTYRDOM OF PERPETUA AND FELICITY

SAHARA DESERT IN TUNISIA

RUINS OF THERMAL BATHS IN CARTHAGE

Cyprian of Carthage

[Jesus said to His disciples], "You shall receive power when the Holy Spirit has come upon you; and you shall be witnesses to Me in Jerusalem, and in all Judea and Samaria, and to the end of the earth." (Acts 1:8)

If you travel to the northernmost tip of Africa, you will find the ruins of the ancient city of Carthage. Today, this area of Africa is called Tunisia. While not as famous as Rome, Carthage became one of the most important cities of the ancient world. This city plays an important part in the history of Africa. Sometime between 800 and 900 BC, the Phoenician people founded the city. Through the years, Carthage became a wealthy and strong city-state, controlling much of the Mediterranean Sea.

At the same time, across the sea, another city-state was growing in power. It was the Republic of Rome (located in modern-day Italy). Eventually, these two city-states, Rome and Carthage, would clash in an epic struggle for power over the Mediterranean world. Between 246 and 146 BC, these two powers fought three major wars. They are called the Punic Wars. At the end of it all, Rome won the wars and destroyed the city of Carthage.

The Romans pronounced a curse upon the city, with the hopes that it would never be rebuilt. God had further plans for this city, though. The Romans and other peoples began to resettle in the broken-down ruins of Carthage. Over time, they rebuilt the city. Once again, Carthage became an important city on the coast of Northern Africa.

The Spirit of God came upon the apostles of Jesus on the Day of Pentecost. Right away, these men took the good news of Christ's resurrection everywhere, starting in Jerusalem and Judea. Eventually, the faith made its way to Carthage. By the

LOCATION OF CARTHAGE IN TUNISIA

mid-200s AD, the Christian faith was firmly established in much of North Africa, including Carthage.

FIRST RECORD OF CHRISTIANITY IN AFRICA

You shall have no other gods before Me. (Exodus 20:3)

For the first 600 years after Jesus Christ rose from the dead, the faith grew quickly in North Africa. The rest of Africa was harder to reach with the gospel message. A 3000-mile wide desert region called the "Sahara Desert" separates North Africa from the rest of the continent. It would not be until the 1750s (about 250 years ago) that the Christian gospel finally made it to central and southern Africa.

The first record of Christians in North Africa is found in an old writing called Acts of the Scillitan Martyrs. According to this account, twelve Christians were put to death for their faith in AD 180. The spokesman for the twelve was named Speratus. The Roman proconsul had commanded the Christians to "swear by the genius of the emperor," but they refused. (The word "genius" means a deity.) The Romans were trying to turn their king into a god or a higher power. Of course, Christians cannot accept this idolatry. These brave Christians told the Roman official that their loyalty was to the King of kings and Lord of lords. They declared that Jesus Christ "is the emperor of kings and of all nations."[1] They died for this testimony.

ILLUSTRATION OF CYPRIAN OF CARTHAGE

These twelve courageous Christians stood strong for their belief that Jesus is King of kings and Lord of lords. In the centuries that followed, many more African Christians would die for this faith. They would not bow the knee to any earthly authority as some earthly deity. They were committed to the exclusive Lordship of Jesus Christ.

THE EARLY LIFE OF CYPRIAN

Before I formed you in the womb I knew you; Before you were born I sanctified you; I ordained you a prophet to the nations. (Jeremiah 1:5)

Cyprian of Carthage is another example of a bold and brave man who went through

---
[1] Mark Shaw, *The Kingdom of God in Africa: A Short History of African Christianity* (Grand Rapids: Baker, 1996), 43.

very great persecution for Christ. His full name was Thascius Caecilius Cyprianus, but we usually just call him Cyprian. All Christians around the world should know of this great man of God. He lived and died as a disciple of our Lord Jesus Christ in North Africa.

Cyprian was born into a rich family in Carthage around AD 200. His family was not Christian. The faith was still new in this part of the world in these early days. It is possible that his family was part of the ruling class in Carthage. We don't know much about Cyprian's early life. We do know he went to school as a young boy and studied books written by the Greeks and Romans. He was trained in pagan, non-Christian literature and speeches.

Later, when Cyprian became a pastor, he realized that the pagan schools had trained him in the wrong way. He had to change the way that he spoke to God's people in the church. He wrote about this in a letter. When preaching, he said he didn't want to "charm a popular audience with cultivated rhetoric." He did not want to speak to impress people anymore. He didn't need people to clap for his wonderful speeches. Now he would speak in a simple way and would rely on the power of God to change people's hearts. Although Cyprian knew all about Greek and Roman writings, he did not quote from them very much. For Cyprian, the Bible was the place to find God's truth for man.

CYPRIAN'S CONVERSION

The wind blows where it wishes, and you hear the sound of it, but cannot tell where it comes from and where it goes. So is everyone who is born of the Spirit. (John 3:8)

Although Cyprian was raised in a rich home and given a good education, he was still missing one thing. One day he discovered "the pearl of great price." His eyes were opened, and he trusted in Jesus Christ as his Lord and Savior. It happened while he was hearing about the Book of Jonah. A pastor in the early church in Carthage named Caecilius discipled the young man. This pastor became Cyprian's "parent in the faith." Caecilius and Cyprian became good friends. When Pastor Caecilius died, he entrusted the care of his family to Cyprian.

The story of Jonah made a big impression on the young man. The Lord saved Jonah when he was inside the big fish at the bottom of the sea. This meant that the Lord could save Cyprian from sin and death too. This story reminds us that the Word of God is "living and active" (Heb. 4:12). It works in us and changes us. And faith comes by hearing the Word of God (Rom. 10:17). As time went by, Cyprian began to see the emptiness of his worldly life. He left behind much of his wealth. He got rid of his purple robes which marked him as a rich person. Then he gave away much of his wealth to the poor. He turned away from his old pagan beliefs and followed Jesus.

Cyprian gave all praise to God for his new life. He knew that this life in Christ could only come by the Holy Spirit of God. He wrote to his friend Donatus, "All our power is of God; I say, of God. From Him we have life, from Him we have strength." The Spirit produced in Cyprian new desires for holy things. He no longer loved the things of the world. He loved God.

Cyprian was well known in the community of Carthage because of his family ties and wealth. But when he became a Christian, he wasn't interested in becoming big and famous in the church. He spent his time reading the Bible, meditating on the Word, fasting, and praying.

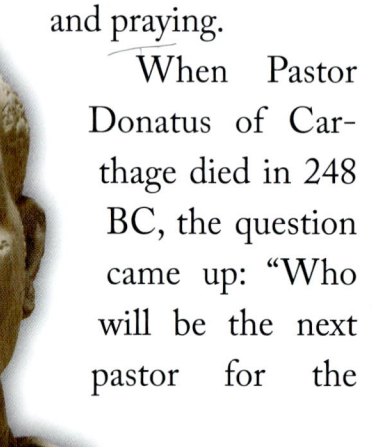

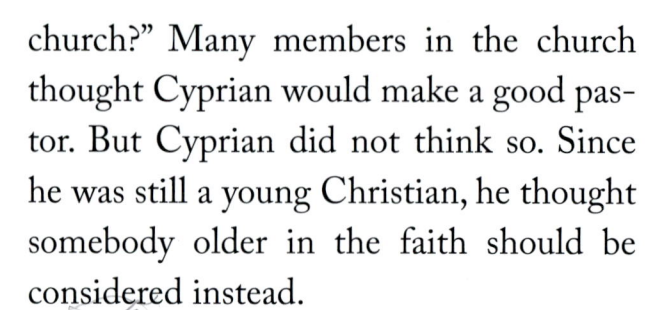

When Pastor Donatus of Carthage died in 248 BC, the question came up: "Who will be the next pastor for the church?" Many members in the church thought Cyprian would make a good pastor. But Cyprian did not think so. Since he was still a young Christian, he thought somebody older in the faith should be considered instead.

But the community of believers loved this man so much that they quickly elected Cyprian as their pastor. He had been a believer for only two years. It would not be long before this young pastor would face very difficult trials. God would send a big test of faith to him and his fellow believers in Africa.

PERSECUTION DURING THE REIGN OF EMPEROR DECIUS

Do not fear any of those things which you are about to suffer. Indeed, the devil is about to throw some of you into prison, that you may be tested, and you will have tribulation ten days. Be faithful until death, and I will give you the crown of life. (Revelation 2:10)

Carthage was under the control of the Roman Empire. This was the case with all the lands around the Mediterranean Sea at this time. In AD 249, Emperor Decius took the throne after the reign of Philip the Arab. The Emperor Philip had treated Christians kindly, probably because he was raised in a Christian area just east of the sea of Galilee in Palestine. However, Decius was not at all kind to Christians.

Rome had just celebrated its thou-

BUST OF THE EMPEROR DECIUS

sand-year birthday in the year AD 248 when Decius took the throne. It was a big year for the empire. The Romans held many games in the coliseums where thousands of gladiators were killed. People watched these horrible events with a wicked excitement. Since this was the thousand-year birthday for Rome, the celebrations were more violent and wicked than ever. Over a thousand gladiators died in the celebration of 248.

Yet Rome was not doing well. God was not blessing this wicked nation. The farms and businesses were losing money. Emperor Decius thought he had lost the favor of the false gods. He blamed the Christians for it, because he did not believe in the true and living God. Decius wanted to regain the favor of his false gods. Therefore he made a law to try to force everybody to sacrifice to these gods. If anybody refused to make the sacrifices, that person would be put to death. Everyone who did make the sacrifice would receive a certificate. Anyone who did not have a certificate could get in trouble with the Roman authorities. This trouble could result in death.

This presented a problem for Christians. Would they sacrifice to the false gods of Rome and break God's commandments? Of course not. They would have to break the king's law. They had to obey God rather than man. Peter and the other apostles faced the same problem in Jerusalem 200 years earlier.

Then the captain went with the officers and brought them without violence, for they feared the people, lest they should be stoned. And when they had brought them, they set them before the council. And the high priest asked them, saying, "Did we not strictly command you not to teach in this name? And look, you have filled Jerusalem with your doctrine, and intend to bring this Man's blood on us!" But Peter and the other apostles answered and said: "We ought to obey God rather than men." (Acts 5:26-29)

Cyprian and his fellow Christians in Carthage refused to obey Emperor Decius' orders. Many Christians in Carthage and throughout the Roman Empire were killed. They bravely committed themselves to obey Christ and only worship the one true God.

About this time, Cyprian decided to go into hiding. Some called him a coward. But he thought it would be better to guide the church by writing letters from his place of hiding than by being killed.

After eighteen months of persecution, God brought Decius' life to an end. The emperor died in battle. This also ended the persecutions against Christians. During the persecution, the church in Carthage and everywhere else had been damaged. Many Christians had been killed. Others were scarred from having been tortured. Some had left the church and denied Jesus. Under heavy pressure, they gave in and sacrificed to the false gods. These were hard times for the church. Such times required wise shepherds to guide the flock of God to green pastures. Pastor Cyprian returned from hiding. He began to minister again to a wounded and divided church. As pastor, it was his job to mend the wounds and encourage unity.

Some believers who offered sacrifice and rejected the faith wanted to return to the church after the persecution. This was hard for families who had lost fathers, mothers, brothers, and sisters through martyrdom. How could they sit in church with those who had given in to Caesar and offered sacrifice? Cyprian wanted to be patient with those who had fallen down. He would wait to see if they felt bad about their sin. If they truly repented, he would restore them back into the church. With Jesus, there is always forgiveness of sins for those who repent. Even if they denied Christ (just like Peter did), they could be forgiven. There was still time to repent of that sin and find mercy in Christ.

Just as the Lord Jesus had restored Peter, Cyprian wanted to offer forgiveness for those who had denied Christ in Carthage. As it turned out, many did repent of their sin and returned to the church. Cyprian's patient work with the church after the persecution was a good model for other situations like this.

PLAGUE COMES TO CARTHAGE

**He has shown you, O man, what is good;
And what does the Lord require of you
But to do justly, to love mercy,
And to walk humbly with your God? (Micah 6:8)**

The persecution had ended. But more suffering was ahead for the church at Carthage. God sent a major plague across the whole Roman Empire. The sickness was so bad in Rome that 5,000 people were dying every day. It was a tough judgment on Rome. But it was also a trial for the church at Carthage. Cyprian took this as the right time to preach the gospel. When people are close to death, they are often more open to hearing the good news of Christ and His heaven.

Cyprian and the church at Carthage worked hard providing medical care, food, and clothing to those in need. Cyprian used much of his own money to help the needy. Many unbelievers left the city to preserve their own lives. Yet the Christians stayed to show mercy to the sick. Cyprian urged his fellow brothers and sisters not to

COINAGE DEPICTING THE EMPEROR VALERIAN

fear death. He told them that the Christian still wins in death, and he will go to be with the Lord.

Cyprian's leadership through the plague was a great example of mercy. The brothers and sisters in the church acted out the part of the Good Samaritan in Jesus's parable. They were willing to help those suffering from the plague—even though it could have cost them their own lives.

Then Jesus answered and said: "A certain man went down from Jerusalem to Jericho, and fell among thieves, who stripped him of his clothing, wounded him, and departed, leaving him half dead. Now by chance a certain priest came down that road. And when he saw him, he passed by on the other side. Likewise a Levite, when he arrived at the place, came and looked, and passed by on the other side. But a certain Samaritan, as he journeyed, came where he was. And when he saw him, he had compassion. So he went to him and bandaged his wounds, pouring on oil and wine; and he set him on his own animal, brought him to an inn, and took care of him. On the next day, when he departed, he took out two denarii, gave them to the innkeeper, and said to him, 'Take care of him; and whatever more you spend, when I come again, I will repay you.' So which of these three do you think was neighbor to him who fell among the thieves?" And he said, "He who showed mercy on him." Then Jesus said to him, "Go and do likewise." (Luke 10:30-37)

CYPRIAN'S MARTYRDOM

Beloved, do not think it strange concerning the fiery trial which is to try you, as though some strange thing happened to you; but rejoice to the extent that you partake of Christ's sufferings, that when His glory is revealed, you may also be glad with exceeding joy. (1 Peter 4:12-13)

Two years after Decius' death, the Emperor Valerian (253-260) came to power. This king followed in the footsteps of the wicked Decius. Valerian also thought the problems in the Roman Empire were due to false gods who were upset with Rome. Once more, Valerian commanded Christians to offer sacrifice to the gods. He told them they could worship Jesus Christ as long as they sacrificed to the false gods as well. This time, Pastor Cyprian decided to remain in Carthage. He would continue pastoring his church to the end. When he refused to sacrifice to the false gods, he was arrested.

Cyprian was put on trial before the proconsul Galerius Maximus of Carthage. The Roman official asked the courageous pastor if he would make the required sacrifices. Cyprian simply replied, "I will not do it." He was then sentenced to death. Cyprian requested that he be allowed to die alongside his fellow Christians. His wish was not granted. The Romans wanted to make an example of him for anybody else who refused to obey the emperor's edict.

On September 14, 258, Cyprian left his earthly tent behind and went to be with Christ. He remained faithful unto death as a shepherd of God's flock.

STATUTE OF ATHANASIUS

Athanasius of Alexandria

The land of Egypt played an important role in the early church in North Africa. Many famous church leaders were from the city of Alexandria. Alexander the Great founded the city in 331 BC. For the next 300 years, it remained the capital of the Greek Ptolemaic kingdom. Then, in 30 BC, Rome took control of Egypt.

Alexandria became a major center of learning and business. It was the second largest city of the Roman Empire. Ships carried grain and other goods from its busy harbor throughout the empire. It housed the Library of Alexandria. This was the largest and most important library of the ancient world. The city was a center of Greek philosophy. It was also home to a large Jewish community.

In the 1st century AD, John Mark, the author of the Gospel of Mark, preached the gospel in Egypt and founded the church there. The church in Egypt grew rapidly, and Alexandria became an important center of Christianity. By the early 4th century, the majority of Egyptians were Christians.

In 303, Emperor Diocletian started a major persecution of Christians. Christians were required to sacrifice to Caesar. Those who refused to do so suffered terribly. They were imprisoned, tortured, and killed. Churches were destroyed and copies of the Scriptures were burned. The persecution hit Egypt especially hard. But, in 312, the Emperor Constantine converted to Christianity. He ended the persecution of Christians the next year.

THE EARLY LIFE OF ATHANASIUS

Athanasius (pronounced "ath-uh-ney-shuh-s") was born in Egypt about AD 298. We know little about his family. They

LOCATION OF ALEXANDRIA, EGYPT

EGYPT

EMPEROR DIOCLETIAN

were probably native Egyptians. During the terrible persecution of Diocletian, Athanasius was just a boy. What he saw must have affected him deeply.

At this time, the bishop of Alexandria was the chief pastor and leader of the church in Egypt. During the persecution, Bishop Peter was martyred for the faith. Alexander succeeded Peter as bishop.

One day, Alexander looked out his window and saw some boys playing on the beach. These boys were pretending to hold a church service. One of the boys was leading the service and baptizing the others. Alexander feared the boys might be treating baptism as a game, so he called them and asked them questions. By their answers, he realized that the boy who had been leading the play understood the truth about baptism. Alexander saw the potential in this young man. He decided to take him under his wing and mentor him. The young man was Athanasius. Alexander discipled Athanasius in the faith as his spiritual son. He taught him the Bible and prepared him to be a leader in the church. Around 319, Athanasius became a deacon.

> **And the things that you have heard from me among many witnesses, commit these to faithful men who will be able to teach others also. (2 Timothy 2:2)**

Until Alexander's death, Athanasius served as an assistant to the bishop. Under Alexander's teaching, Athanasius was prepared for future ministry. Soon Athanasius would be called to lead the church in Alexandria through hard times.

THE ARIAN CONTROVERSY

> **Now I urge you, brethren, note those who cause divisions and offenses, contrary to the doctrine which you learned, and avoid them. For those who are such do not serve our Lord Jesus Christ, but their own belly, and by smooth words and flattering speech deceive the hearts of the simple. (Romans 6:17-18)**

While Alexander was bishop in Alexandria, a presbyter named Arius began teaching a false doctrine. This unbiblical teaching would soon divide a large part of the church. Arius declared that Jesus must have had a beginning since He is the Son of God. He did not believe that the Son

ILLUSTRATION OF THE COUNCIL OF NICAEA (325)

of God had existed eternally with the Father. This meant that Jesus the Son was not equal with the Father in His divine nature. In Arius' view, Jesus was actually a creature, not God. Arius could not understand how Jesus could both be equal with the Father and yet be the Son of God. Arius believed the Bible taught that Jesus had a beginning. But other Christians ably showed that the Bible teaches that the Son of God is not created. The Son of God is eternal. All things were created through Him (Col. 1:16).

Arius' teaching contradicts the teaching of the Bible. The Word of God teaches that Jesus is equal in nature to the Father. The Bible also teaches that there are three persons in the Godhead: the Father, the Son, and the Holy Spirit. The three persons of the Godhead have different roles in the work of salvation. But they are equal in nature. All three persons of the Godhead are equally God.

The following Bible verses clearly teach that the Son of God has existed eternally with the Father. They teach that Jesus is God just as the Father is God.

In the beginning was the Word, and the Word was with God, and the Word was God. He was in the beginning with God. (John 1:1-2)

> **And now, O Father, glorify Me together with Yourself, with the glory which I had with You before the world was. (John 17:5)**
>
> **. . . of whom are the fathers and from whom, according to the flesh, Christ came, who is over all, the eternally blessed God. Amen. (Romans 9:5)**
>
> **. . . looking for the blessed hope and glorious appearing of our great God and Savior Jesus Christ. (Titus 2:13)**

Alexander and Athanasius did not agree with Arius' teaching about Jesus Christ. Alexander asked Arius and his followers to leave the church in Alexandria. Their false doctrine was creating division. Arius refused. He kept teaching throughout Egypt. His teachings were even made into songs. People in the streets of Egypt debated this theological issue. The debate even spread to other parts of the empire. This was a very important point in history. Since Jesus Christ is our Lord and Savior, it is important that we know who He is. If Jesus is not God, then He cannot be worshiped. If Jesus is not both God and man, then He cannot save us from our sins.

The controversy continued to grow throughout the empire. Eventually, Emperor Constantine heard about the disagreements in Alexandria. He wrote a letter to the church in Egypt. His letter called for peace. But the controversy only grew worse. In order to restore peace to the empire, Constantine called for a church council. This council gathered in the year AD 325 in the town of Nicaea (in modern-day Turkey). Hundreds of church leaders gathered to discuss the matter. The council met from May to August 325.

At the council, leaders of the church debated the meaning of biblical passages. Arius argued for his position. Eusebius, bishop of Nicomedia, was also one of his supporters at the council. Others argued for the view that Jesus is equal in nature with the Father as God. Some disagreed with both positions and wanted to hold a middle ground. Eventually the council determined that the teaching of the Scriptures is that Jesus is equal in nature with the Father. The council then drafted the "Nicene Definition." This document is also known as the Nicene Creed.

Arius and his followers were exiled because they did not accept this definition. Even though the council set forth a definition that was biblical, this did not bring peace to the church. Bishop Alexander died in 328. At this time, the Arians and those who held to the Nicene definition continued to argue. When Alexander died, Athanasius seemed to be an obvious choice to serve as a replacement. But the Arians didn't want Athanasius to become bishop. They fought against his election and ordination. But, in June 328, Athanasius become bishop in Alexandria. He would serve as bishop in Alexandria for forty-six years. However, he would be exiled from Alexandria repeatedly. Athanasius was unwilling to give up the Nicene definition of Christ's nature. He knew that much was stake in understanding who Jesus Christ is. For this reason, he would never compromise what the Bible taught about Jesus.

FIRST EXILE FROM ALEXANDRIA

Emperor Constantine had banished Arius and many of his followers from their posts in the church. But later Constantine relented and allowed Arius to return to Alexandria. In 330, Arius and some of his followers entered the city. Because Athanasius saw Arius' teaching as heretical and dangerous, he refused to allow Arius to enter the church. Athanasius wrote to Constantine telling him about his decision to refuse Arius. Constantine was not happy about Athanasius' decision. Constantine threatened Athanasius with exile if Athanasius did not obey his orders. It is important to remember that the authority of the church and the authority of the state are separate. Rulers in the state cannot tell the church what to do. Church leaders cannot force the state to change its laws. The church is under its only head, Jesus Christ. Our Lord is the head of the church. Pastors in the church must obey the Lord and protect the peace and unity of the church. For this reason, Athanasius would not submit to Constantine's orders. He refused to allow Arius into the church.

The Arians wanted to see Athanasius gone. Various plans were soon hatched in order to get rid of Athanasius. Slander and false accusations were brought against the bishop. Some of the charges were quite silly or ridiculous. Some accusations were very serious. At one time, Athanasius was even accused of murdering a bishop named Arsenius. It was rumored that Athanasius murdered Arsenius, cut off his hand, and used it for magical purposes. Athanasius' accusers even found a hand they used as "proof." But, in reality, Arsenius was alive and in hiding. Athanasius began a search for Arsenius so he could answer these charges. Constantine called for a meeting in the port-city of Tyre to hear these charges. In God's providence, Arsenius was hiding in Tyre at this time. He was eventually discovered.

Arsenius was brought before the council with Athanasius present. His identity was revealed by some people who knew him. When Athanasius was accused of cutting off one of his hands, Athanasius proved that he was innocent by showing them Arsenius' two hands. The charges against Athanasius were proved false. Athanasius was declared "not guilty."

But the false accusations against Athanasius continued. He was soon accused of stopping the corn shipments from Alexandria to Constantinople. (Alexandria was a port-city that supplied much food to Constantinople.) This accusation was also a lie. Once Constantine heard about it, however, he ordered Athanasius into exile. By order of the emperor, he was sent to Treves in February 335. (Treves was located in modern-day Germany.)

THE NILE RIVER

For the next two years, Athanasius lived in Treves. Though he was in exile, he was still the bishop of Alexandria. He continued to write letters to the church and shepherd them from a distance. Each year, Athanasius would write a "festal letter" on Easter. In these letters, he would instruct the congregation on matters of Christian faith and practice.

While Athanasius was living in Treves, Arius died of sickness. Some believed Arius' death was an act of divine judgment. Even though Arius was dead, his teaching continued to divide the church. Another death also occurred while Athanasius was in exile. Emperor Constantine died on May 22, 337. The empire was divided among his sons Constantine II, Constantius, and Constans. The Arian doctrine even divided Constantine's sons. Constantine II held to the Nicene view of Christ. He allowed Athanasius to return to Alexandria in AD 337. The people of Alexandria received their beloved pastor back with great joy and celebration. But the Arians did not want to see Athanasius return. The city and much of the empire was still bitterly divided over the Arian controversy.

SECOND EXILE FROM ALEXANDRIA

Even though Constantine II was favorable to Athanasius, Constantius was in control of the region in which Alexandria was located. The enemies of Athanasius convinced Constantius that Athanasius was a troublemaker. They blamed the local violence and division on the bishop. Constantius decided to send a new bishop to Alexandria. This man hoped to take over the church by force. Gregory, a man who held Arian views, was sent to the city. A host of troops were sent with him. In order to save his life, Athanasius fled to Rome. From AD 340-346, he lived in Rome, teaching and preaching. In Rome, Athanasius was well-received by the Christians. The bishop of Rome, Julius I, also agreed with the Nicene Creed.

Constantine II died in AD 430. His brother Constans then took control of the Western portion of the empire. He threatened war against Constantius if he would not allow Athanasius to return to Alexandria. In order to avoid conflict, Constantius agreed to allow Athanasius to return. The bishop was once again welcomed back to Alexandria in 346. The people of Alexandria celebrated his return. They even came to meet him a hundred miles outside of the city. For the next few years, Athanasius enjoyed a time of peace while serving the church.

But the challenges were not over. In 350, Constans died. This made Constantius the only emperor of the empire. Constantius was always hostile to Athanasius. He forced many church leaders in the western part of the empire to reject the Nicene Creed. Anyone who would not submit to his authority was banished or imprisoned. Many leaders refused. They suffered for their decision, but they remained faithful to the truth. Athanasius also refused to submit to this decree. He would not give up the truth in order to protect himself.

In February 356, Constantius sent soldiers to the church to arrest Athanasius. Thousands of soldiers surrounded the church as Athanasius led an evening service. The people were frightened. But Athanasius led the people in reading Psalm 136. Together they recited the repeated phrase "For His mercy endures forever." Once the soldiers broke into the church, Athanasius' friends smuggled him out of the church. He later escaped into the desert.

THIRD AND FOURTH EXILE FROM ALEXANDRIA

Athanasius was no stranger to trials and persecutions. Even though he suffered much, he knew that God would remain faithful. He was convinced by the Word of God that "nothing can separate us from the love of Christ" (Rom. 8:35-39). From 356 to 362, Athanasius lived in the desert of Egypt with other Christians. We believe that during this time he wrote many important books. Athanasius' writings are still read by some Christians today. His book *On the Incarnation of the Word* explained why it was necessary for Jesus the Son of God to become man. The Son of God became man in order to save us through His sacrificial death and resurrection. Athanasius also wrote a book on the Holy Spirit. In this book, he argued that the Holy Spirit was also equal in nature with the Father. Athanasius helped Christians to better understand the biblical doctrine of the Trinity.

In the year 360, Constantius died. He was succeeded by the Emperor Julian (360-363). Julian was the nephew of Constantius. The Christian church eventually called Julian "the apostate" because he rejected Christianity. He became a promoter of the old Roman gods. He didn't set out to destroy the church. But he did persecute Christians in some ways. He did not want to see the church's influence grow. Athanasius returned to Alexandria in 362. Once he returned to the church, he resumed his preaching ministry. Influential citizens in the city began to convert to Christianity. This angered Julian and he ordered Athanasius to leave. Soldiers were sent to find the bold pastor.

Thus began Athanasius' fourth exile from his beloved home. He once again fled to the desert of Egypt for refuge. Soldiers roamed through Egypt trying to find Athanasius. But he was able to escape. One day he was traveling in a boat down the Nile with his companions. Roman soldiers in another boat called out to Athanasius, "Have you seen Athanasius?" Athanasius replied, "He is not far from here." This was true. Athanasius was right in front of them. But the soldiers didn't know what Athanasius looked like. They continued on without capturing the bishop.

Once again, Athanasius was protected by the Lord. Soon Julian's reign came to an end. In 363, while Julian was fighting the Persians, he died in battle. Jovian, the next emperor (363-364), was a Christian. He was favorable towards Athanasius. But Jovian only reigned for eight months before he died. The empire was then divided. Valentinian ruled in the West and Valens ruled in the East. Since Alexandria was in the eastern part of the empire, Valens ruled it. Valens was an Arian and did not agree with Athanasius. He affirmed Constantius' decision to expel any bishops who did not agree with Arianism. For a time, Athanasius went back into hiding. But soon Valens became busy with other matters. Athanasius was able to continue his work as bishop.

FINAL YEARS

Athanasius' last years were spent in peace in Alexandria. He returned to the city in 364 and served the church until his death on May 2, 373. Athanasius pastored the church and wrote commentaries on Scripture and letters to the church. One of his most important letters was his festal letter written in 367. This letter is known as "Festal Letter 39." The reason this is an important letter is because Athanasius lists the books of the New Testament canon within it. The list of books in the letter is the same twenty-seven books of the New Testament we have today. The church did not create the canon. Instead the church recognized the books inspired by God that make up the canon. Athanasius' letter is an important early witness to the New Testament canon.

After Athanasius' death, the church still struggled with the Arian controversy. But, in 381, a council in Constantinople reaffirmed the teaching of the Council of Nicaea. This council also affirmed that the Holy Spirit was equal with the Father as God. This helped to bring greater unity around the truth. The church now saw that the Father, Son, and Holy Spirit are the three persons in the Godhead.

What lessons can we learn from Athanasius' life?

First, we must stand for God's truth no matter what the cost. Athanasius would not deny the teaching of the Bible. For a time, it seemed that everyone was out to stop him. But that didn't stop Athanasius. He went into exile many times because he would not bow to the demands of the emperors. He fought for the truth that Jesus is both God and man. We also should not be afraid to stand for the teaching of Scripture, even when it is unpopular.

Second, biblical doctrine is important. The Christian faith is based on the teaching of the Bible. We must know the truth and believe it in order to be saved. False doctrines that pervert the gospel can bring eternal ruin to those who adopt them. Therefore it is important to study your Bible and know the true doctrines of the Word. The truth sets us free (John 8:32). ■

> **Beloved, while I was very diligent to write to you concerning our common salvation, I found it necessary to write to you exhorting you to contend earnestly for the faith which was once for all delivered to the saints. (Jude 3)**

BASIC FACTS ABOUT ARAB REPUBLIC OF EGYPT

Total Population:	94 million
Total Area:	390,121 square miles
Capital:	Cairo
Official Languages:	Arabic
Primary Religion:	Islam, Christian minority

TAKING AFRICA FOR JESUS

THE WESTERN ROMAN EMPIRE (AD 395)

THE EASTERN ROMAN/BYZANTINE EMPIRE

9. ATHANASIUS OF ALEXANDRIA 95

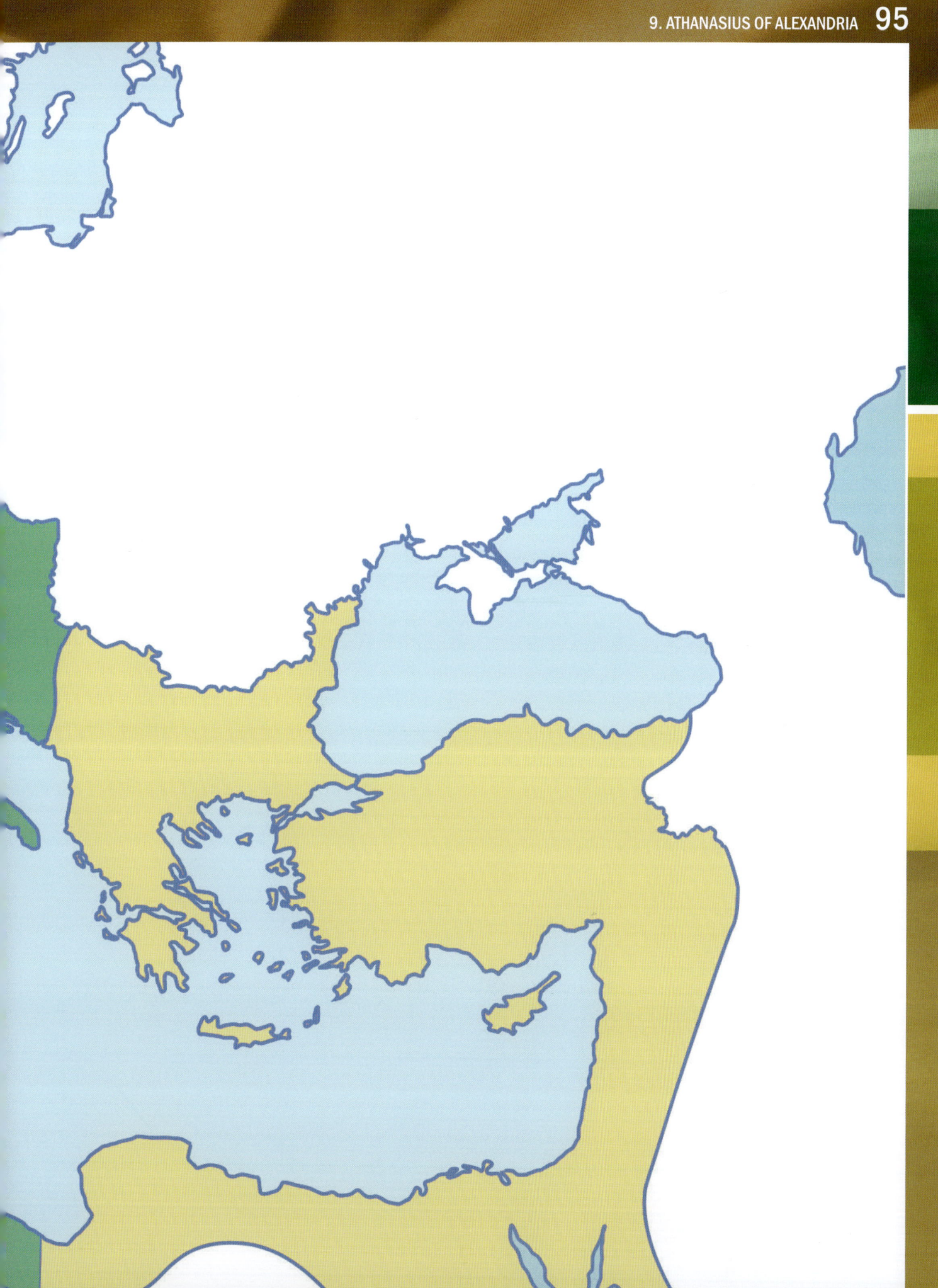

COLUMNS IN HIPPO

Augustine of Hippo

This is a faithful saying and worthy of all acceptance, that Christ Jesus came into the world to save sinners, of whom I am chief. However, for this reason I obtained mercy, that in me first Jesus Christ might show all longsuffering, as a pattern to those who are going to believe on Him for everlasting life. (1 Timothy 1:15-16)

The Bible says in Psalm 111: "The works of the LORD are great, studied by all who have pleasure in them" (Psalm 111:2). We can learn about God's great works by studying history. Sadly, the history of the early church in North Africa is often forgotten. But, since Christians should take pleasure in knowing God's works, we should study this important period.

The early church in North Africa left a legacy of faith for future generations. When we talk about the early church, we usually refer to the first five centuries after the ascension of our Lord Jesus Christ (AD 33-500). Many pastors, theologians, missionaries, and everyday Christians in North Africa served Christ faithfully during this time. One of these men whom the Lord gave to His church was named Augustine. He lived from AD 354 to 430. Most of his life was spent in North Africa. But he also lived in Milan (in modern-day Italy).

EARLY LIFE IN THAGASTE

Do not be deceived: "Evil company corrupts good habits." (1 Corinthians 15:33)

Augustine was born in the small village of Thagaste. This little village is now part of the country of Algeria. Thagaste was located about 60 miles south of the Mediterranean coast. Augustine's father was a man named Patrick. His mother's name was Monica. Monica was a believer, but Patrick was not. Monica would frequently pray for Augustine and exhort him to believe in the

AUGUSTINE AND HIS MOTHER MONICA

97

LOCATION OF THAGASTE IN ALGERIA

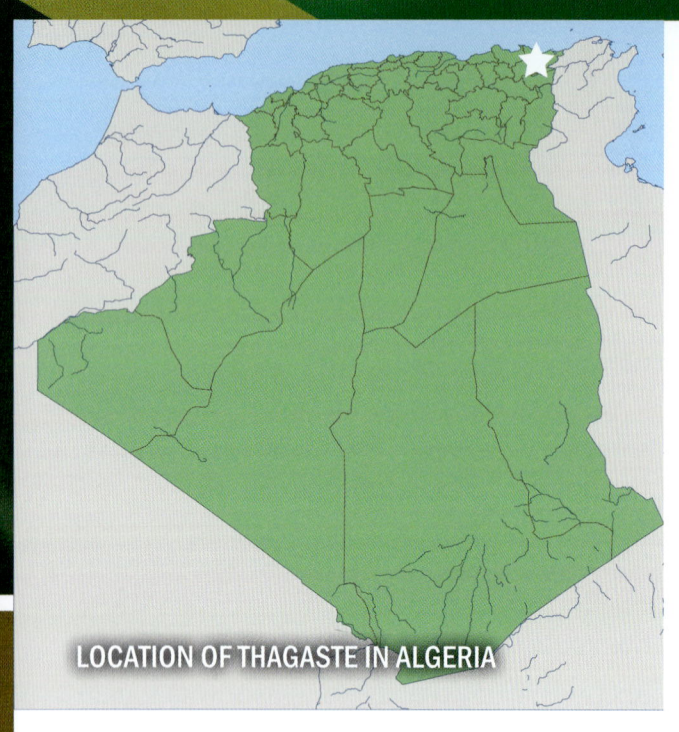

Lord Jesus. But pagan Patrick had worldly ambitions for his son. He wanted Augustine to be rich and successful. Patrick did not raise Augustine in the fear and admonition of the Lord. But the Lord is merciful. And, in the years that followed, the Lord showed mercy to Augustine. The Lord would save Augustine.

The small village of Thagaste was located in the ancient Roman province of Numidia. Augustine came from the people group known as the Berbers. Since the Romans conquered the region, Latin became the dominant language. Augustine grew up speaking Latin. But, since he was a native of Africa, he probably spoke the Punic language as well. Augustine spent his childhood in Thagaste. In his autobiography, *The Confessions*, Augustine says his years at school were very difficult. Schoolmasters were very harsh. They punished wrong answers with harsh floggings. He had to learn his lessons under these conditions.

In school, Augustine learned to read the Greek and Roman classics. He also learned logic. But the most important subject in his school was oratory. Oratory is the subject that teaches how to speak persuasively. It is also known as *rhetoric*. Later, Augustine would become a teacher of oratory or rhetoric himself.

When Augustine was sixteen, his father Patrick died of sickness. About this time, Augustine became very rebellious. He fell into bad company with friends from school. These young boys frequently broke God's commandments. Augustine enjoyed his life of sin. Because he didn't love God, he loved to please himself. When he later became a Christian, he deeply regretted his past sins.

Once Augustine and his friends stole pears from someone's orchard. They didn't steal the pears because they were hungry. They stole the pears because it was fun to steal. Augustine had a wicked heart. He needed God's grace to save him from his love of sin. He needed a new heart.

After his father's death, Augustine moved to Carthage to continue his school studies. There he indulged in more sin. Augustine learned the truth of Jesus' words: "whoever commits sin is a slave of sin" (John 8:34). He broke God's commandment to be pure with his body. He moved in with a young woman at age 17, but he did not marry her. Together, Augustine and the woman had a son named Adeodatus (which means "God's gift"). While he lived in Carthage, Augustine sometimes attended church services. But he didn't go to hear the preaching of God's Word. Instead, he was more interested in seeing the young women at church.

THE MANICHEE CULT

Beloved, do not believe every spirit, but test the spirits, whether they are of God; because many false prophets have gone out into the world. (1 John 4:1)

While Augustine lived in Carthage, he joined a cult called the Manichees or Manicheans. The name of the group came from its founder Mani. This man did not believe God's Word. Instead, he took ideas from many different religions, including Christianity and Buddhism. Mani mixed the ideas of these religions together to create his own religion. Mani used part of the New Testament for his false ideas. But he completely rejected the Old Testament.

Though he claimed to be an apostle of Jesus Christ, Mani was a false teacher. He taught his followers that God and evil both existed eternally. Since the beginning, God has been at war with evil. In this battle Mani taught that God had lost parts of himself to the powers of darkness. These fragments of God are now imprisoned in the bodies of men and animals. By following Mani's teachings, the "divine light" in men could be set free. Mani taught that God is a spiritual being and evil is physical matter. This meant that all physical things were evil. Physical things imprisoned God's nature.

Mani's teachings were not biblical. The Bible teaches that God created all things "very good" (Gen. 1:31). The Bible also teaches that God is not contained in His creation. God is above His creation.

But will God indeed dwell with men on the earth? Behold, heaven and the heaven of heavens cannot contain You. How much less this temple which I have built! (2 Chronicles 6:18)

Mani required strict obedience to his teachings. His followers were divided into two groups. The first group were the

MOSAIC OF AMBROSE OF MILAN

"Elect." This group of Manichees were not allowed to eat meat and could not marry. The second group were the "Hearers." This second group was allowed to marry, but they were forbidden to have children. Having children meant more of God's divine spirit would be imprisoned in bodies. This was a bad thing. Therefore, children were forbidden. But the Bible teaches that marriage, children, and food are blessings from God.

Augustine became a "hearer" in the cult for ten years. Augustine's mother Monica was heartbroken. As a Christian, Monica desperately wanted her son to walk with the Lord. She often wept as she prayed for her son. A godly pastor once encouraged Monica about this. He told her that "a son of so many prayers cannot be lost." After ten years of being a "hearer" in the Manichee cult, Augustine left the group. He couldn't find answers to life's hardest questions there. The Manichee cult did not possess the truth.

CONVERSION TO CHRIST

And the grace of our Lord was exceedingly abundant, with faith and love which are in Christ Jesus. (1 Timothy 1:14)

RUINS IN OSTIA

After Augustine finished his education in Carthage, he moved to Milan (in modern-day Italy). In Milan, he became a teacher of rhetoric. This move occurred in AD 384. Augustine was still not a Christian. But, in God's providence, there was a pastor in Milan named Ambrose. This pastor was well known for his powerful preaching. Since Augustine liked good rhetoric, he decided to visit the church to hear Ambrose. At first, he didn't believe the words Ambrose spoke. But he was impressed with Ambrose's speaking abilities. Eventually Augustine began to receive the message Ambrose preached. Ambrose's sermons addressed his objections to the Christian faith.

While living in Milan, Augustine separated from the woman he had lived with for many years. Augustine should have married her. But he was dealing with the pressures of Roman law. According to Roman law, people in different classes could not legally marry. The woman was born a servant. Augustine was born in a higher class. Therefore the law did not allow them to marry.

Augustine had a long, hard struggle with sin. In some ways, he wanted to part with his sins. He sometimes prayed to the Lord to set him free. But he still loved his sin. He didn't want to turn away from his sins. But one day everything changed. One day, Augustine and his friend Alypius spent the day with a man named Ponticianus. This man was a Christian working in the palace at Milan. While visiting together, Ponticianus shared a story about St. Anthony, a Christian monk who gave up his wealth to serve God. The story gripped Augustine and Alypius. They were astounded by Anthony's devotion to serve God.

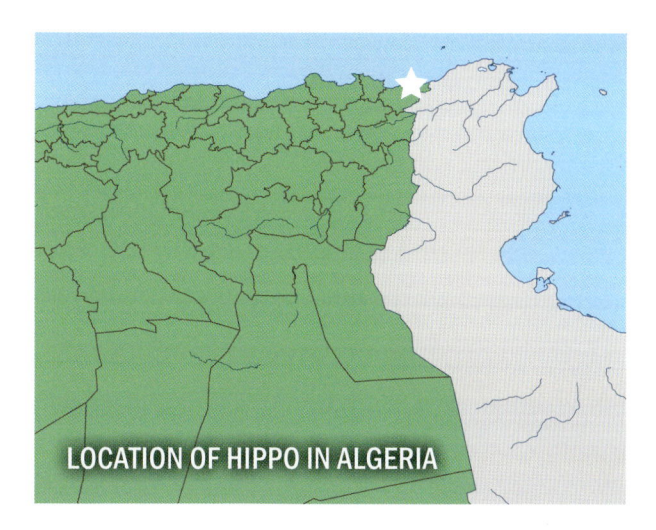

Augustine then went out to the garden to be alone. He wept over his sin. As he was crying, Augustine heard the voice of a boy or girl telling him to "take up and read, take up and read." Looking at the ground, Augustine found a book containing some of the letters of the Apostle Paul. Augustine held the book and opened it at random. The first words his eyes saw were from Romans 13:

Let us walk properly, as in the day, not in revelry and drunkenness, not in lewdness and lust, not in strife and envy. But put on the Lord Jesus Christ, and make no provision for the flesh, to fulfill its lusts. (Romans 13:13-14)

This was a word in season for Augustine. He says in his Confessions that he was

LOCATION OF HIPPO IN ALGERIA

converted by reading these verses from God's Word. The light of God's peace flooded Augustine's heart. He says that the "darkness of doubt was dispelled." This story teaches us that the Word of God is living and active, sharper than a two-edged sword (Heb. 4:12). Augustine went to his mother Monica and told her that he was now a follower of the Lord Jesus Christ. The many tear-filled prayers of Monica had been answered. Augustine was baptized by Ambrose in AD 387. The Lord mercifully saved Augustine from his sins.

RETURNING TO AFRICA

And they continued steadfastly in the apostles' doctrine and fellowship, in the breaking of bread, and in prayers. (Acts 2:42)

Now that he was a disciple of the Lord Jesus Christ, Augustine gave up his desire for power and success. At the time, he was a teacher of rhetoric in Milan. As a Christian, though, Augustine didn't want to use persuasive speech to lie or to be unjust. Many of his students used their skills in rhetoric to do just that. Augustine knew that his speech should be used to glorify God and to tell the truth. He decided to leave his post at Milan and return to Africa.

Augustine, with his mother Monica and a group of friends, began their journey back to Thagaste. But their plans were halted for a time. Civil war broke out in the summer of AD 387. This prevented Augustine from traveling back to Africa. He stayed in the seaside town of Ostia. While in Ostia, Monica became ill and died. She was 56 years old. Her work on earth was done. And she departed in peace, knowing that her prayers for Augustine had been answered.

For a time, Augustine stayed in Rome with his friends. Once the fighting died down, the sea-routes to Africa reopened. With his Christian friends, Augustine returned to his hometown of Thagaste. He arrived in August 388. From this date until his death, Augustine never left Africa again. He and his friends gathered as Christian laymen and devoted themselves to lives of meditation and prayer. They lived together in Augustine's home. Augustine did not call his group a "monastery." But the group lived together much like monks would in a monastery.

Augustine was not a pastor or a deacon in the church. But he became well-known in the Christian community in Thagaste and the nearby town of Hippo. One day, Augustine was invited by the bishop of Hippo to visit the church. In Numidia, the town of Hippo Regius was second in size to Carthage. This town was forty miles away from Thagaste. Hippo was a large town for its day.

The bishop (pastor) in Hippo was a man named Valerius. When Augustine arrived during the Sunday service, Valerius publicly welcomed Augustine. Valerius then informed the congregation that he needed an assistant in the ministry. Valerius and the congregation urged Augustine to become a presbyter (assistant pastor) in the church. Augustine was very reluctant. He did not think he was wise enough for such a high calling. But he accepted the call of the church. Augustine only asked that Valerius allow him to return to Thagaste to study and pray for a few months. Valerius gave Augustine permission for this time of preparation.

MINISTRY IN HIPPO

This is a faithful saying: If a man desires the position of a bishop, he desires a good work. (1 Timothy 3:1)

Augustine began his ministry in Hippo in AD 391. He lived near the church building and devoted time to prayer, Scripture study, and memorization with the other men in the monastery at Hippo. For six years, Augustine labored in the ministry alongside Bishop Valerius. However,

MODERN DAY MILAN, ITALY, WHERE AUGUSTINE BECAME A CHRISTIAN

in AD 397 Valerius went to be with the Lord. Augustine became the sole bishop of Hippo.

In Augustine's time, many Christian churches drew a distinction between a "pastor" and a "bishop." The office of bishop was above the office of "presbyter" or "elder" in the church. However, the Bible does not draw this distinction. It mentions two church offices: elder and deacon (Phil. 1:1).

Augustine served as bishop from the death of Valerius until his own death in AD 430. As a bishop, Augustine had special responsibilities in Hippo. Bishops were often called on to judge court cases. They were also expected to show hospitality to large groups of people. Some bishops lived in luxury. But Augustine did not fall into this temptation. He refused to accept bribes. He was committed to using any money he received for the poor. He did not keep money on the church property. Any extra money was immediately given away to those in need.

By the end of the 4th century, the church of Jesus Christ was making significant progress in its spread throughout North Africa. As the church grew, the culture of the Roman Empire also changed. In his lifetime, Augustine saw the pagan temples empty. During the reign of Emperor Theodosius I (392-395), pagan sacrifices were forbidden throughout the empire. However, this was not often enforced.

During his time as bishop, Augustine worked to see the people of Hippo converted to the faith. He became well-known throughout the region as a faithful preacher in the church. He also wrote many books. Many of his writings are still read by Christians today. His most popular book is *The Confessions*, in which he describes his past life. The book is written in the form of a prayer. Augustine confesses his past sins and tells how God was merciful to him. Augustine also wrote a book on how to interpret and teach the Bible. This book is called *On Christian Teaching*.

As pastor in Hippo, Augustine also helped in matters of justice. In a letter he wrote to his friend Alypius, Augustine urges freedom for a group of slaves. Augustine mentions slave traders who were kidnapping women and children in North Africa in order to sell them into slavery. Apparently, the church at Hippo stopped one shipment to Galatia and redeemed a boatload of slaves. Augustine explained:

> I myself asked one girl of a crowd which had been freed by our Church from this miserable captivity, how she came to be sold to the slave traders. She told me she had been seized from her parents' house . . . Some four months ago, there were people brought together from different places, but especially from Numidia, to be deported from the port of Hippo. This was done by Galatians, for it is only they who, out of greed, engage in such

business. A member of our church became aware of it, and knowing our policy of helping with money in such circumstances, wished to tell us. I was not in Hippo at that time. But immediately our faithful liberated one hundred and twenty people, some from the ship on which they were already embarked ... Here in Hippo at least, by the mercy of God, the church is on its guard, so that unfortunate people are rescued from this type of captivity.

In his letter, Augustine argued that every pastor is should speak about these social issues:

> **For if we, that is, the bishops, do nothing, will there then be anyone, who has power on the shore, who will not sell these most cruel cargoes, rather than remove one of these unfortunate people from captivity, or stop someone from being put in chains, out of Christian or human compassion?**

This is a beautiful example of how early Christians redeemed slaves. Where Christianity has operated throughout the ages, it has always worked toward this end.

In AD 410, the city of Rome fell to an invasion of barbarian tribes from northern Europe. Alaric and his Goths sacked the city on August 24, 410. Many Christians throughout the Empire were alarmed when Rome fell. Some, like Jerome, thought the end of the world was near. Others blamed the Christians for the fall of Rome.

To answer this charge, Augustine penned the largest book he ever wrote: *The City of God*. In this massive book, Augustine argued that the fall of Rome was God's judgment for the many sins of the Empire. Augustine also explained that two cities have existed since creation: the city of God and the city of man. The city of man is devoted to the glory and praise of man. But the city of God is devoted to the glory and praise of God.

Augustine also played an important role in a doctrinal dispute in the early church. This dispute was known as the Pelagian Controversy. A British monk named Pelagius taught that the human race did not fall with Adam when he ate the forbidden fruit. Pelagius argued that men are not born with sin. All people are born innocent, but they become sinners through imitating other sinners.

Augustine argued against Pelagius' teachings. He showed that Scripture teaches that all mankind fell into sin with Adam (Romans 5:12). Augustine taught that we are all born with a sinful nature (Psalm 51:5). He explained that only the grace of God can give us spiritual life. Only God can grant us faith to believe. It is only through His grace that any one of us can be saved (Ephesians 2:8-9). Augustine and Pelagius argued over the question "How is man saved?" Augustine affirmed what the Bible clearly teaches. We can't save ourselves. We are born sinners. And we need a redeemer who will save us from our sins. That is why Jesus came (Matthew 1:21).

The Bible teaches that God resists the proud but gives grace to the humble (1 Peter 5:5). Augustine showed that he was a humble man when he wrote a book called *Retractions*. He finished the book in AD 427, three years before his death. This book was a review of ninety-three of his own writings. Augustine defended some of his previous writings. But he also said that some of his past writings were wrong. He withdrew the statements he believed were in error. He wrote, "I think that by God's mercy I have made progress in my writing, but not at all that I have reached perfection." By publicly stating he was not perfect in his writings, Augustine left a good example of humility.

In the years that followed, the barbarian tribes continued to invade parts of the Roman Empire. By AD 430, the Vandals were besieging the city of Hippo. Inside the city, Augustine lay mortally ill. In his last months, Augustine asked his friends to hang copies of the seven penitential Psalms (psalms of confession) on his wall. These are Psalms 6, 32, 38, 51, 102, 130, and 143. Augustine spent his last days reading these beautiful psalms and praying over them. To his dying day, he knew that he was a sinner in need of God's grace.

Before he died, he instructed his brothers and sisters to preserve the library at the church in Hippo. Of course, this library included Augustine's own writings as well. Augustine died and entered the joy of his Master on August 28, 430. He was 75 years old. Shortly after his death, the Vandals captured Hippo and destroyed most of the city with fire. But, in the providence of God, the church and Augustine's library were not destroyed. Augustine's many writings were preserved for future generations.

Today, Christians can read Augustine's many works and benefit from his teaching. As Augustine himself confessed, he was not a perfect man. He was a sinner saved by grace, as all true Christians are. Let us learn from Augustine's example to walk humbly with our God. ∎

BEACH NEAR HIPPO, ALGERIA

CAVE OF HIRA, LOCATION OF MUHAMMAD'S FIRST REVELATION

The Rise of Islam

Beloved, do not believe every spirit, but test the spirits, whether they are of God; because many false prophets have gone out into the world. (1 John 4:1)

The rise of the religion known as Islam plays a big part in Africa's story. There are more Muslims living in America, Europe, and other nations now than ever. The influence of Islam on Europe during the Middle Ages was massive. Therefore Christians should know something about the origins and beliefs of Islam. Today, most of the people living in North Africa and the Middle East are Muslim. How did this happen? This chapter will help you understand the rise of Islam.

MUHAMMAD – AD 570-632

The story of Islam begins with its founder, Muhammad. This man was born in the city of Mecca around AD 570. Muhammad became a successful merchant and traveled widely in the regions of Arabia, Palestine, and Syria. Throughout his travels, he came in contact with both Jews and Christians. He learned about the Christian faith, but he did not use this knowledge for good. Muhammed would eventually reject the teaching of the Bible and would invent his own religion. This new religion would borrow a little from the Old and New Testaments but would not accept them as God's Word.

In AD 610, Muhammad claimed to receive a number of revelations from Allah. "Allah" is the Arabic word for "God." Muhammad said he received visions through the angel Gabriel. This was the same angel who had come to visit Joseph to announce the birth of the baby Jesus. However, what this "Gabriel" brought to Muhammed was very different from the truth revealed in the Bible.

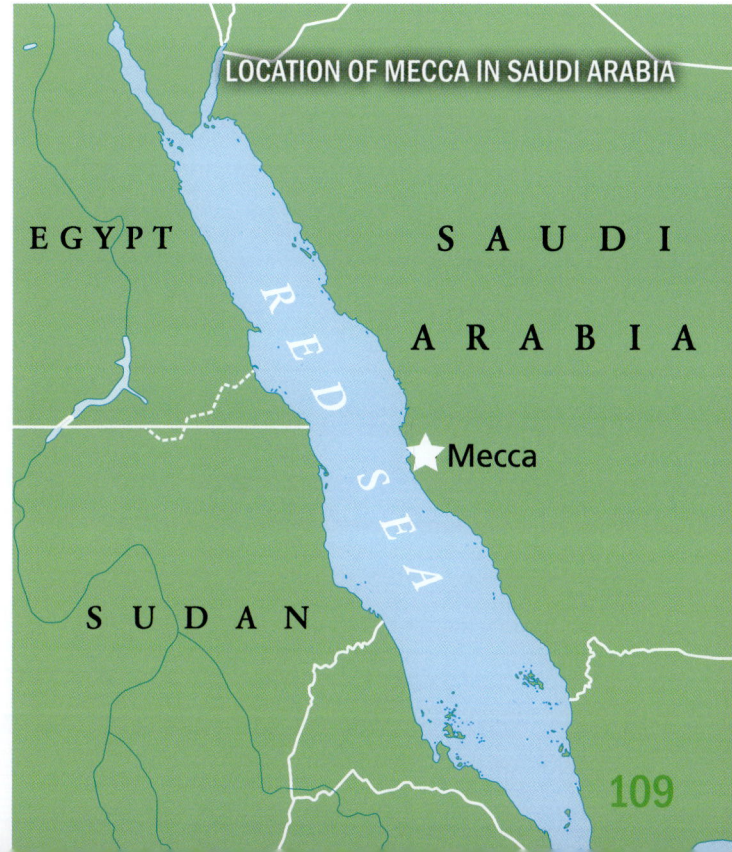

LOCATION OF MECCA IN SAUDI ARABIA

109

MUSLIMS WORSHIPPING AT THE KAABA ON PILGRIMAGE (HAJJ)

Muhammed's dreams were collected in a book called "the Quran." The Bible declares that Jesus, the Son of God, was the final prophet of God. But Muhammed now claimed that he was the final prophet. He said the Bible had been corrupted since the time of the prophets and apostles.

Cave of Hira, location of Muhammad's first revelation

Muhammed said there is one god, and his name was "Allah." For three years he shared his visions with family and immediate friends. Then, in 613, he began to preach his message in the town of Mecca. He was concerned with "impurity" and the idolatry of the people in his area. Mostly the people rejected his message, and some wanted to kill him. So he ran away to Medina in AD 622. This is where more people began to follow his teaching. His early converts to Islam were Abu Bakr (the first caliph of Islam) and his son-in-law Othman (the third caliph). "Caliph" is the Arabic word for "ruler."

THE BELIEFS OF ISLAM

The word "Islam" means "submission" or "to submit." The followers of Islam are called "Muslims." This religion does not believe that Jesus Christ is God. Muslims do not believe that the Holy Spirit is God. They believe that God is one, but they do not believe that there are three persons in the Trinity. Proud men will always turn away from doctrines they cannot fully understand.

Muslims mostly focus on the power of God. They do not teach the love of God, nor do they speak of loving God.

Muslims are required to do five basic things. They are called "the five pillars of Islam."

1. The *Shahadah* is the basic creed of Islam: "There is no God but Allah and Muhammad is his prophet."
2. The *Salah* is prayer required five times a day, facing Mecca.
3. The *Zakah* is giving to the poor.
4. *Sawm* is fasting from eating, which is required during the holy month of Ramadan.
5. *Hajj* is the pilgrimage to Mecca, to be made at least once in a lifetime.

This religion is mainly about telling people what to do. Muslims believe that these are the things you need to do in order to make God happy with you.

The Bible says that we are saved by grace through faith. Faith is a gift of God. This is the basic truth of the Bible. We must believe in Jesus Christ who saves us from sin by His death and resurrection. Jesus' death is the way that God is made happy with us. But Muslims try to save themselves. They try to make God happy with them by their prayers, fasting, and giving to the poor.

For by grace you have been saved through faith, and that not of yourselves; it is the gift of God, not of works, lest anyone should boast. For we are His workmanship, created in Christ Jesus for good works, which God prepared beforehand that we should walk in them. (Ephesians 2:8-10)

The false religion of Islam grew quickly in Arabia. By AD 700, it became the most popular religion in Arabia, Persia, and North Africa. There was also one more part of this religion—a 6th pillar. It was called jihad or "holy war." Muhammed taught his followers to spread the "bad news" of Islam by killing people. He wanted to force people into submission. Either the people of the world must become Muslims, or they must pay the Muslims a special tax. Remember, the word islam means "submission." This is the part of the Quran that talks about jihad:

But when the forbidden months are past, then fight and slay the Pagans wherever ye find them, and seize them, beleaguer them, and lie in wait for them in every stratagem (of war); but if they repent, and establish regular prayers and practice regular charity, then open the way for them: for Allah is Oft-forgiving, Most Merciful. (Surah 9:5)

Fight those who believe not in Allah nor the Last Day, nor hold that forbidden which hath been forbidden by Allah and His Apostle, nor acknowledge the religion of Truth, (even if they are) of the People of the Book, until they pay the Jizya [the tax] with willing submission, and feel themselves subdued. (Surah 9:29)

This fighting-and-killing religion was powerful. Over time, the Muslims took over a large part of the world. Today, Islam is very powerful in North Africa, the Middle East, Indonesia, and Malaysia.

THE CONQUEST OF NORTH AFRICA

Muhammad died in AD 632. Just eight years after his death, Muslims had taken over large portions of the Middle East, North Africa, Cyprus, and portions of Spain. By 636, Damascus had come under Muslim control.

Sadly, the Christian faith was not very strong in this area of the world. This is a lesson we have learned over many, many years. Wherever the Christian faith was weak, Muslims rushed in and took over. Muslims conquered Persia (modern-day Iran and Iraq) about the same time (AD 636). Two years later, Jerusalem was captured by Muslim armies. The caliph (ruler) Umar allowed the Christians to continue living in Jerusalem, but he would not allow the Jews to live there.

The first African land to be conquered by the Muslims was Egypt. Egypt fell to the Muslims in AD 641. Half the city of Alexandria was destroyed, many people were killed, and homes were robbed. It was a terrible time for Christians living there. Eight years later, the Muslims conquered Cyprus. They were getting very close to Italy and the Christian people of Europe.

Then the Muslims moved into North Africa. One by one, they conquered the coastal cities in the north. In AD 698, the great city of Carthage fell to the Muslims. From this time until the present day, Muslims have controlled most of North Africa

BATTLE WITH MUSLIMS AT TOURS, FRANCE, AD 732. THE MUSLIM ADVANCE INTO EUROPE WAS STOPPED BY CHARLES MARTEL.

and the Middle East.

The Muslim armies continued their mission to take over the world. They crossed the Strait of Gibraltar from Morocco in AD 711. At its closest point, there are just nine miles of ocean between Spain and Morocco. For the next seven years, the Muslims gained control of much of Spain. These Muslim invaders were called "Moors" because they came from Morocco.

Muslims forced people to either convert to Islam or submit to paying taxes to their Islamic rulers. Most of the time, Christians and Jews just paid the tax. Over the centuries, though, most people in these countries became Muslim.

Finally, the Muslim armies were stopped at the Battle of Tours in AD 732. Charles Martel conquered the Muslim armies at Tours by sneaking up on them and taking them by surprise. According to God's sovereign purpose, the Muslims were stopped in their advance. By God's grace, the Christian faith would continue to grow throughout Europe. Muslims would be stopped once more during the Reformation in AD 1565 in the Battle of Malta. Once again, the Lord Jesus Christ (who is Lord of all) wanted to complete His work in Europe. He would use the Muslims to discipline His people from time to time. But the Muslims would never stop the work our Lord Jesus Christ was doing around the world.

Jesus Christ has always been true to His Word. He will not fail in building His church. Truly the gates of hell and the armies of Islam cannot overcome the true church of Christ.

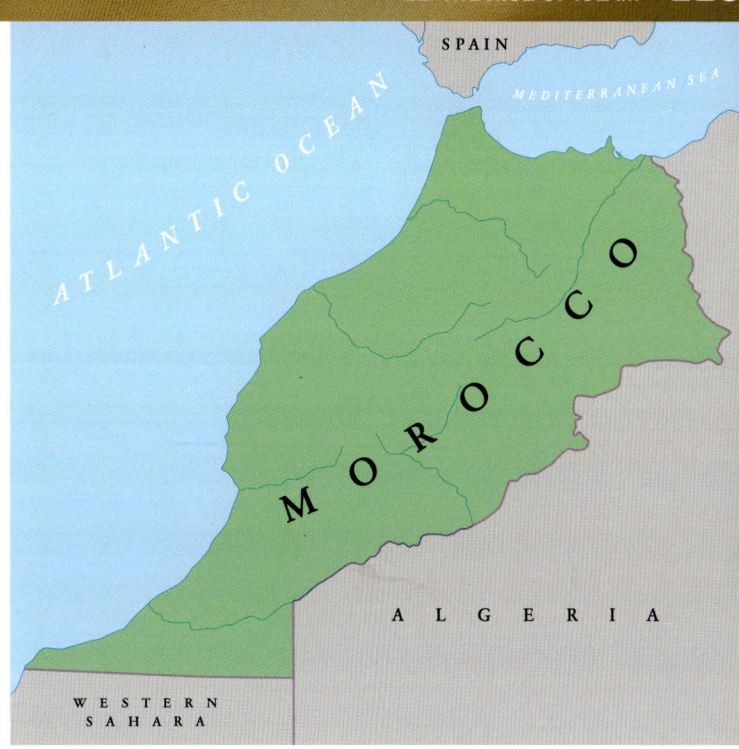

LOCATION OF MOROCCO

[Jesus] said to them, "But who do you say that I am?"
Simon Peter answered and said, "You are the Christ, the Son of the living God."
Jesus answered and said to him, "Blessed are you, Simon Bar-Jonah, for flesh and blood has not revealed this to you, but My Father who is in heaven. And I also say to you that you are Peter, and on this rock I will build My church, and the gates of Hades shall not prevail against it."
(Matthew 16:16-18)

For 800 years, the Muslims would continue pushing against the Christians in the north. They would fight the Byzantine

Empire (in modern-day Turkey) for hundreds of years. The European Christian countries would try to push them back with the Crusades, beginning in AD 1095.

THE CHURCH UNDER ISLAMIC RULE

> **And who is he who will harm you if you become followers of what is good? But even if you should suffer for righteousness' sake, you are blessed. "And do not be afraid of their threats, nor be troubled." (1 Peter 3:13-14)**

After the Muslims took over North Africa, the Christians lived under Islamic rule. This brought a lot of changes to the church in North Africa. Today, the majority of North Africa is Muslim. The largest Christian populations in Africa live south of the Sahara Desert.

The Quran talks about two kinds of people—the idolatrous pagans and the "people of the book." The people of the book are Jews and Christians. They were called "people of the book" because they followed the teachings of the Old and New Testaments.

Jews and Christians sometimes died by the sword during Muslim conquests. But most of the time they were allowed to live as second-class citizens under their Muslim rulers. They had to pay the extra tax and were forced to wear different kinds of clothing from the Muslims. Also, they could not own swords or horses. Without weapons, the Muslims knew that Christians would never be able to fight against

ROMAN AMPITHEATRE IN ALEXANDRIA, EGYPT

their Muslim rulers. They could not announce their church services with the ringing of bells, and they were not allowed to marry Muslims.

Jews and Christians were also told not to evangelize Muslims. Any Muslims who became Christians would be put to death. Even today, people in Islamic countries who convert to the Christian faith are put to death. Thus, true Christians have always suffered in Muslim countries. This was the same situation faced by Peter and John in the Book of Acts. When these disciples of Jesus preached the Gospel publicly, they got in trouble with their rulers.

And the high priest asked them, saying, "Did we not strictly command you not to teach in this name? And look, you have filled Jerusalem with your doctrine, and intend to bring this Man's blood on us!" But Peter and the other apostles answered and said: "We ought to obey God rather than men." (Acts 5:28-29)

While the church never disappeared from North Africa, the Christian faith grew weaker. Sadly, many Christians did not stand strong for Jesus in the face of persecution and death. They converted to Islam.

Some Christians did evangelize. Others served in the courts of Muslim rulers. Muslims would often employ Christians to work for them. They were seen as more faithful and trustworthy than others, like Daniel and Joseph in the Bible. They were trusted by their Muslim employers.

Servants, be submissive to your masters with all fear, not only to the good and gentle, but also to the harsh. (1 Peter 2:18)

Very little missionary work was done in North Africa from AD 670 until the present day. There were few from Europe who had the courage to bring the Gospel to these Muslim lands. Raymond Lull is one man who had the courage to go and speak of Jesus in North Africa.

THE CRUSADES

For rulers are not a terror to good works, but to evil. Do you want to be unafraid of the authority? Do what is good, and you will have praise from the same. For he is God's minister to you for good. But if you do evil, be afraid; for he does not bear the sword in vain; for he is God's minister, an avenger to execute wrath on him who practices evil. (Romans 13:3-4)

God has put the church and the civil government in place. These are both institutions made by God, but they have different purposes. The state carries the sword and defends a nation from evil. The church preaches the gospel and disciples the nations in everything Jesus has commanded us to do. The church is not supposed to do what the state government does. And the state government is not supposed to do what the church does.

Sadly, the Roman church became more involved in the government of the nations after AD 1000. The pope and other church leaders became very power-hungry. They wanted to control kings. They didn't see the difference between the church and the civil government. The church and the civil government became mixed in the Middle Ages.

The Crusades were a series of military campaigns fought over many centuries. Many kings and the pope were hoping to keep the Muslims from taking over the Byzantine area (in Turkey) and Western Europe. They also wanted to take back control over Christian lands in the Middle East and Africa.

The main problem with the Crusades is that they were mostly inspired and encouraged by the pope. This was the man who was supposed to be the leader of the Roman Catholic Church. He was not a king. He was supposed to be a pastor of a church. The many cities and nations throughout Europe did not want the Muslims to take over. So, many kings thought it was a good idea to oppose the Muslim armies.

For many centuries, Christians had gone on pilgrimage to visit Jerusalem and the rest of the Holy Land. This was supposed to be an act of devotion. Sometimes Christian pilgrims were mistreated by Muslims in control of the area. This persecution got worse when the Seljuk Turks conquered Palestine in the 11th century.

The Byzantine emperors asked for help from their Christian brothers in the West. It was mainly the Roman Catholic church that responded.

In the year 1095, Urban II spoke up at the Council of Clermont. He encouraged the church to support a Crusade against the Turks and other Muslims in the East. The crowd responded so strongly that they began to chant "Deus vult." This means "God wills it." Church leaders were claiming that the first crusade was the very will of God. Pope Urban II went so far as to promise forgiveness of sins for those who would go on this great crusade

THE CRUSADES

First Crusade	1095-1099
Second Crusade	1147-1150
Third Crusade	1189-1192
Fourth Crusade	1202-1204
Fifth Crusade	1217-1221
Sixth Crusade	1228-1229

to retake the holy land. Of course, forgiveness of sins is not something that we earn by good works. It is the gift of God. This promise made by the pope was a terrible error. It is false teaching like this that produces bad fruit.

A series of crusades took place over the next 200 years. The First Crusade was the most successful. The crusaders were successful in recapturing Jerusalem and a large part of the Holy Land (by AD 1099). For the next 100 years, Christians from Europe had control over Jerusalem. After that, the crusader kingdom fell to the Muslim leader Saladin. The Third Crusade (1189-1192) was led by three important kings of Western Europe. These kings were Richard the Lionhearted of England, Frederick Barbarossa of the Holy Roman Empire, and Philip II of France. But this crusade ended in failure and defeat. The next three crusades were mostly failures. The Fifth Crusade did involve a direct attack on Egypt— the only crusade to enter Africa.

How should Christians view the Crusades? First, the unjust shedding of blood must be condemned. In many cases, innocent people were killed by both sides in the wars.

Second, the confusion of the church and the state was harmful. In many ways, it was the same mistake the Muslims had made. Christians do not spread the faith by offensive warfare. A state government has a right to defend its nations and cities by fighting. But this is not the role of the church. When the church gets involved in warfare, it sends the wrong message. But it is also a distraction. The most powerful thing the church does is to preach the gospel, which is the power of God unto salvation. This is 100 times more powerful than fighting with guns and swords.

Also, Muslims were often viewed as enemies to be killed and destroyed rather souls that needed the love of Christ and His salvation.

Finally, kings still have a role to defend themselves from imperialistic attackers. Even though many injustices were committed, the crusades may have helped to defend Europe. If the crusades had not happened, it is possible that more of Europe would have been conquered by the Muslims.

In God's providence, the Christian faith was preserved in Europe. Then, after the Reformation, the faith was taken into the Americas and Asia. Another great work of the Holy Spirit would return to the Middle East and to North Africa much later in the 21st century. This was all in God's good timing. ∎

And [Jesus] said to them, "It is not for you to know times or seasons which the Father has put in His own authority. But you shall receive power when the Holy Spirit has come upon you; and you shall be witnesses to Me in Jerusalem, and in all Judea and Samaria, and to the end of the earth." (Acts 1:7-8)

LEADERS OF THE FIRST CRUSADE

Raymond Lull: First Missionary to the Muslims

**Sing to God, you kingdoms of the earth;
Oh, sing praises to the Lord.
(Psalm 68:32)**

From 1095 to 1270, European Christians fought many wars against the Muslims. These wars are known today as "the Crusades." Hostility between the Muslims and Christians was already running high during the Middle Ages. The Crusades increased this hostility. At this time, very few Christian missionaries took the gospel to the Muslims. The Muslims learned about the Christian faith through the sword. Yet Jesus Christ called His disciples to preach the gospel to the world and disciple the nations. This doesn't happen by the power of the sword. It comes about by the power of the Spirit through the preaching of God's Word.

Raymond Lull was one of the first missionaries to the Muslims. When almost no one was willing to confront Muslims with the truths of Christianity, Raymond Lull went alone. His life is a testimony of faith-filled courage. In this chapter, you will learn his story.

THE LORD CALLS RAYMOND LULL

**Before I formed you in the womb I knew you;
Before you were born I sanctified you;
I ordained you a prophet to the nations.
(Jeremiah 1:5)**

Raymond Lull was born in the city of Palma on the small island of Majorca (also called Mallorca today). Majorca is an island in the Mediterranean Sea, east of Spain. The native language of Majorca is Catalan. This is one of the official languages in Spain. Lull was born in the year 1235.

RAYMOND LULL

He was born into a wealthy and distinguished family. His family had many connections to the Spanish royalty. From the time he was born, he enjoyed the privileges of wealth. His family owned a large estate in Palma.

Before he was awakened to his sinful state by the Spirit of God, Lull lived a sinful life. Like most Europeans, he grew up in the church. But the church was deeply corrupt during the late Middle Ages. The popes residing in Rome were known for their immorality, sinful lifestyles, and greed. Knowledge of the Word of God was rare. Many people professed Christianity but did not have the saving work of God's Spirit. The church was in need of reformation.

Raymond Lull married at a young age and moved to Spain. He was made a "seneschal" in the royal court. A seneschal was the chief official in the household of a medieval prince or noble. This was an important position in the royal household. Lull attended many feasts and ceremonies. For many years, Raymond served in this important position. He enjoyed the pleasures and entertainments of this world. Lull was also a talented artist. He wrote many poems in Catalan. He also played music on the cittern. This is a stringed instrument similar to a guitar or lute. His skills in music and poetry made him famous, and his Catalan poetry is still read today.

When Raymond was thirty-two years old, he returned to Palma. One night, when he was at home in Palma, he was writing poetry and playing his cittern. He

MALLORCA, PART OF MODERN-DAY SPAIN

was writing a love song for a woman who was not his wife when his mind began to focus on the Lord Jesus Christ hanging on the cross. It seemed as if Jesus was looking right at him. Raymond was startled by this convicting sight and immediately stopped playing the cittern. He then retired to bed, hoping that sleep would clear his mind.

Eight days later, Raymond Lull began working on the song again. Once more the sight of Jesus Christ crucified flashed into his mind and stayed there. Lull saw the Savior dying on the cross, looking at him. The Savior seemed to call him to turn aside from his sinful life and receive Jesus as Lord. Lull immediately cast his instrument aside and laid on his bed thinking about this tremendous scene of Christ, the Son of God dying on the cross. He was filled with remorse because of his sins. From that point on, he committed his life to the service of Christ.

Just a few years before Lull was born, the kingdom of Aragon had regained control of Majorca. Before that time, the island Majorca and the smaller Menorca were under the control of the Muslim Moors. Muslim religion and culture had made a significant impact on Majorca. This was part of Raymond Lull's background living in Palma. He did not live very far from the Muslim-dominated lands of North Africa. Lull also knew about the Crusades. Those bloody conflicts had failed to conquer the Muslims. Lull thought it was time for a spiritual crusade. Instead of wielding a sword, he wanted to take the powerful gospel of Jesus to the Muslims.

As Lull contemplated this missionary call, he went to a nearby church and poured his heart out to God in prayer. He prayed, "Lord, if this is what You would have me do, make a way for me to carry out this mission." He continued to pray for three months. The confirmation came one day when a preacher came to the church at Palma and preached a sermon. The preacher told a story of a man who had lived a life of wealth. But, in the midst of war, this man was taken prisoner in Perugia. While suffering in prison, the man saw visions of Christ and the world to come. Once he was set free, he became a preacher. In 1219, this man went to Damietta, a Muslim stronghold, and preached Christ before the Sultan. He declared to the Muslim ruler, "I am not sent of man, but of God, to show you the way of salvation."

Upon hearing this sermon, Raymond Lull made up his mind. He would become a preacher and missionary. He sold all his property and reserved just a small amount of money for his wife and children. He consecrated his life to the Lord in these words: "To you, Lord God, do I now offer myself and my wife and my children and all that I possess. And since I approach You humbly with this gift and sacrifice, may it please You to accept all that I give . . . that I and my wife and my children may be Your humble slaves." He laid aside his

THE CATHEDRAL OF SANTA MARIA OF PALMA

wealthy clothes and wore the clothes of a monk. His life was now dedicated to the service of the Lord Jesus.

PREPARATION FOR MISSIONARY WORK

And a servant of the Lord must not quarrel but be gentle to all, able to teach, patient, in humility correcting those who are in opposition, if God perhaps will grant them repentance, so that they may know the truth, and that they may come to their senses and escape the snare of the devil, having been taken captive by him to do his will. (2 Timothy 2:24-26)

Most Christians in the 13th century did not show love to Muslims. Centuries of war and bloodshed had soured the relationship between these opposing religious groups. The Samaritan woman speaking to Jesus said, "Jews have no dealings with Samaritans" (John 4:9). This was also true of Christians and Muslims in the 13th century. Christians had no dealings with Muslims. Because of this, most Christians did not understand the Islamic faith. Few Christians had ever read the Muslim holy book, the Qur'an. The first Christian to translate and study the Qur'an in Europe was Petrus Venerabilis. He translated the Qur'an so that Christians could study the book and refute it. He believed that the Qur'an should be a weapon used against Islam. Petrus knew that using swords and spears against the Muslims wouldn't do any good. He said, "Not with arms but with words, not by force but by reason, not in hatred, but in love." Petrus was a forerunner who prepared the way for Raymond Lull.

Raymond Lull believed the same as Petrus did. Lull explained his strategy: "I see many knights going to the Holy Land beyond the seas and thinking that they can acquire it by force of arms; but in the end all are destroyed before they attain that which they think to have. It seems to me that the conquest of the Holy Land ought not to be attempted except in the way in which the Apostles acquired it, namely by love and prayers, and the pouring out of tears and blood." Lull knew that only prayer, the preaching of the Word, and martyrdom would bring the Muslims to Christ.

If Lull would preach the gospel to Muslims, he would have to speak their language. He needed to learn Arabic. At first, he thought he would go to Paris and study at the university. But he instead took the advice of a friend and stayed in Palma. In order to learn Arabic right where he lived, he purchased a Muslim slave. For the next nine years, this young slave taught Raymond Arabic. Lull longed to see this slave come to faith in Jesus Christ. But, instead, the Muslim became hardened to the gospel message. One day, while studying together, the young man blasphemed the name of Christ and then attacked Raymond Lull. The authorities seized the slave and threw him in prison. The Muslim was afraid he would be executed. For this reason, the young man committed suicide rather than face justice.

This tragic event grieved Raymond Lull very deeply. If he could not reach a young man whom he studied with for nine years, could he really reach the Muslims? For eight days he retired to a mountain to pray. He asked himself, "Is this truly what the Lord wants me to do?" But after eight days of prayer and meditation, Lull was still convinced of his mission.

After nine years of study, Lull was now proficient in Arabic. He decided to write a book that would compare Christianity and Islam. This would be a book for other Christians to learn how to debate Muslims. The book would provide arguments Christians could use to refute Islam. When Lull wrote the book, he was forty-one years old. He spent four months in Palma writing this book, and completed it in 1275. He

KING JAMES II OF MAJORCA

then went before the King of Palma and asked for his help to publish the book. After the book was published, Lull traveled and taught others about Islam.

For the next twenty years, Raymond Lull traveled to different parts of Europe. He taught other Christians about Islam. He also urged Christians to consider the call to Muslim missions. With the help of King James II of Majorca, a monastery was founded on the island. This monastery was unique. Here the monks learned Arabic so that they would be prepared for debates with Muslims. The curriculum of the monastery even included a study of the geography of the Muslim world. Lull understand that it was important for missionaries to know the geography, customs, and language of the people they would reach. Lull also spent a number of years in Montpellier. While there, he taught students and also wrote numerous books. Lull was a gifted theologian. But he also wrote books on medicine, science, mathematics, and other subjects.

Raymond Lull was a man filled with passionate love for the Lord. He preached to others, calling them to lay their lives down for Jesus Christ. He once preached, "I find scarcely anyone, O Lord, who out of love for You is ready to suffer martyrdom as You have suffered for us." By this time, Lull was about sixty years old. But he had not yet embarked on a journey to Muslim lands. He had spent decades preparing. Now he tried to raise support for his missionary efforts. He went to the popes residing both at Rome and Avignon. (At this time in church history, there were two popes, both claiming to be the only true pope. One pope lived in Rome and another lived in Avignon.) Each time Lull brought the missionary cause before the popes, the popes didn't want to help him. They were too busy securing their own power and wealth. They didn't care about reaching the Muslims.

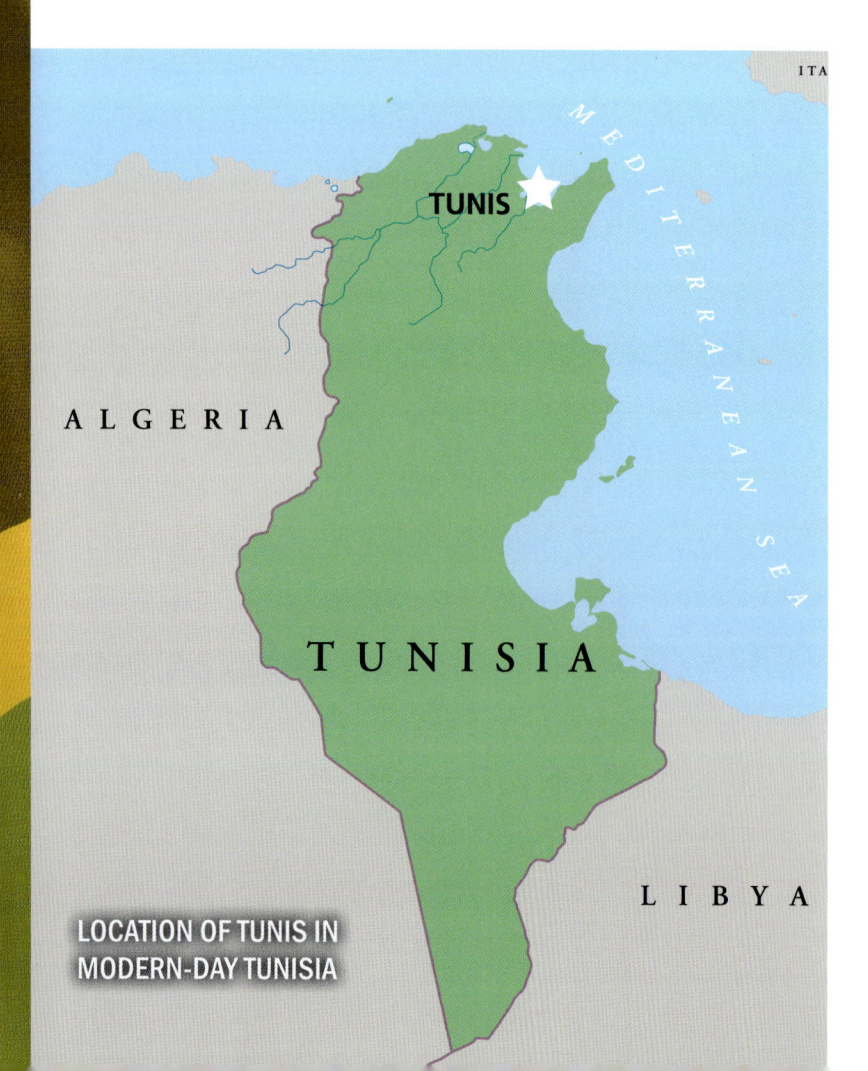

LOCATION OF TUNIS IN MODERN-DAY TUNISIA

MISSIONARY JOURNEYS TO AFRICA

The wicked flee when no one pursues, But the righteous are bold as a lion. (Proverbs 28:1)

With little support from the church, Raymond Lull set out for Africa on his own. From Genoa, he found passage on a ship headed to Tunis. The ship was loaded with Lull's missionary books, and everything was made ready for his journey. But, before the ship left the harbor, Lull became terrified at the thought of what might happen to him. Would the Muslims kill him immediately? Even though he had spent his life preparing for this moment, Lull still struggled with his fears. He said he was "overwhelmed with terror at the thought of what might happen to him in the country where he was going. The idea of enduring torture or lifelong imprisonment presented itself with such force that he could not control his emotions." But, by faith, he overcame his fears and went anyway.

Raymond Lull reached Tunis in 1292. This port city on the coast of North Africa was established by Carthage. It became a very important city after it was conquered by Arabian Muslims. From Tunis, the Muslims traveled back and forth to Spain. Tunis was also the location where the Seventh Crusade had ended in failure. Now, Raymond Lull wanted to embark on a new spiritual crusade where the last military crusade had ended. Once he arrived in Tunis, he began speaking about Christianity and Islam to the local residents. He exposed the errors of Islam. Not surprisingly, the local Muslim leaders would not allow this to continue. They took Raymond Lull and threw him in a dungeon. Local authorities wanted to put him to death, but a merciful man stopped them and had Lull set free. He was banished from Tunis and told never to return. Lull then returned to Europe and traveled to a number of other locations in the East, seeking to reach Muslims.

After fifteen years of banishment from North Africa, Lull returned in 1307. This time he went to the city of Bugia. This city was not far from Tunis. It is located in modern-day Algeria, west of Tunis. Immediately when he arrived in Bugia, Lull went to a public place, stood up and began to preach boldly. Speaking in Arabic, Lull declared that Christianity was the only true faith. He called all Muslims to debate with him. He said he would prove to them that Islam was a false religion. A Muslim cleric rushed to him and urged him to stop preaching. He warned Lull that death would soon follow if he continued his open-air proclamation. To this Lull replied, "Death has no terrors at all for a sincere servant of Christ who is laboring to bring souls to a knowledge of the truth."

The Muslim religious leader then asked Lull to prove the superiority of

BUGIA IN MODERN-DAY ALGERIA

Christianity. Lull used a variety of arguments to disprove Islam. One of these arguments used the Ten Commandments. Lull would prove that the Ten Commandments were the eternal and perfect law of God. Then he would demonstrate that Muhammad, the chief prophet of Islam, broke all of the Ten Commandments. The Muslims were not convinced by his arguments. In Bugia, Lull was once again cast into the dungeon. For six months he suffered in prison. The Muslims gave him

BASIC FACTS ABOUT TUNISIA

Total Population:	11,400,000
Total Area:	63,100 square miles
Capital:	Tunis
Official Languages:	Arabic, Berber, French
Primary Religion:	Islam

an opportunity to be set free if he would become a Muslim. They offered him wealth and power if he would reject Jesus Christ. But Lull did not care about earthly rewards. He said, "You offer a poor prize, as all your earthly goods cannot purchase eternal glory."

Eventually, the Muslims decided to let Raymond Lull return to Europe. He left Bugia imprisoned on a Muslim ship. But during the voyage home, a storm arose and the ship was almost lost. But, in the providence of God, Lull was rescued. He had been shipwrecked near the town of Pisa. Now that Lull was back in Europe, he continued his work of preaching and writing. He was now in his mid-seventies. He did much good in teaching others in Europe, but his heart was constantly drawn back to the Muslims perishing in North Africa.

At age seventy-nine Lull decided to set out for Africa once again. He didn't fear martyrdom. Most of all, he wanted to glorify God and to see the Muslims saved. In 1314, Lull set out for Bugia. He arrived on August 14 and began his gospel labors. For a year he quietly shared the gospel and gathered a small group of converts. But he became tired of remaining quiet. He did not want to hide any longer. So he went into the open market of Bugia once again. He began preaching and reminded the people that he was the one who had previously been banished. But he had now returned. He pleaded with them in love to receive Jesus Christ as the true Messiah. The people seized him, dragged him out of town, and killed him. He died on June 30, 1315.

Raymond Lull was a unique man. There were few like him in the 13th and 14th centuries. He was a man who loved Jesus Christ. He also cared deeply for the Muslims. He knew that without Christ they would perish in their sins. He did not fight the false religion of Islam with a sword. Instead, he took the gospel, which

BASIC FACTS ABOUT THE PEOPLE'S DEMOCRATIC REPUBLIC OF ALGERIA

Total Population:	42,000,000
Total Area:	919,500 square miles
Capital:	Algiers
Official Languages:	Arabic, Berber
Primary Religion:	Islam

is the power of God for salvation, to the Muslim world. He was just one man against millions of Muslims. But he carried with him the sword of the Spirit: the Word of God. He was not afraid to follow Christ, even when faced with death. He was willing to give everything for the cause of His Lord. May we also learn from such sacrifice. May we labor for our Lord and share with others the good news of salvation. ∎

> Now then, we are ambassadors for Christ, as though God were pleading through us: we implore you on Christ's behalf, be reconciled to God. (2 Corinthians 5:20)

PRAYER POINTS: ALGERIA

- **Growth of the Church:** The Christian church in Algeria makes up a small percentage of Algeria (about 0.28% of the population). Pray that the church would grow and become a greater light in Algeria. Pray that Christian fathers and mothers would faithfully pass on the faith to their children. Pray that the church would faithfully disciple those who profess the name of Jesus.

- **Bible Distribution:** The government of Algeria has banned the import of Bibles. This makes it difficult to get copies of the Scriptures into the hands of Algerians. Pray that the Scriptures would be distributed widely throughout Algeria despite the government ban.

PRAYER POINTS: TUNISIA

- **Religious Freedom:** The government of Tunisia forbids Christian churches from owning their own property. Churches are not allowed to have bank accounts. Pray that the Lord would provide freedom to the Tunisian Christians. Even while oppressed, pray that the Lord would enable these Christians to remain faithful.

- **Missionaries:** Pray that the Lord would send more missionaries into this land. It has been about 700 years since Raymond Lull preached in Tunis. Today, most Tunisians have still not heard the gospel of Jesus Christ. Pray for an evangelistic heart for Tunisia in the worldwide church.

12. RAYMOND LULL: FIRST MISSIONARY TO THE MUSLIMS

MALLORCA

ARAB MUSLIMS OPERATED SLAVE TRADE OUT OF AFRICA FOR CENTURIES

The African Slave Trade

If a man is found kidnapping any of his brethren of the children of Israel, and mistreats him or sells him, then that kidnapper shall die; and you shall put away the evil from among you. (Deuteronomy 24:7)

This chapter records a heartbreaking story. But the history of Africa would not be complete without telling this story. This is the history of the Atlantic slave trade. It lasted from the mid-1400s to the early-1800s. During this time, around 11 million Africans were removed from Africa. They were carried to other parts of the world. Such a large forced migration is a major event in world history. The slave trade changed Africa's populations. It also changed the rest of the world's populations. The slave trade reshaped the history of Africa, Europe, and the Americas.

Ever since the fall into sin, slavery has existed in many cultures. But slavery has taken many forms. In some cases, men and women became slaves in order to pay off debts. This is called "indentured servitude." But, in other cultures, people were kidnapped and enslaved against their will. This is wrong. The law of God forbids kidnapping and enslavement (Deuteronomy 24:7). The Apostle Paul also described kidnapping or manstealing as a sin.

But we know that the law is good if one uses it lawfully, knowing this: that the law is not made for a righteous person, but for the lawless and insubordinate . . . for kidnappers, for liars, for perjurers, and if there is any other thing that is contrary to sound doctrine, . . . (1 Timothy 1:8-10)

It is a sin against God to take a person captive and sell him into slavery. Human beings are made in the image of God. They cannot be owned as property like any other object. This form of slavery is known as "chattel slavery."

By God's mercy, chattel slavery is uncommon in Western nations today. But forms of slavery still exist in many parts of the world. Even though it is illegal in Western nations, evildoers still practice slavery secretly. Christians should pray that God would stop such evildoers. We can also support the government and local law enforcement in stopping slavery.

THE BEGINNINGS OF THE AFRICAN SLAVE TRADE

Slavery has existed in Africa for thousands of years. African tribes enslaved each other. Muslims have also engaged in the slave trade for centuries. Europeans became involved in the mid-1400s. The nations of

Europe were looking for ways to increase their wealth and strengthen their nations. Portuguese and Spanish ships began sailing to Africa and Asia. They found many natural resources along the coast of Africa. They also found slaves.

An African might become a slave by being kidnapped from his local tribe or kingdom. War was another way Africans were enslaved. If a kingdom fought against its neighbors, the victors would kill some of their enemies. But they would often take their defeated enemies captive. The captives would be kept or sold as slaves.

Europeans did not start the slave trade in Africa. But they did help the slave trade grow. Africans saw slavery as a way to make more money. Europe was a new market. Its nations wanted slaves. Many Africans were more than happy to kidnap and enslave other Africans. Europeans did not normally travel into the African interior to find slaves. The risks of disease or attack were too great. Instead, they sailed to ports on the coast. Then Africans brought captured slaves and sold them to the Europeans. European slave traders would bring items of interest to the Africans. This was their form of payment. The slaves were then loaded onto a ship and taken to Europe or the Americas.

Christians in North Africa often spoke out against slavery. They condemned the unjust treatment of human beings who were slaves. Slaves were not treated with as much dignity as those who were free. Christians knew that all people are made in the image of God. All deserve respect and just treatment.

THE SLAVE TRADE EXPANDS

In 1444, the first African slaves were taken to Europe. The Portuguese brought them to serve as household slaves. Columbus discovered the Americas in 1492. Afterward, the Spanish and Portuguese founded colonies in the New World. They created colonies in South America, Central America, and the Caribbean. These colonies produced goods to send to Europe. However, it was difficult to find laborers to work in these colonies. European laborers were usually too expensive. There were also many risks to colonial life. The new climate and diseases could be

SLAVE-TRADING PORT OF ZANZIBAR

SUGAR PLANTATION

deadly for Europeans. If pay was low and dangers were high, Europeans did not want to go. For this reason, Europeans decided to use African slaves.

From the mid-1400s to the 1600s, millions of Africans were taken to the Americas. Most of these were purchased by the Portuguese and Spanish. The slaves worked on sugar plantations in the Caribbean. They also worked in Spanish settlements further south. Some islands had more African slaves than Spanish or native peoples. This included islands such as Jamaica and Haiti.

In the 1600s, other nations in Europe began purchasing African slaves. These nations included the Dutch, French, and English. Most African slaves were shipped to Central and South America. But by the 1700s, a large number were transported to the English colonies as well. It was these colonies that would eventually form the United States.

THE MIDDLE PASSAGE

Before the days of modern airplane travel, crossing the Atlantic Ocean could be very dangerous. Many slaves died on the voyage. The journey from Africa to the Americas became known as "the middle passage." Over a period of months, European slave ships would go up and down the African coast. The ship would travel from port to port collecting slaves. In each port, a slave trader might pick up a few slaves. The captain would go ashore to purchase his "cargo." A ship's doctor would often go with the captain. The doctor would physically examine the slaves. If a slave had a health issue or was unfit for labor, the captain might refuse to purchase the slave. Generally, the most desirable slaves were adult males. They costed the most since they were the most productive for farm labor. Women and children would also be purchased. But they were purchased at a lower cost.

The largest slave ships could hold up to 500 slaves. Others would hold 200-300. Often, only a few slaves were purchased at each African port. This meant that it could take months to fill the ship's hold with slaves. Once the ship was full, the slaves would be transported to the Americas. The journey across the Atlantic could take anywhere from 1-3 months. The length of the voyage depended on the destination and weather conditions. Tight quarters and living conditions often resulted in the death of slaves and sailors.

Europeans purchased African slaves from other Africans. Because of this, a slave ship captain did his best to keep his slaves alive and healthy. If he lost slaves during the voyage, he would have a smaller profit in the Americas. Unhealthy slaves also resulted in a loss because they would have to be sold at a lower price.

The percentage of slaves who died on the passage is not known with certainty. The mortality rate varied from one century to the next. In the early years of the slave trade, as many as 10% to 20% of the slaves might have died. But, in later centuries, the number was much lower. Regardless of the percent, it was still a dangerous journey and led to the death of many innocent people. The more tightly a slave ship was packed, the more likely that the death rate would be higher. The death of slaves was usually caused by diseases such as dysentery and fever. In some cases, slave riots on board would also result in the loss of life. Slaves were also frequently beaten and abused by sailors. Some governments intervened to make the trade safer. For example, in 1788 and 1799, the British Parliament established a law that limited the number of slaves based on a ship's size. But these laws did nothing to end the sin of chattel slavery.

At its height, the slave trade was a massive enterprise. In England, the city of Liverpool might have seen 50,000 slaves pass through its port. In Britain, up to 5,500 sailors were employed in the industry. By 1801, Barbados had 250,000 slaves working its sugar plantations. This sugar was exported to Britain. Wealthy men and women of Britain enjoyed sugar in their tea and coffee at the price of these slaves' freedom. Between 1690 and 1770, Virginia received 100,000 slaves. Eventually the slave population in North America was so large that they no longer needed to import slaves. The slave population grew on its own.

THE CAMPAIGN TO END SLAVERY

**Is this not the fast that I have chosen:
To loose the bonds of wickedness,
To undo the heavy burdens,
To let the oppressed go free,
And that you break every yoke?
(Isaiah 58:6)**

GEORGE WHITEFIELD

For centuries, the slave trade continued with little opposition. Even many Christians did not see anything wrong with the trade. Many Christians did not know the horrors of the trade firsthand. But the Lord saw the sin of slavery. Even if Christians did not realize how wicked this trade was, God knew. And He heard the cries of the oppressed. In His mercy, He opened the eyes of His people to see the sin in their land.

In the 1730s and 1740s, God began to awaken His people. His Spirit convicted them of sin. Many came to saving faith in Jesus Christ. This happened through a movement called the Great Awakening. The Great Awakening was a spiritual revival that touched churches of England and its colonies. Men such as George Whitefield (1714-1770), John Wesley (1703-1791), and Gilbert Tennent (1703-1764) preached the gospel to millions. This spiritual revival had many blessed results. Churches increased in number. Spiritual fruit began to flourish in the homes of many. This awakening was a marvelous work of God.

God's Spirit brought spiritual life to His people. Now they looked at the world through new eyes. They began to see others as God saw them. These Christians had a greater concern for the good of their neighbor. These neighbors included the slaves living in Britain and America. Many Christians began trying to end the slave trade. At first, they worked to abolish the slave trade. Once the slave trade ended in Great Britain and the United States, they tried to end slavery itself.

In the late 1700s, the movement against slavery grew. People who opposed slavery began to form groups in England and North America. Some groups, such as the Quakers, had always wanted to end slavery. Now others joined the Quakers in opposing slavery. In 1774, John Wesley wrote a pamphlet called *Thoughts on Slavery*. In this work, he explained why he believed slavery was wrong. Wesley's writing strongly influenced other Christians.

A Christian man named Granville Sharp (1735-1813) also became committed to abolition. In 1767, Granville Sharp met a slave from Barbados. The slave had been beaten so violently by his master that he was almost blind. The slave asked Sharp to help him become free. Granville fought for the slave's freedom in the court. In God's providence, Granville helped the slave gain his freedom. From then on, Granville Sharp campaigned for freedom for slaves in England. Sharp and others with him pointed to the many abuses suffered by slaves. They used this unjust treatment to campaign for abolition.

John Newton (1725-1807) was a famous hymn writer. Before his conversion, he served on a slave ship. In God's amazing grace, Newton repented of his sinful life. He began to serve the Lord as a pastor in Olney, England. He wrote with horror of experiences on British slave ships. In his later years, he joined the cause of abolition in England. In 1788, Newton wrote a book called *Thoughts Upon the African Slave Trade*. He deeply regretted his past involvement with the slave trade. He frequently spoke about this topic with his friends. Newton wrote his book as a "public confession." In his book, he told of some of the evil episodes he witnessed firsthand. Slaves were often treated in barbaric and wicked ways. Newton's book was given to every member of the British Parliament. Thousands of copies sold throughout Great Britain. His harrowing firsthand testimony helped to turn the British against the slave trade.

The man most responsible for ending the slave trade was William Wilberforce (1759-1833). He was born in the town of Hull in England. At the age of 21 he became involved in politics. He served in Parliament from 1780 to 1825. Wilberforce grew up in a home where he learned a little about Christianity. But very little real faith or conviction existed in the Wilberforce home. However, in 1785, God saved him. William became deeply committed to the gospel of Jesus Christ. Due to his new convictions, he worked in Parliament to reform his nation.

WILLIAM WILBERFORCE

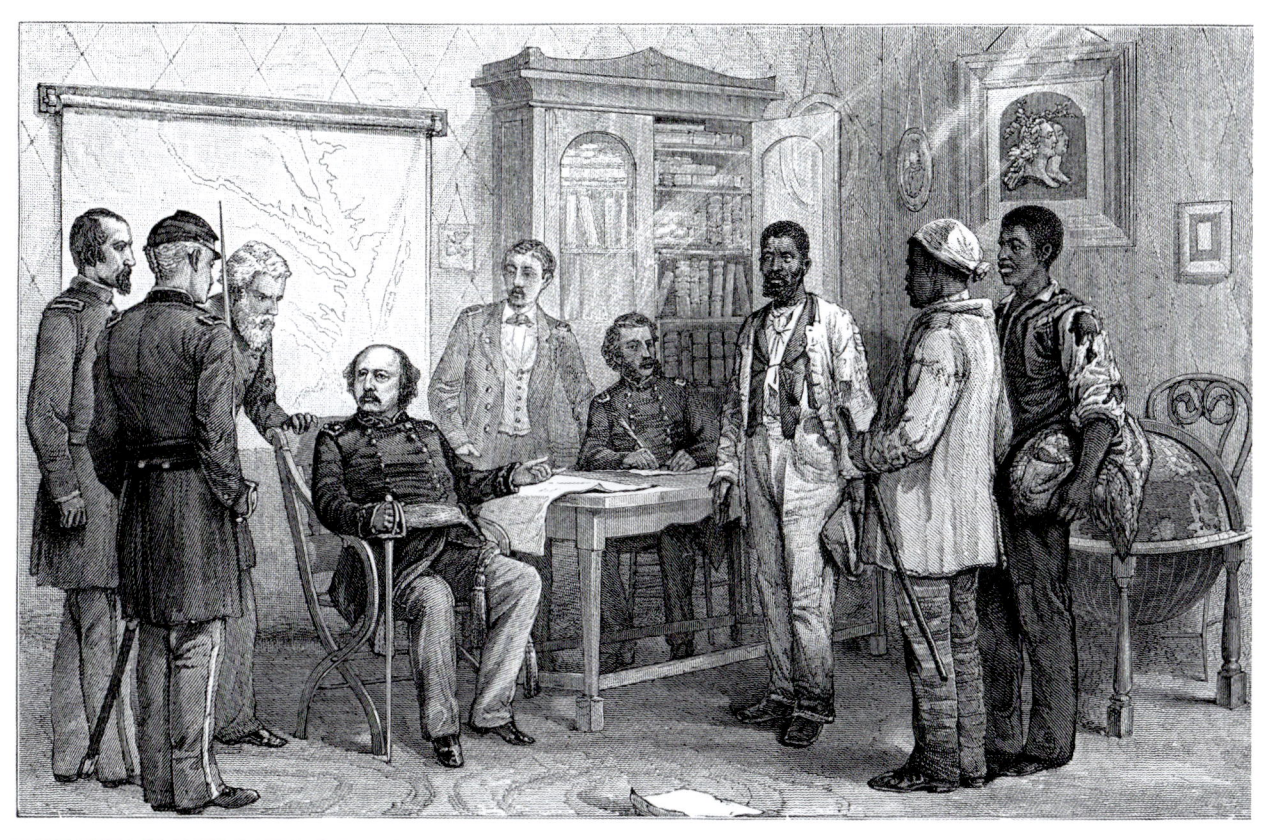

AMERICAN SLAVES DURING THE CIVIL WAR

Wilberforce also became a friend of John Newton. In 1785, he contacted John Newton. He asked the older pastor to give him some advice. William was unsure whether he should stay in Parliament. Was it wrong for a Christian to be in politics? Would he be a more faithful Christian if he became a pastor instead? Pastor Newton encouraged Wilberforce to stay in politics. Newton believed that the man was a good politician. Wilberforce could serve the Lord Jesus faithfully in Parliament. God-fearing Christians should be involved in every area of life, even in government. Newton's counsel changed the course of history. William followed Newton's advice and continued to serve as a member of Parliament.

Wilberforce worked for decades to end the slave trade. He wanted to abolish slavery itself. But the first step was to end the buying and selling of slaves. Newton frequently encouraged Wilberforce. John Wesley also supported him. Wesley wrote to him in 1791, "Go on, in the name of God, and in the power of his might, till even American slavery (the vilest that ever saw the sun) shall vanish away before it."

Wilberforce was joined by other activists in England. This tight-knit group was known as the "Clapham sect." They were called the "Clapham" sect because they met together in the Clapham region of London. Wilberforce and his friends met in the home of banker Henry Thornton. Together, they fought for the end of slavery.

In 1789, Wilberforce tried to pass laws that would end the slave trade. He was vigorously opposed. But, in time, the opinion of the British people changed. In 1807, a bill passed in Parliament that made the slave trade illegal in the British Empire. Now that the slave trade was illegal, Wilberforce kept fighting to abolish slavery itself. On March 2, 1807, bringing slaves into the United States was also made illegal. The law went into effect on the very same day as the British law. The date was January 1, 1808. By this time, the slave population in the United States was growing on its own. Many in the Southern states did not think the slave trade was even necessary. But, even though the slave trade had ended, slavery still continued. These laws did not free the Africans who were already slaves.

Wilberforce retired from Parliament in 1825. Slavery was still legal in the British Empire when he left office. Even though he was retired, he kept fighting to end slavery. Because of his diligent labors, he became known around the world. Even in Jamaica, a slave song said, "Oh me good friend, Mr. Wilberforce, make we free!" After Wilberforce retired, Mr. Thomas Buxton (1786-1845) continued the fight against slavery. Finally, in 1833, slavery was abolished throughout the British Empire. Parliament declared that all slaves must be set free by August 1, 1834. This included slaves in England and in all England's colonies. Wilberforce was near death when he received the good news. He died just three days after the bill passed in Parliament. His lifelong mission was accomplished!

The end of slavery in the United States came by a much bloodier route. The Civil War began in the United States in April 1861. Many disagreements existed between the Southern and the Northern states. Slavery was not the only issue people were fighting over. But it was one of the reasons that caused the war. In 1863, President Abraham Lincoln published an order that became known as the "Emancipation Proclamation." This order declared that all slaves living in the Southern states were free. After the Civil War ended, Congress freed all slaves in the United States. They passed the 13th Amendment in 1865. This amendment made slavery illegal in the United States. Sadly, the end of slavery in this nation came through much bloodshed. ■

PRAYER POINTS: ALGERIA

- **Praise God for the end of the slave trade in America and Europe:** Give thanks to God for freeing those who were oppressed through the slave trade. Give thanks to God for bringing freedom to Africans living in the Americas.

- **Pray for challenging racial divisions**: Men's hearts are sinful. Because of this, people of different nations and skin color sometimes mistreat each other. It is only the gospel of Jesus Christ that can bring ultimate healing to racial conflict. Pray that the gospel would break down these barriers in your nation.

- **Pray for justice for those in slavery:** Slavery ended in the Western world as a legal institution. But slavery still exists in our world. Pray that the Lord would stop evildoers who treat human beings as property. Pray that God would give freedom to those in chains.

ATLANTIC COAST IN SENEGAL

CAPE OF GOOD HOPE

Exploration and Colonization of Africa (1400-Present)

> Be still, and know that I am God;
> I will be exalted among the nations,
> I will be exalted in the earth!
> (Psalm 46:10)

For thousands of years, Africa below the Sahara Desert was unknown to the world. This area of Africa is called "sub-Saharan" Africa. People from Europe had never been here. North Africa had frequent contact with Europe. These lands were only separated by the Mediterranean Sea. Ships easily sailed from ports in Europe to ports along the north African coast. But other parts of Africa were unknown to the people of Europe. In the 1400s, that began to change. Europeans began traveling further by sea. Portugal and Spain led the way in this time of exploration.

Henry the Navigator (1394-1460) began what many call the Age of Discovery. Henry was one of the leading explorers of Portugal. He was one of the first to explore the coast of West Africa. He also discovered many islands in the Atlantic. His voyages were the first of many European explorations of Africa.

When Europe began visiting Africa, the continent changed forever. Many men followed in Henry's footsteps. From now on, Africa would no longer be isolated from the people of Europe.

PORTUGUESE EXPLORATION AND MISSIONS

The Portuguese were some of the first to explore the African interior. In 1485, a Portuguese man named Diogo Cao reached the Congo. The next year, Bartholomew Diaz reached the Cape of Good Hope. This cape is located near the southernmost tip of Africa. Then, in 1498, Vasco da Gama discovered Mombasa, Zambezi, and Malindi. Soon, the Roman Catholic Church was sending missionaries to Af-

HENRY THE NAVIGATOR

141

JAN VAN RIEBEECK LANDS IN AFRICA, 1652

rica. Most of these Africans had never heard the name "Jesus" before.

In 1491, an influential African leader in the Congo embraced the Christian faith. This happened the year before Columbus sailed to the Americas. A ruler named Mvemba Nzinga and his people confessed Jesus Christ. On May 3, 1491, Portuguese missionaries baptized natives who had turned to Christ. There were so many people to baptize that the missionaries' hands became sore and tired. Mvemba's new adopted name was Alfonso. Alfonso declared "we definitely renounced all errors and idolatries which our ancestors thus far had believed in." He confessed that God had worked greatly among his people. He said, "The grace of the Holy Spirit enlightened us, by a unique and special favor, given to us by the Holy Spirit – we received the Christian doctrine so well that by God's mercy, it was from hour to hour and from day to day better implanted in our heart."

In 1506, Alfonso ascended to the throne in the Congo. He launched a plan to destroy the pagan temple in the capital city. The name of this capital city was Mbanza Kongo. After the temple was destroyed, a church was built. The city was renamed São Salvador. But some people opposed Alfonso's efforts. Alfonso's successor tried to return the people to paganism. Sadly, as more missionaries and priests came from Europe, many openly disobeyed God's commandments. They did not repent. This brought shame to the name of Christ. Other priests joined in the slave trade with the rest of the Portuguese. These church leaders were not faithful in following Christ.

DUTCH EXPLORATIONS AND MISSIONS

**Sing to the Lord a new song,
And His praise from the ends of the earth,
You who go down to the sea,
and all that is in it,
You coastlands and you inhabitants of them! (Isaiah 42:10)**

The Dutch were the next group to colonize Africa. The modern-day nation of South Africa traces its roots back to Dutch settlers. South Africa sits at the southern tip of the African continent. For this reason, it has always been an important location for trade. The Cape of Good Hope was a key location for European explorers. In 1652, a Dutchman named Jan Van Riebeeck landed at the Cape with a hundred employees. Van Riebeeck was a businessman, not a missionary. He worked for the Dutch East India Company. He sailed to the Cape to start a business. He did not have much interest in sharing the Christian faith with the local Khoisan tribe.

After their arrival, Van Riebeeck and his employees built a fort at the Cape. They did this to protect themselves. Tension and hostility already existed between them and the native tribes. However, the Dutch settlers depended on the Khoisan for supplies. These people traded together, and peace lasted for a time. But, in 1659, the Dutch established farms in Khoisan territory. This led to fighting between the "boers" and the Khoisan people. The word "boer" in Dutch means "farmer." Van Riebeeck did not understand God's view of mankind. He had a very ungodly view of the Khoisan people. He once wrote that the Khoisan were "dull, stupid, and odious." He described them as "black stinking dogs." Other Dutch settlers sometimes thought like Van Riebeeck. They did not respect the native Africans as people made in the image of God.

Many Dutch who came to South Africa desired to see the local people saved. Dutch missionaries also wanted to spread the faith to native tribes. They hoped to preach Jesus Christ to the Africans. People from other nations settled in South Africa, too. French Protestants (known as Huguenots) were being persecuted in France at this time. The king of France took away many of their freedoms in 1685. Many French Christians fled their country to escape persecution. They looked for lands where they could worship God in freedom. They traveled to places likes North America and South Africa. Some of them joined the Dutch East India Company. This company sent them to South Africa. The Huguenots brought their biblical faith with them. Most of them joined Christian Dutch congregations.

By the 1700s, other Christian groups

arrived in South Africa. This included the Lutherans and the Moravians. A Moravian missionary named George Schmidt dedicated himself to work among the Khoisan. Schmidt arrived in South Africa in 1738. He criticized the Dutch Reformed Church for their lack of zeal for evangelism. The Dutch Reformed were not pleased with this criticism. Because of this, they forced Mr. Schmidt to end his mission work in 1748. This was a tragic example of a lack of love among Christians. Instead of wanting to preach Christ to the lost, the Dutch were concerned with themselves. They did not possess a love for those who are lost in their sins. Christ says that love is something all of His disciples should possess. He says, "By this all will know that you are My disciples, if you have love for one another" (John 13:35). Love for each other and love for the lost should be a mark of all Christians. George Schmidt would not be the last missionary to South Africa with a love for the local people groups. Many others would follow in his courageous footsteps. Robert Moffat is one such missionary. You will read about his life in a future chapter.

BRITISH AND AMERICAN COLONIZATION

Were you called while a slave? Do not be concerned about it; but if you can be made free, rather use it. (1 Corinthians 7:21)

The English also founded colonies in Africa. Through the years, they governed large portions of the continent. They ruled over many African nations. (In the 20th century, many of these British colonies became independent nations.) The British influence on Africa was truly enormous. England influenced Africa in many, many ways.

Some colonies were created as a new home for freed slaves. Many English and Americans desired to see the end of slavery. But how could these former slaves be a part of society as free people? Some who opposed slavery thought it was best to send the slaves back to Africa. Two colonial efforts began as a result of this plan.

In 1787, the colony of Sierra Leone was formed by some 400 settlers. Most of these colonists were freed slaves from Britain. The first years of the colony were full of hardship. Disease and famine faced the settlers. British abolitionists such as Granville Sharp wanted to see the colony survive. He and his friends prayed that God would sustain the young colony. Their prayers were answered in 1792. That year, 1,200 additional freed slaves arrived to reinforce the colony. As the former slaves arrived on the shores of Sierra Leone, they sang praises to God. "The day of jubilee is come; return ye ransomed sinners home."

Eventually the settlement was called Freetown. This new name was chosen because this was a colony of freed slaves. With each passing month, more and more rescued slaves were brought to Freetown.

British men-of-war watched the coast of Africa for slave ships. They captured these ships and brought the freed slaves to safety in Freetown and nearby villages. The British hoped this area of Africa would provide a safe place for freed slaves to begin a new life. They gave the Africans free land and food. They hoped this would turn the people into honest, productive citizens. However, they were terribly mistaken.

Many of the rescued Africans belonged to heathen tribes of Africa. These tribes practiced witchcraft and other evils. When the British placed these people together in a clean new home, the Africans quickly returned to their old ways. Soon murder, violence, and disease spread through the settlement. The British thought this problem might be caused by a lack of education. They sent schoolteachers to educate the freed slaves. But this didn't change the wickedness and problems in the community.

The British were forced to learn what Job 14:4 teaches: "Who can bring a clean thing out of an unclean? No one!" England thought that cleaning up the Africans' environment would make them good. But this is not enough to change a person's heart. Only the power of God can take an unclean heart and make it clean.

GRANVILLE SHARP

Finally, Christian missionaries arrived in Sierra Leone and Freetown. They began preaching repentance to the freed slaves. God's Spirit worked mightily among the Africans. Many turned to the Lord. They left their old ways and embraced Christ. Soon immorality and violence disappeared. The Africans were transformed by the power of Christ. In God's mercy, Freetown and other local villages took on a new appearance. People began obeying the laws. They stopped fighting and stealing from each other. They treated Sunday as a holy day. Soon the cities and villages were quiet, peaceful places to live. In 1822, the Lord Chief Justice stated that, among a population of 10,000, there were only six criminal cases awaiting trial.

Members of the British government watched this change in astonishment. The freed slaves in their colony became honest and hard-working. They were now faithful, law-abiding citizens. The power of man had failed to make any change. But the power of God was far greater than any human power that could be imagined. It transformed soci-

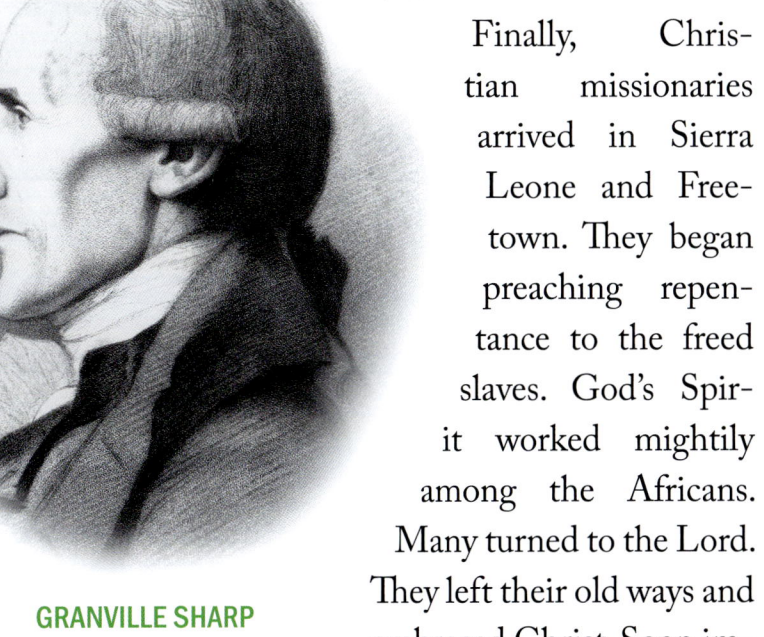

LOCATION OF SIERRA LEONE AND LIBERIA

ety when nothing else could. Sir Charles MacCarthy, the British military governor of Sierra Leone, noticed the change. He knew how important Christianity was for Africa. He wrote: "Witnessing, as I have done, the sufferings of our Black brethren, [I know] it is the influence of Christianity alone which can make them civilized and happy in this life."

The Christian residents in Freetown worked to transform their city into a godly society. They wanted to establish a beacon of light for the rest of Africa. Today, Sierra Leone's population is mostly Muslim. However, there is still a strong Christian presence in the country.

Southeast of Sierra Leone, another colony for freed slaves began. This was the colony of Liberia. Many Americans wanted to end slavery. They started this colony in Africa as a place to send freed slaves. The colony was established in 1820 by Pastor Samuel Bacon. With Pastor Bacon, some eighty freed slaves arrived on the shores of West Africa. In 1847, Liberia became an independent nation. By 1866, the colony had grown to a population of 18,000. The Lord had sustained the budding colony. Today, Sierra Leone and Liberia are both independent nations in West Africa.

THE SCRAMBLE FOR AFRICA

By 1870, Europeans had explored large portions of Africa. But most European colonies were still on the coast of Africa. They were not located in the interior of Africa. This meant that most of Africa was untouched by Europe. In 1870, only about 10% of the continent was under foreign rule. But that would soon change. This change is what historians call "The Scramble for Africa."

Between 1881 and 1914, European powers took control of about 90% of Africa. Nations such as Britain, Germany, Italy, and France began taking large swaths of African land. They tried to get as much land as possible to increase trade. They also wanted to use the land as strategic military locations. Soon, these nations were "scrambling" to take Africa for themselves. Each nation began taking as much land as they could. Sometimes they made treaties with African leaders. Sometimes they seized control without asking permission. In many cases, foreign powers took over local governments. This continued throughout much of Africa until 1950. Many Europeans traveled to Africa to take part in these colonial efforts. Some went to Africa for business. Others went as missionaries seeking to spread the gospel. Some came for both reasons.

THE SHIFT TOWARDS INDEPENDENCE

**Do not fret because of evildoers,
Nor be envious of the workers of iniquity.
For they shall soon be cut down like the grass,
And wither as the green herb.
Trust in the LORD, and do good;
Dwell in the land, and feed on His faithfulness. (Psalm 37:1-3)**

European control of Africa continued from 1914 until about 1950. In 1945, World War II ended. This war brought many changes throughout the world. It changed things in Africa, too. From 1950 to 1975, colony after colony in Africa became independent nations. These

EUROPEANS SCRAMBLE FOR AFRICA (THE BERLIN CONFERENCE)

ROBERT MUGABE

colonies had been ruled by nations in Europe. But now the continent quickly became independent. African nations began to rule themselves. Through these changes in government, the African map changed. Countries were renamed.

In some cases, nations that were now independent went through difficult times. Some tyrants and dictators took advantage of this shift in power. They seized power for themselves and used it for wicked purposes. Sadly, many African nations suffered severe violence and famine because wicked men took control.

One example of dictators taking power is the small nation of Equatorial Guinea. In 1968, this nation became independent from Spain. A free election was held. Francisco Macias Nquema was elected president. But, in 1971, President Nquema seized the powers of government. He decreed that anyone who threatened the president would be put to death. Anyone insulting him could be put in prison for up to 30 years. During his presidency, about one third of the population was executed or exiled. Today, citizens of this small country face tyranny, violence, and poverty.

In 1979, a civil war broke out and the president's nephew took power. As of this writing, Teodoro Obiang is the president of Equatorial Guinea. He holds complete power, just like his uncle did. While most of the nation lives in poverty, President Obiang enjoys a wealth of $600 million. This is no surprise to Christians. Fallen man, apart from God's grace, wants power and wealth for himself. He does not care about others. These modern dictators will face God's judgment unless they repent and put their trust in Jesus Christ.

**When the righteous are in authority, the people rejoice;
But when a wicked man rules, the people groan. (Proverbs 29:2)**

Another modern dictator of Africa was Robert Mugabe. In 1987, Robert Mugabe became president of Zimbabwe. Like other wicked rulers, he took all power for himself. In the years that followed, he won every election. He probably won because he controlled the elections. He did not win because the people loved him. During his iron-fist rule, Zimbabwe faced massive unemployment. Its citizens could not find work. They had trouble providing food for their families. By the 1990s, the nation's economy had almost completely collapsed. Those who opposed Mugabe were sent to prison camps. Today, the average person in Zimbabwe has a personal wealth of about $1500. When he died, Robert Mugabe held tens of millions of dollars in personal wealth. Mugabe died in 2019. But his past abuses of power continue to harm the people of Zimbabwe.

Other people groups in Africa suffered at the hands of ungodly leaders in the 20th century. However, the church would continue its rapid growth in Africa during this time. God's purposes were coming to pass. The Bible promises that the "meek will inherit the earth" (Psalm 37:11). Wicked leaders may rule for a period of time. But one day the nations must all bow to the King of kings and the Lord of lords: Jesus Christ.

In the chapters that follow, you will learn more about how Jesus Christ's reign has expanded in Africa since the 1700s. ■

GIRAFFES IN ZIMBABWE

LIONS HEAD MOUNTAIN, CAPE TOWN, SOUTH AFRICA

The Moravians in South Africa

Surely you shall call a nation you do not know,
And nations who do not know you shall run to you,
Because of the LORD your God,
And the Holy One of Israel;
For He has glorified you. (Isaiah 55:5)

In 1722, a small Christian community was founded in Germany on the land of Count von Zinzendorf.[1] It was given the name Herrnhut. Moravians from the land of Bohemia (modern-day Czech Republic) took refuge on Zinzendorf's land. Fleeing persecution in Bohemia, they found a place of refuge at Herrnhut. This Christian community grew rapidly. It was a community of prayer, Bible-reading, and Christian service. It was also a community of Christians who had a great interest in seeing our Lord's Great Commission advanced.

Within ten years, the first Moravian missionaries were sent out to take the good news about Jesus to distant lands. The first mission was the Caribbean Island of St. Thomas. Moravian missionaries reached St. Thomas in 1732. St. Thomas was only the beginning. Moravians went to all different parts of the world. They deployed to Greenland, North America, Canada, Australia, South America, and Africa.

One of the first Moravians to reach Africa was a man named George Schmidt. In the previous chapter, we learned about his conflict with the Dutch who settled in South Africa. In this chapter, we resume Schmidt's story. We will also learn about the Moravian missionaries who followed him.

On March 13, 1737, Schmidt set sail from Amsterdam for South Africa. After a voyage of a few months, he arrived in Cape Town, on the coast of South Africa.

George learned something the first evening he was in Cape Town. On that night, July 9, 1737, he was in the public room of the inn in which he was staying. There a few farmers were discussing his arrival. His coming was now public knowledge, but none of the farmers knew who he was.

One of the farmers said, "I hear that a

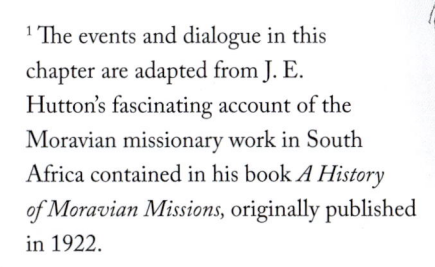

COUNT VON ZINZENDORF

---

[1] The events and dialogue in this chapter are adapted from J. E. Hutton's fascinating account of the Moravian missionary work in South Africa contained in his book *A History of Moravian Missions*, originally published in 1922.

151

LOCATION OF CAPE TOWN, SOUTH AFRICA

parson has come here to convert the Hottentots."

"A parson?" said another man. "The young man is no parson at all. What good can he ever do to the Hottentots? They have no money. And this man plans to pay for all his own expenses? The poor fool must have lost his head."

A servant in the inn, hearing the conversation between the two farmers, turned to Schmidt and said, "And what, sir, do you think?"

Schmidt answered, "I am that man."

The word "Hottentot" was a term used of some of the natives of South Africa. Today, the word is often considered offensive, much like the word "negro." The people group that the word "Hottentot" was usually applied to were the nomadic tribe of the Khoekhoen. At the time George Schmidt arrived, it was a word regularly used to describe the Khoekhoen.

When Jan van Riebeeck began his colonization efforts in South Africa, he established a school for slaves. Some of the Dutch pastors preached to the Hottentots and baptized some of them. Even though some efforts were made to share the Christian faith with the native peoples, many of the Dutch had little to no love for the native peoples around them. The Dutch settlers were often more interested in making money than sharing the gospel. Part of the reason for this was that many of the Dutch farmers were Christians in name only. Many did not have a real love for Christ. Because of this, many of the Dutch were angered by Schmidt's efforts to do so much for the "Hottentots."

Some of the Dutch farmers acted wickedly toward the natives around them. Some called the Hottentots "children of the devil." Some said they were no better than "black cattle." And others even boasted of how many Hottentots they had shot.

Driven by his love for Christ and love for his fellow man, Schmidt came to love the native peoples known as the Hottentots. As the Lord Jesus once said, "the Son of Man did not come to destroy men's lives but to save them" (Luke 9:56). This was George Schimdt's desire: to see the native peoples saved from their sins by the power of God.

Schmidt set up a mission station about one hundred miles east of Cape Town. He built a house there, planted a pear tree, and dug a garden. Then he invited the natives to visit him regularly at his home. He taught boys and girls how to read and write in the afternoons. Each evening, he invited the natives to come and hear the Word of God. He shared the gospel from portions of Scripture such as the Book of Romans.

In his diaries, Schmidt detailed what the natives were like. He observed that the native people lived in villages in wooden huts that looked much like beehives. They made their own pots and pans. They ate primarily meat, milk, roots, and various fruits. They also took marriage quite seriously. Any unfaithfulness on the part of a husband or wife was severely punished. Each village had a "headman." The headman would lead the villagers in battle and administer justice within the village.

The native people believed in a god

COASTLINE OF CAPE TOWN, SOUTH AFRICA

named Toiqua. They claimed this god lived above the moon but did not care about what was happening on earth. They believed in a second god they called Gauna. Gauna was the cause of all evil in the world. They also believed in a third god they called Heitsi-elib who was a friendly god. They worshiped the moon and thought it had power to control the weather. They also revered witch doctors and sought help from the witch doctors in times of need or suffering.

As with many early missionary efforts, it was many years before Schmidt began to see conversions take place among the natives. But through the power of God, the day did come in which the native peoples confessed that Jesus is Lord. In 1742, Schmidt baptized the first few converts to Christ.

Sadly, the Dutch pastors did not rejoice over the sinners who were repenting and finding salvation in Jesus Christ. Instead, they saw George Schmidt as a threat to their church. Since Schmidt was a Moravian, he was not a pastor in the Dutch State Church established in South Africa. The Dutch pastors told Schmidt he had robbed them of "their converts." This did not stop George Schmidt. He kept baptizing. The Dutch pastors were upset over Schmidt's refusal to stop his ministry. They appealed for help to the Netherlands to stop Schmidt. Due to the persecution of the Dutch pastors, Schmidt was eventually accused of illegal action. Because of the continual legal opposition, in 1744 Schmidt left South Africa to labor elsewhere.

Despite the conflict, Schmidt's labors for the Lord were not in vain. His work among the same native people would be resumed by others within a few decades.

THE THREE MUSICIANS

**Sing to the LORD, all the earth;
Proclaim the good news of His salvation from day to day.
Declare His glory among the nations,
His wonders among all peoples.
(1 Chronicles 16:23-24)**

In 1792, the Moravians sent out three men to pick up the mission work that Schmidt had left. These three Christians were gifted musicians. Henry Marsveld sang. Daniel Schwinn played the flute. And John Kühnel played the violin. They brought together their musical talents and preaching gifts to carry the gospel mission forward.

Many of the Dutch farmers (known as Boers) still opposed evangelizing the Hottentots. But this did not stop the Moravians from picking up the work once again. On December 24, 1792, the three brethren visited the same location where George Schmidt had once labored. George's pear tree was still standing and thriving. Part of Schmidt's house was still there as well. Nearby, the three brethren met an old woman named Helena. She was now eighty years old and was losing her sight. The brethren learned that she was one of

GENADENDAL, SOUTH AFRICA

Schmidt's original converts. She still remembered George Schmidt and all he had done among her people.

Marsveld asked Helena, "Is it true that George Schmidt baptized you?"

"Yes, it is true."

"And what name did he give you?"

"Helena."

"And do you remember anything George Schmidt taught you? Do you remember what he said about Jesus?"

Helena responded with joy, "Jesus! Jesus! Oh, yes! I remember that."

Marsveld told Helena, "We are George Schmidt's brethren, and we have come to tell your people how to be saved."

"Thank God! Thank God!" Helena said. She then showed the brethren a copy of a book given to her by George Schmidt. It was a copy of the New Testament in Dutch. Helena told the brethren that she was unable to read. But she loved to hear the Bible read to her by those who could read.

The brethren were overjoyed to see how George Schmidt's work had endured. They decided to reestablish the mission station. In January 1793, they built a mission house and started a day school. Once the school was opened, the native people eagerly came to learn. The brethren taught them how to read and write while teaching them the Word of God. The brethren also required strict discipline in the school. Immoral behavior was not allowed. Through the teaching of God's Word, the native peoples grew in faith and holiness.

Since the brethren were gifted in music, they also taught the natives how to sing and play instruments. Now, for the first time, the praises of God ascended to heaven from the mouths of the Khoekhoen as they sang hymns to the Lord. The mission work progressed, and within a few years' time, there were many additional conversions and baptisms.

Nevertheless, the Dutch pastors continued to oppose the Moravians. At a few points, the work almost ceased entirely. But things began to change when Great Britain took over colonial rule of South Africa in 1806. Under British rule, freedom for different Christian groups expanded. This allowed the Moravians to continue their missionary work with much less opposition. In fact, some government officials lent direct financial support to the Moravian mission.

As the decades passed, the gospel transformed the native people. By God's grace, once selfish, proud, and unloving people became generous, humble, and selfless in their behavior.

Such blessings of the gospel also

MORAVIAN MISSION STATION IN GENADENDAL

brought about a much healthier society. When George Schmidt first arrived, the native people were lazy and did little with their hands. Now, through the influence of Christianity, they became hard workers. In fact, they became so industrious that the mission settlement became one of the largest towns in South Africa for a time. Beehive huts were traded for brick homes, where the natives were given an acre of land to farm and develop. They learned industry and trade. The mission station, now a town called Genadendal, became a marvel to many in South Africa. Visitors from Cape Town would remark on its beauty and order. The natives called it "God's Home."

In the spring and early summer, beautiful red flowers dotted the hills. Peaches, oranges, and tomatoes were in abundance in the gardens. A South African poet by the name of Pringle who witnessed the community wrote a poem to describe it:

> In distant Europe oft I've longed
> To see this Vale of Grace; to list the sound
> Of bubbling brooks and morning twitters round
> The apostle Schmidt's old consecrated tree;
> To hear the hymns of solemn melody
> Rising from the sequestered burial ground,
> To see the heathen taught, the lost sheep found,
> The blind restored, the long-oppressed set free.
> All this I've witnessed now, and pleasantly
> Its memory shall in my heart remain.

This is what happens when the salvation of God visits a people. As Psalm 85 says, when God speaks peace to a people, abundant blessings flow through Jesus Christ.

**Mercy and truth have met together;
Righteousness and peace have kissed.
Truth shall spring out of the earth,
And righteousness shall look down from heaven.
Yes, the LORD will give what is good;
And our land will yield its increase.
(Psalm 85:10-12)**

MORAVIAN MINISTRY TO THE LEPERS

Another important part of the Moravians' ministry was among the lepers. In cooperation with the government, the Moravians provided physical and spiritual care to the "least of these" who were often neglected. The first leper colony was established just a few miles south of Genadendal. The government built a hospital and a church for the lepers. A doctor visited twice a week to assess the medical needs of the lepers. A Moravian minister named Peter Leitner was there as a general manager of the ministry. He made sure that every patient was fed and washed. He also assisted the lepers in taking a daily bath in the sea. During the course of his ministry, he baptized some ninety-five lepers. Though the doctor could not heal the lepers, yet many received the gospel before they parted from this earthly life. Pastor Leitner conducted many funerals among the lepers. But because of the gospel, he and the others did not grieve without hope. He knew that many of the lepers were asleep in Christ and would rise again on the day of the resurrection.

**The Spirit of the Lord GOD is upon Me,
Because the LORD has anointed Me
To preach good tidings to the poor;
He has sent Me to heal the brokenhearted,
To proclaim liberty to the captives,
And the opening of the prison to those who are bound;
To proclaim the acceptable year of the Lord,
And the day of vengeance of our God;
To comfort all who mourn. (Isaiah 61:1-2)**

THE MISSION CONTINUES

As the 19th century ended, the Moravians continued their work among the native people group. However, significant challenges arose when many of the natives moved to the larger cities such as Cape Town. There they encountered many worldly temptations. Much to the sorrow of the Moravian missionaries, some of the natives left behind their profession of Christ and began to love this present world. Thankfully, by this time other natives were firmly rooted and grounded in Christ's truth. The native people then pursued evangelizing their own people within the cities, turning them back to the Lord Jesus Christ. This was a testimony to the strength of Christ's church as it grew in South Africa. ■

PRAYER POINTS: SOUTH AFRICA

- **Communities of Prayer:** Thank God for the movement of prayer that began in South Africa known as the Global Day of Prayer. This prayer movement has spread to other parts of the world as well. God's people are to be a praying people, and there has been much of this in South Africa.
- **Ethnic Divisions and Conflict:** South Africa is a diverse nation made up of many different tribes and ethnicities. Some ethnic groups are of European origin (from Britain and the Netherlands) while others are native to Africa. Over the centuries, there has been much hatred and strife between these different people groups. The gospel of Jesus Christ is the only hope to heal these wounds permanently. Pray for the gospel to break down barriers between people groups.

DRAKENSBERG AMPHITHEATRE IN SOUTH AFRICA

BOTSWANA, WHERE ROBERT MOFFAT MINISTERED, IS STILL KNOWN FOR ITS WILDLIFE AND OPEN SAVANNAS

Robert Moffat: Missionary to South Africa

**The people who walked in darkness
Have seen a great light;
Those who dwelt in the land of the shadow of death,
Upon them a light has shined. (Isaiah 9:2)**

Today, South Africa is one of the most important countries in Africa. It has a very large population. The country is also made up of many ethnic groups. It has eleven official spoken languages. But there are actually many more languages spoken in different regions of the nation. These languages came from the many different tribes in South Africa's past. Additionally, both the British and the Dutch colonized the region. This made Dutch, English, and a Dutch-derived language known as "Afrikaans" common languages in South Africa.

South Africa's diversity came at a cost. When the British and Dutch colonized the region, conflict and even bloodshed in some cases followed. Sometimes relationships between colonists and the native peoples were healthy. But at other times they turned deadly. Godly missionaries helped to keep peace. But other colonists were only interested in money. They often took advantage of the native peoples. When we look at the work of missionaries, we see that only the gospel of Jesus Christ brings lasting unity and peace. Today, South Africa is still in need of more gospel work.

The life of Robert Moffat (1795-1883), missionary to South Africa, gives us one window into South Africa's past. This faithful man labored for over fifty years among the tribes of South Africa. His entire life work was dedicated to establishing the kingdom of Christ in South Africa. He was a faithful and humble man. The Lord always uses faithful and humble servants to expand His kingdom.

CALL TO THE MISSION FIELD

**I will praise You, O Lord, among the peoples;
I will sing to You among the nations.
For Your mercy reaches unto the heavens,
And Your truth unto the clouds.
(Psalm 57:9-10)**

Robert Moffat was born in 1795 in Scotland. He grew up in a humble family. His parents were not wealthy, but they gave Robert something more important than money. They taught Robert the Christian faith. When Robert was fourteen years old, he became an apprentice in gardening. He labored in gardening for a few years. Afterward he moved to Cheshire, England

MAP OF SOUTH AFRICA

to work as a gardener. As he departed, his mother gave him wise counsel. She told young Robert, "O, my son, read much in the New Testament. Read much in the Gospels, the blessed Gospels. Then you cannot well go astray. If you pray, the Lord himself will teach you."

In Cheshire, Robert Moffat worked for a wealthy man named Mr. Leigh. While working on Mr. Leigh's estate, Robert met some very zealous Christians who were Methodists. He attended their meetings and became convicted of his sin. The Word of God pierced Moffat's heart. The Christian training of his parents was not in vain. Those early seeds sown in his heart now began to bear fruit. Moffat was twenty years old when he embraced the faith. He became a zealous man who desired to bring others to a saving knowledge of the Lord Jesus.

In God's providence, Robert attended a missionary convention in Manchester. It was at this meeting that he felt the call to mission work. He believed he was called to serve as a foreign missionary, but he wasn't

16. ROBERT MOFFAT: MISSIONARY TO SOUTH AFRICA

ROBERT MOFFAT

MISSIONARY LIFE AMONG THE KURUMAN

And a servant of the Lord must not quarrel but be gentle to all, able to teach, patient, in humility correcting those who are in opposition, if God perhaps will grant them repentance, so that they may know the truth, and that they may come to their senses and escape the snare of the devil, having been taken captive by him to do his will. (2 Timothy 2:24-26)

On September 30, 1816, Robert Moffat was ordained to missionary work. He was sent to South Africa. In January he and a team of missionaries arrived in Cape Town in the Cape Colony of South Africa. This faraway land was a treacherous wilderness. The missionaries faced many dangers. Robert and his fellow missionaries didn't travel with any modern con-

ROBERT MOFFAT AND HIS WIFE MARY

sure how to become one. He had not received much education. Most missionaries had received more training. Moffat wasn't sure if a missionary society would accept him. But, in faith, he offered his services to the London Missionary Society. Even though Moffat did not have a very strong education, the London Missionary Society accepted him. They were impressed with his knowledge and zeal. The Lord gave Robert favor with the organization. When the Lord would have any of us work in a particular field, he will make a way for us to do it. We just need to trust Him and take the next step. The Lord can open doors for us.

LOCATION OF KURUMAN IN SOUTH AFRICA

veniences like cars or air conditioning. A journey across South Africa could mean death by wild beasts or attacks from local tribes. Even though it was dangerous, the mission was worth it. Moffat and the other missionaries counted the cost. They would make this sacrifice for the Lord Jesus Christ. Moffat eventually settled into a mission station in the northern portion of South Africa. At that time, the region was known as "Bechuanaland." Here, Moffat served for most of his life.

When Moffat left England, he planned to bring his fiancée with him. He wanted to begin missionary work with a faithful wife. Before he left England, Robert had become engaged to a young lady named Mary Smith. But when Mary's parents learned about Robert's plans to go to Africa, they would not permit Mary to marry Robert. They feared that if their daughter married Robert, they would never see her again. Living in Africa was a dangerous life. Many missionaries never came back. So for the first few years Robert labored without a close companion. He patiently waited for an opportunity to marry the young lady. This time of waiting had a purpose. It was a lesson in patience. God had a plan for Robert and Mary. Both of them would have times of patient waiting in the future.

My brethren, count it all joy when you fall into various trials, knowing that the testing of your faith produces patience. But let patience have its perfect work, that you may be perfect and complete, lacking nothing. (James 1:3-4)

After two and a half years of waiting, Mary's parents gave her permission to marry Moffat and go to South Africa. Mary boarded a ship and made the three-month journey to the southern tip of Africa. In December 1820, Robert and Mary were married in Cape Town. Together, they set out for Bechuanaland to see the gospel of Jesus and the kingdom of God established.

For some time Moffat's headquarters were in the village of Kuruman. The word "Kuruman" was the name of an African tribe. It was also the name of the village where Moffat lived. The first years of missionary work among the Kuruman were difficult. The local peoples received the missionaries because they brought valuable technology and training. The Africans mostly cared for the things of this life. They did not want to listen to eternal things. This was discouraging to Mr. and Mrs. Moffat. But, by faith, they labored on, waiting for the working of God's Spirit.

The ravages of sin were evident everywhere in Bechuanaland. In most of the tribes, women did most of the work. The men were very lazy. Old people were often abandoned, left to die alone. Children were also frequently abandoned and left to die. Robert Moffat rescued many children from this fate. These native peoples needed God's mercy to fall on their land.

Moffat also found it challenging to learn the language. The people of Kuruman spoke the Tswana language. It took many years for Robert and his wife to learn this language. Pioneer missionaries are those who go to lands never yet evangelized. These pioneer or "frontier" missionaries do a lot more than just preach the Bible. Their main calling is to teach Jesus Christ's commands to the nations (Matt. 28:19). But they often have to do a lot more than discipleship. Many had to build homes, dig wells, and cultivate farms. Like other missionaries, Robert Moffat learned a variety of practical skills. During his years as a missionary, he became skilled in carpentry, translation, printing, and blacksmithing.

In 1823, Moffat became a military leader when a war broke out among the natives. This event was known as the "Mantatee Invasion." The Mantatee people ravaged the countryside of South Africa. They would pillage and burn any village they came across. The Mantatee were now approaching the Bechuanas. Robert Moffat led group of one hundred armed men to meet the violent tribe. Moffat wanted to negotiate peace. But the Mantatee were not interested. The Mantatee didn't want peace. They attacked the Bechuanas. Yet the Lord protected Robert Moffat and the Bechuana people. They drove back the Mantatee invasion. The mission work in Kuruman was preserved. This battle strengthened the relationship between Moffat and the Bechuana. But there was little spiritual fruit. Moffat was faithful to preach the gospel, but he knew that the Lord also had to grant a change of heart to the people.

1826 brought more trials to the Moffat family. In that year, Robert and Mary lost a baby boy. Robert also lost one of his brothers. Mary's mother died as well. It was a hard year. But Moffat made good progress in the mission work. He had now mastered the language. He created a spelling book and also translated a catechism (a manual of Christian doctrine). He translated portions of the Bible, too. These printed resources in the Tswana language would be important tools for communicating the gospel.

GOD'S SALVATION VISITS THE KURUMAN

**Therefore I will look to the Lord;
I will wait for the God of my salvation;
My God will hear me. (Micah 7:7)**

Finally, in 1829, the Spirit of God brought awakening to the Kuruman. The Moffats had waited patiently for the salvation of the Lord. The Lord heard their prayers and brought a spiritual awakening. Many of the Kuruman confessed their sins and put their trust in Jesus Christ. Moffat had prayed for this very thing to happen for many years. But he admitted that he was surprised when his prayers were answered. Sometimes we are surprised when God answers our prayers. This is especially true if we have prayed for a long time. But our Lord does not forget His people's prayers.

When men and women are converted, the Bible says that they become a "new creation" (2 Cor. 5:17). The work of Jesus begins to transform every aspect of their lives. People have new attitudes and new habits. They learn new priorities. There was evidence of these new creations everywhere among the Kuruman. Times of worship and prayer were held by the natives throughout the week. These meetings would often last through the night until dawn. These people now loved to worship God. They hungered and thirsted for God (Psalm 42:1-2). A new church building was erected. New homes were built by the natives to provide for the needs of others. The gospel was transforming the Kuruman people.

The changes among the Kuruman were so drastic that other tribes came to see whether the news was true. Two men came from over seven hundred miles away. They were sent by King Mosilikatse, a great king in the east. These men were shocked to see the Kuruman people transformed. One of the most obvious changes was that the Kuruman were now wearing clothes. Before the gospel took root, most of the Kuruman were naked. Of course, the most important changes were spiritual changes. But there were also many improvements to public life and industry. The Spirit brings about the fruit of the spirit. Christian character brings blessings to the life of a community. The men from King Mosilikatse invited Robert Moffat to journey back with them and meet this warlord from the east. This king was known as a powerful king all over South Africa. Even tribes such as the Kuruman, seven hundred miles away, knew about him. Moffat agreed to make the long journey. He hoped to save the Kuruman people from any wars. And, perhaps, the Lord would save this king from his sins.

After a long journey, Moffat arrived at the court of King Mosilikatse. This man was known as the "Elephant," the "Lion's Paw," and the "King of Heavens." The king reigned over the Matabele tribe. The two men testified before the king about the Kuruman and Robert Moffat's leadership among them. Then, for ten days, Moffat and the King talked together. The men in King Mosilikatse's court were amazed by Robert Moffat's boldness. The missionary rebuked the king for his attacks on neighboring tribes and his disregard for human life. Moffat also proclaimed the gospel of Jesus to the king, hoping that the Lord would work in the king's heart. Though the king could have killed Moffat, he did not. Instead, he became friends with the missionary. Moffat's words even changed the king's behavior. The king became more merciful and lenient with his servants. Robert Moffat was a man filled with the Spirit of God. For this reason, he was bold in his dealings with the king. The Lord protected him and gave Moffat a friendship with the king that lasted many years.

Twenty-three years passed and Robert Moffat had not visited his homeland. But in 1838 Robert and Mary returned to England for some much-needed rest. By this time, Moffat had completed his translation of the New Testament into Tswana. The translation was then printed in England. During his rest in England, two more missionaries for the Kuruman were sent out. The two missionaries were William Ross and David Livingstone. Soon David Livingstone, the well-known African explorer, would marry Mary Moffat. She was the firstborn of the Moffat's ten children. Livingstone and Ross went ahead of the Moffats and took the translation of the New Testament back to the Bechuanas. Though the Moffats did have a time of rest in England, Robert was very busy with speaking engagements. The Moffats remained in England until late 1843, when they returned to the Kuruman. One of the most important gifts left to future generations by Robert Moffat is his translation of the Bible into the Tswana language. It took him over thirty years to complete the entire Bible. The completion of this work in 1857 is a testimony to Moffat's perseverance. Moffat also completed a translation of John Bunyan's classic book *The Pilgrim's Progress*.

DAVID LIVINGSTONE

LAST YEARS IN SOUTH AFRICA

I have fought the good fight, I have finished the race, I have kept the faith. (2 Timothy 4:7)

South Africa was colonized by the British and Dutch. This resulted in many conflicts between colonists and the native peoples. In 1848 conflicts between the Bechuana peoples and the Dutch farmers (known as the "Boers") became increasingly hostile and violent. The Dutch farmers and the missionaries came to South Africa for different reasons. The Dutch farmers were interested in making a profit. The missionaries wanted to see the native tribes converted to Christ. Because they had different purposes, they treated the native tribes differently. The Dutch Boers often invaded tribal territories and took the land by force. Many missionary stations were also raided by the Boers. David Livingstone and his wife Mary lost their missionary station to the Boers. The violence and theft of the Dutch farmers turned the natives against any white foreigners. Eventually, the conflict between the Dutch Boers, the English, and the native tribes became so fierce that the English government stepped in to defend the English.

ROBERT MOFFAT IN LATER YEARS

By 1860, Robert Moffat had served for over forty years as a missionary to the Bechuanas. He was now over sixty years old. Moffat had already enjoyed a long life. But he endured the sorrow of losing many of his children before he went to glory. His firstborn daughter, Mary Livingstone, died in 1862. Through trials and tribulations, Moffat continued to faithfully disciple the Kuruman. Finally, in March 1870, he preached to the Kuruman for the last time. At seventy-five years of age, he and his wife returned to England. Their good deeds in South Africa were told throughout the world. Many English people wanted to meet these faithful missionaries. Even though Robert was now retired to his homeland, he continued to plead the cause of the mission work. He raised funds to build a seminary in Kuruman. Moffat knew that the church in South Africa needed native students to continue the work of the gospel. In 1871, Robert lost his dear wife Mary when she went to be with her Lord. Though he was without his earthly companion, the Lord Jesus was with him.

Moffat's son-in-law, David Livingstone, continued to do missionary work in Africa after the death of his wife Mary in 1862. Though Livingstone was a missionary, he dedicated much of his time to exploration into the interior of Africa. He was one of the first Europeans to venture into the deep interior of Africa. His explorations of Africa helped to fill in the maps of European explorers. This pioneer work paved the way for future missionaries. While exploring Africa, Livingstone died in 1873 from malaria. He left this earthly life while in present-day Zambia. In 1874, his body was brought back to England. Moffat also led his funeral service at Westminster Abbey. It was at this historic church that David Livingstone's body was laid to rest.

ROBERT MOFFAT IN LATER YEARS

Robert Moffat spent his last years in the small English town of Leigh. Then, on August 10, 1883, he finished the race of faith and entered into paradise. He was eighty-eight years old. The day after he was buried, the *Times* of London honored him with this tribute:

> We owe to our missionaries that the whole region (South Africa) has been opened up. Apart from their special service as preachers, they have done important work as pioneers of civilization, as geographers, as contributors to philological [language] research. Of those who have taken part in this, Moffat's name is not the best known, Livingstone—Speke—Stanley, (coming after him, because of him) have become household names. In his own simple words, it never occurred to him while working among the Bechuanas that he should obtain the applause of men. His one care was for those among whom he had cast his lost.

Another newspaper, the *Brighton Daily*, said this of Moffat:

> Robert Moffat belonged to no sect or party. To better the world, and advance the one church formed the sole end [purpose] of his being.

Robert Moffat was a servant of Jesus Christ. We all have something to learn from Jesus' servants, who are given to the church as a gift (Eph. 4:11). From Robert Moffat, we see a true example of perseverance through hardships. Moffat endured trial after trial, but he pressed on. He didn't give up on the work Jesus gave him to do. He finished translating the entire Bible. Moffat also gives us an example of boldness. He traveled seven hundred miles to confront a dangerous African king. He led the Kuruman into battle to defend their lands against invaders. And he preached the gospel faithfully, year after year. ∎

BASIC FACTS ABOUT THE REPUBLIC OF SOUTH AFRICA

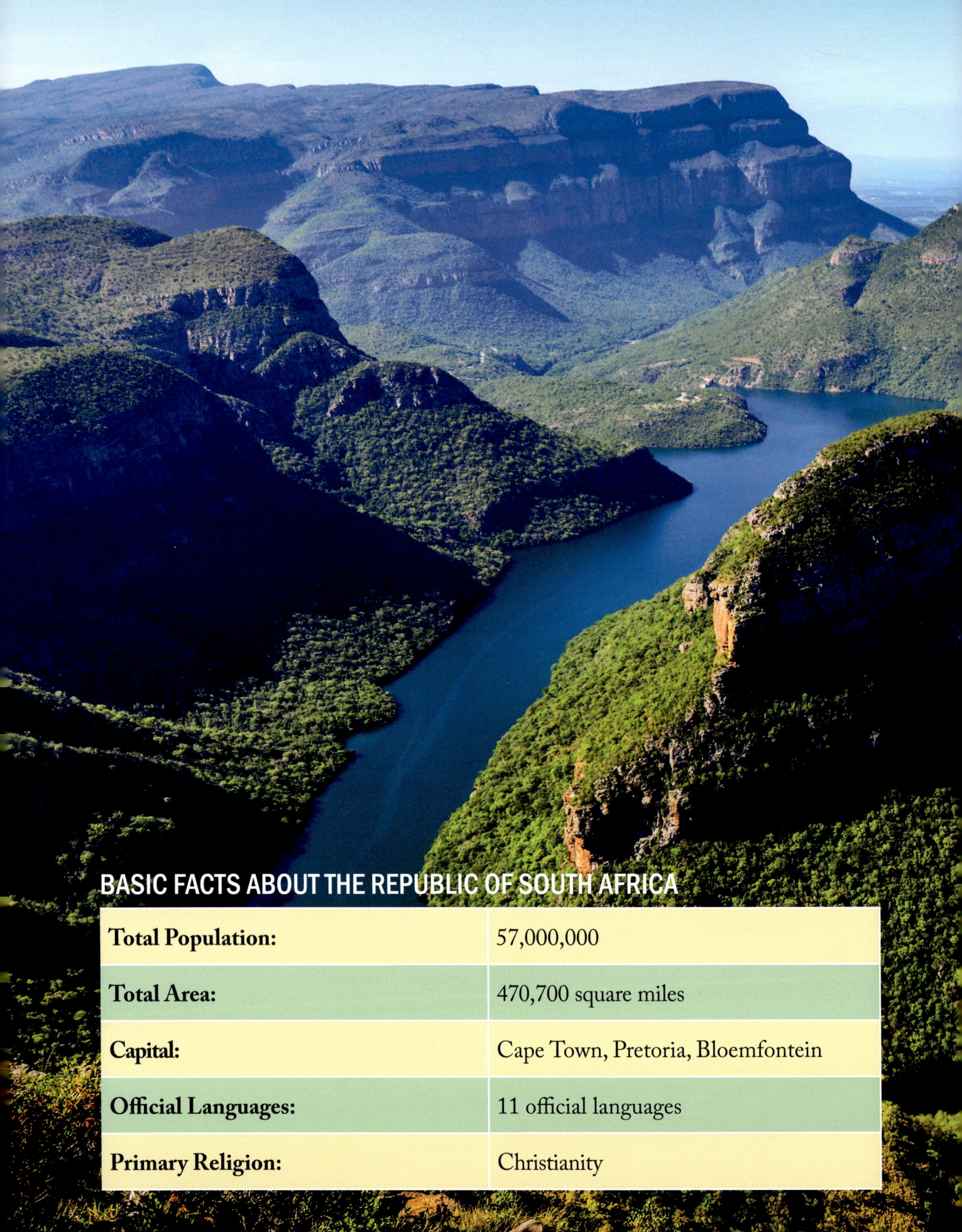

Total Population:	57,000,000
Total Area:	470,700 square miles
Capital:	Cape Town, Pretoria, Bloemfontein
Official Languages:	11 official languages
Primary Religion:	Christianity

BLYDE RIVER CANYON IN SOUTH AFRICA

PRAYER POINTS: SOUTH AFRICA

- **Communities of Prayer:** Thank God for the movement of prayer that begun in South Africa known as the "Global Day of Prayer." This prayer movement has spread to other parts of the world as well. God's people are to be a praying people and there has been much of this in South Africa.
- **Ethnic Divisions and Conflict:** South Africa is a diverse nation made of many different tribes and ethnicities. Some ethnic groups are of a European origin (from Britain and the Netherlands) while others are native to Africa. Over the centuries there has been much hatred and strife between these different people groups. The gospel of Jesus Christ is the only hope to heal these wounds permanently. Pray for the gospel to break down barriers between people groups.

THE NAMIB DESERT IN NAMIBIA BORDERS THE OCEAN.

The Gospel in Namibia: The Salvation of an Outlaw and His Son

The wilderness and the wasteland shall be glad for them,
And the desert shall rejoice and blossom as the rose;
It shall blossom abundantly and rejoice,
Even with joy and singing.
The glory of Lebanon shall be given to it,
The excellence of Carmel and Sharon.
They shall see the glory of the Lord,
The excellency of our God. (Isaiah 35:1-2)

Southwestern Africa was the wild west in the early 1800s. The gospel had not set deep roots into African soil. This is the story of how the gospel of Jesus made it to Namibia or Namaqualand.

The European settlers had not done a good job making disciples for Jesus in Southern Africa. As soon as they got there, Governor Jan Van Riebeeck opened the Cape to the slave trade (1658). Two Dutch pastors, Godefridus Udemans (1581-1649) and Jacobus Capitein (1717-1747), had taught that slavery was a good thing. So the Dutch brought slaves into the colony. The slaves came from Indonesia, India, and other places around Africa. Most of the slaves came from India. By 1710, there were many more slaves than colonials in South Africa. Instead of bringing the message about Jesus to Africans, the Dutch created a slave plantation. Now there were three kinds of people living in this area of Africa—the Europeans (including the French, British, and Dutch), the slaves from India and other countries, and the African blacks.

Some of the slaves escaped from their masters, hoping to find freedom in the wilderness. Sometimes they were set free by Christian farmers. Sometimes freed slaves joined together to form bands of outlaws. That was the story of a young man named Jager Afrikaner. His father Klaas tried farming, but he was driven out by the colonials. So Klaas took up a job with a Dutch farmer named Piet Pienaar, guarding his cattle herds from rustlers. At a time when there were no lawmen or sheriffs to keep order, these men took the law into their own hands. They would chase down the rustlers with guns, dispense with the thieves, and retrieve their animals.

But the Afrikaners did not know Jesus and His ways. So it wasn't long before they became the outlaws. They had learned how to succeed as outlaws from the outlaws they chased down. In 1795, twenty-six-year-old Jager Afrikaner replaced his father as the leader of the family. When the family refused to obey Piet Pienaar's order to go on a dangerous mission, the farmer got angry and knocked Jager to the

NAMIBIAN DESERT

ground. Then Jager's brother Titus shot the farmer. That's when Jager and the family became outlaws. They stole the farmer's cattle and headed north of the Orange River into Namibia.

The family got richer by raiding cattle from the Dutch farms in South Africa. Jager and his men were feared by the African tribes and the Dutch colonials. They were fast on horses and expert with their guns. Governor George Dundas offered a large reward for anybody who would capture Jager Afrikaner and bring him to justice.

Around 1805, two brothers arrived in South Africa with the idea of taking the gospel to Jager's backyard. Christian and Abraham Albrecht built a mission house at a place called Warmbad in 1808. Not long after that, Jager raided the place and burned it down. Abraham died and Christian fled the country.

About this time, another missionary named Johannes Ebner approached a young man named Robert Moffat in Cape Town. He spoke of a dangerous mission—to bring the gospel to the outlaw of Namibia. He told Moffat that he might lose his life if he were to take up this challenge. Moffatt set out on the journey right away to meet the outlaw. At first, Afrikaner was unfriendly towards the missionary, but after a while the two men became friends. Jager attended worship services and learned to read the Bible. By 1819, it was clear to everybody that this outlaw had become a Christian. God had changed the man through the gospel of Jesus Christ.

Robert Moffat decided the time had come to take the outlaw back to Cape Town. Jager was afraid to go because the governor had offered a big reward for anybody who could capture him. Nevertheless, God had already captured this outlaw.

On the way to Cape Town, the missionary and the outlaw stopped overnight at the home of a farmer named Engelbrecht. The farmer told Robert Moffat that he was amazed to see the missionary alive after having spent so much time with the outlaws. When Moffat introduced Jager, all the farmer could do was raise his eyes heavenwards and cry out, "O God, what a miracle of your power! What cannot your grace accomplish!"[1] The Governor forgave the old outlaw and gave him a gift of a wagon. Jager Afrikaner returned to Namibia. He was baptized and changed his name to Christian Afrikaner. His son Jonker was made the head of the clan.

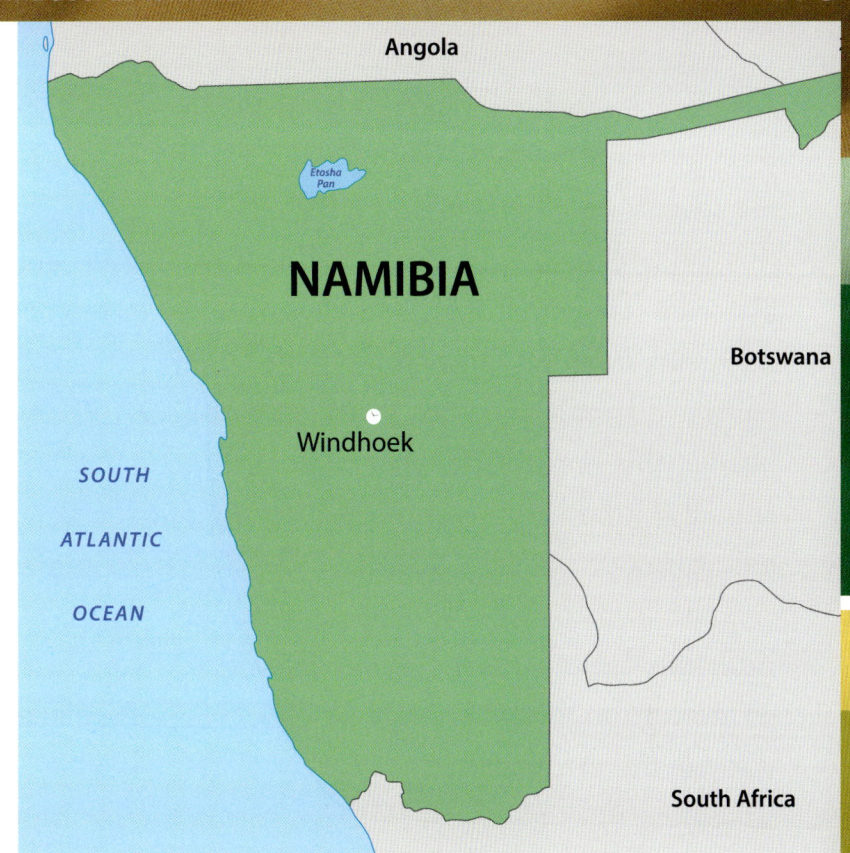

TAKING THE GOSPEL TO NAMIBIA BY OX

Who would bring the gospel to Namibia now? Robert Moffat had married and was called to bring the gospel to the Africans in Botswana and South Africa.

That's when Jesus called another young man to the mission. A German Lutheran, Johann Heinrich Schmelen, made the trek up into Namaqualand in 1812. Johann built the first mission stations in Bethanie and Steinkopf. He was a hardy pioneering sort. He hiked across the country, bringing God's Word to the people. There wasn't much money coming in for his support. At times, he would go without shoes. He couldn't afford a horse, so he resorted to an ox to carry him across the barren lands. All he carried with him was

---

[1] J. Marrat, *Robert Moffat: African Missionary* (London: C.H. Kelly, 1895), 23.

a Bible, a sheepskin for a saddle, and only a little meat for food. He wrote home about his adventures: "I crossed the vast areas of this land to preach the gospel. The Lord blessed my feeble efforts so much. . . . I had no bread, but the Lord strengthened me daily. . ."[2] By the time the missionary had finished his journey, he wore nothing but animal skins. His trousers, shirt, and shoes had worn out.

The Lord blessed this gospel work at Bethanie. Twice a day, Schmelen preached sermons from the Bible, verse by verse. He wanted the Africans to know the whole Bible. Sometimes they would listen, and sometimes they would not. When the people would lose interest in the prayers and singing of hymns, Schmelen would weep before the Lord. He begged God not to withdraw His hand from these people. A deceiver tried to lead the young people away from the church. Schmelen warned the people about the man. He continued to stay faithful, as a faithful shepherd for Jesus. Several African women were saved, and Schmelen married a woman from the Nama tribe named Zara. This wonderful woman of God translated his sermons for him whenever he preached. And she helped translate the Bible into the Nama language.

---

[2] Joachim Rieck, "Johan Heinrich Schmelen (1777-1848)," *Reformation Today* (January-February 2006), 209.

SCHMELEN'S HOME IN BETHANIE, NAMIBIA

CHRIST CHURCH IN WINDHOEK, NAMIBIA

A MISSIONARY MURDERED

Over the next few years, two men joined the mission with Johann Schmelen in Namibia. Both were Methodists from England—Barnabas Shaw and William Threlfall. They built a station at Lily Fountain. This church continues to this day.

In August 1825, young Threlfall set out on a trek up the Orange River to share the gospel. Two young African men, recently converted, joined him on the journey. Disaster struck as they camped out under the stars. Before they bedded down that night, they sang a hymn. The last verse goes like this:

When passing through the shades of death.
When yielding up this fleeting breath,
In need, our only Friend is He,
Who gives the final victory.

As they slept that night, three native guides snuck into the camp and killed them. In his final moments, William Threlfall cried out in a loud voice to God, "Lord, lay not this sin to their charge!" The young missionary was just twenty-six years old when he died.

About this time, Johann Schmelen trekked to a place called Tsebris to visit Jonker Afrikaner. The son of the outlaw was now interested in the gospel. He want-

PRAYER POINTS: NAMIBIA

- **Mixing Religions:** The devil comes to deceive in so many ways. Many Africans including those in Namibia still mix the Christian faith with their old tribal religion. They go to church on Sundays. But they still trust in witchdoctors to help them with sickness. Pray the people of Namibia will trust the true and living God. Pray that they will stop resorting to demons.

- **Faith in Government:** Many Namibians hope the civil government will save them. They are more interested in being saved by powerful dictators than by Jesus. But these governments always make things worse for the people. It is better to trust in God than to put trust in princes (Psalm 118:9). Namibians need to realize their problem is not government. The solution is not government. The problem is sin. The solution is Jesus. Pray that the real gospel would be taught in the churches of Africa.

- **Bad Gospels:** Many Africans are fooled by lies. Some preachers tell them that Jesus has come to make people rich. Many people want to be saved from poverty. They get excited when they hear the false promises from these pastors. Pray that the Namibians will want to hear the real gospel. Jesus has come to give us life. He has come to save us from our sins. He has come to conquer death. We know this because He is risen from the dead!

ed a missionary to serve full time with his tribe of about 1,000 persons. When he set out to build a city called Windhoek, right away he built a stone church big enough for 500 people. A missionary named Franz Kleinschmidt came to help minister to the people at Windhoek in 1842. Franz had married Johann Schmelen's daughter.

These were the beginnings of the Lord Jesus's work in Namibia. Today, the country is 65% Protestant and 23% Roman Catholic. Most of the Christians are Lutheran.

Then the lame shall leap like a deer,
And the tongue of the dumb sing.
For waters shall burst forth in the wilderness,
And streams in the desert.
The parched ground shall become a pool,
And the thirsty land springs of water;
In the habitation of jackals, where each lay,
There shall be grass with reeds and rushes.
(Isaiah 35:6-7)

QUIVERTREES IN NAMIBIA

VICTORIA FALLS

David Livingstone: Explorer of the African Interior

**All nations whom You have made
Shall come and worship before You, O Lord,
And shall glorify Your name.
For You are great, and do wondrous things;
You alone are God. (Psalm 86:9-10)**

David spotted a group of lions nearby. It was February 16, 1844. Scottish missionary David Livingstone was near the village of Mabotsa (in modern-day Botswana). With him was a local villager named Mebalwe. They were protecting a flock of sheep. It was not uncommon in that region to lose sheep to lion attacks. The villagers worked hard to fend off lions to preserve their flocks.

That day, some of the villagers warned David that a pride of lions had been spotted nearby. Livingstone and Mebalwe set out with guns in hand. They were on the hunt. Coming upon the group of lions, Livingstone fired. The shots reached their target. One of the lions was wounded, but the shots did not stop the creature. David reloaded his weapon for another shot. But before he could fire, the lion pounced.

The lion's jaws clamped down on Livingstone's left shoulder. David fell to the

LIVINGSTONE ATTACKED BY A LION

TAKING AFRICA FOR JESUS

DAVID LIVINGSTONE

ground as his bones were crushed in the powerful grip of the beast. He was unable to fight back. Mebalwe saw the lion and took aim. He fired, but both barrels misfired. The lion dropped David and then attacked Mebalwe. Finally, the wounds inflicted by Livingstone's previous shots took effect. The lion dropped to the ground dead.

David and Mebalwe were both alive but injured. David's wounds were severe. For weeks he struggled to recover as he dealt with crushed bones and infection. In time he did recover, though his shoulder would trouble him the rest of his life.

The lion mauling would be just one of many thousands of dangerous events in David's life. For some thirty years, he spent his life exploring Africa and teaching the natives about Christ. Few missionary stories contain such tales of danger and adventure. David was often sick with many strange illnesses. He faced animal attacks and assaults from native tribes. Over the years, he lost many friends and family members to death. Africa was filled with dangers. To spend any length of time there was risky. To explore the deep interior of Africa was even more treacherous. This did not stop David. No European explorer had ever journeyed as deep into Africa as he did. He was a pioneer. He opened new regions in Africa. Many missionaries would come after him. They would preach the gospel in those lands.

CALLED TO BE A MISSIONARY

Better is a little with the fear of the Lord, Than great treasure with trouble. (Proverbs 15:16)

David Livingstone was born in Blantyre, Scotland in 1813. David's family was not wealthy. Yet he was blessed with something more important than money. He was blessed with godly parents. They taught David God's Word. Since his family was so poor, David worked hard as a young boy. He worked in a cotton spinning factory. His work shifts were long, sometimes lasting fourteen hours a day. Not only were the days long, but the conditions were uncomfortable. Temperatures in the cotton spinning factory were often around 80-90°F.

David's years in Africa would also be hot and difficult. In fact, they would be much hotter and much more difficult than the cotton spinning factory. David learned at an early age that God had created him to work hard and to endure difficulty.

As David grew older, he thought about becoming a missionary. To prepare for this, he studied in Glasgow for a few years. There he learned more about the Bible, language, and medicine. David's training in medicine would be a useful tool in Africa. He would use that skill to heal his companions and the natives he met.

In 1840, David was ordained by the London Missionary Society. He left England in December 1840. Boarding a ship, he sailed for Cape Town, South Africa.

EARLY MISSIONARY WORK

Months later, in July 1841, David arrived in the mission station of Kuruman. In a previous chapter, we learned about Robert Moffat. Robert labored in Kuruman for some years before David arrived. Moffat worked hard and waited many years before God changed the hearts of the people. In time, the native peoples of Kuruman began to receive the gospel.

While in Kuruman, David became acquainted with Mary Moffat, Robert's daughter. In a few years, they would be married. In 1843, David joined some other missionaries and journeyed 200 miles northeast to the village of Mabotsa. There he preached the gospel and cared for the medical needs of the local native peoples.

In 1845, David married Mary Moffat. Together they committed their lives to serving the people of Africa. They hoped to bring the gospel to these people. Some years they worked in Africa together. At other times, they would be separated for long periods while David explored new areas. Within a few years, the Lord blessed David and Mary with several children. In total, they were blessed with six children: Robert, Agnes, Thomas, Elizabeth, William, and Anna.

When he was training in Scotland and England, David had struggled with preaching. He did not think he was a very gifted preacher. Yet he always preached God's Word to the natives when he had a chance to do so. He wanted them to understand the love of Christ revealed in the gospel. David wrote:

> For a long time, I felt much depressed after preaching the good news of Christ to hearts that were dead in sin. But now I like to dwell on the love of the great Mediator, for it always

warms my own heart, and I know that the gospel is the power of God. It is the great way God uses to save a ruined world.

One of the Africans David discipled was a tribal leader named Sechele. He was the chief of the Kwena people. This tribe lived in Botswana. Like many tribal leaders of the region, Sechele practiced polygamy. He had five wives. Livingstone worked hard to teach Sechele about the one true God. He told him about Jesus Christ who was sent by God the Father to save us from our sins. Through David's teaching, Sechele began to turn from his sins. He came to Christ and began to do the will of God. As he was taught to read, Sechele began reading the Bible. He loved to read God's Word. He especially found delight in the Book of Isaiah. He led family worship each day, reading the Bible and praying with his family. Sechele did struggle with temptations from his past life. Yet it appears he was truly converted to the Lord. Through his influence, most of the Kwena people received Christ. Other nearby tribes were also changed by this.

PRESSING DEEPER INTO AFRICA

As a missionary, David wanted to take the gospel message to new peoples and places. For this reason, he wanted to explore new parts of Africa. David would chart new paths. He would meet new people groups. And in time, as he learned the languages of each new group, he would preach the gospel to them. This would open the way for others to follow in his steps.

In 1852, David and Mary made a decision. Mary and the children would go back to England. Africa was a dangerous place to live. Exploration in Africa was exceedingly dangerous. While exploring, David faced extreme weather, treacherous landscapes, menacing animals, and threatening people. For this reason, he wanted his family to go home to England. He wanted them to be safe while he explored. David would see his family each time he made a trip back to England. But for many decades he was separated from his wife and children. Sadly, this distance made it difficult for him to be a part of his children's lives. He had a close relationship with some of his children, such as Agnes. But some of his children never got to know their father very well.

Even during these times of separation, David wrote frequent letters to his children. He loved his children. He earnestly wanted them to trust in Christ and walk with Christ. In a letter to his daughter Agnes, David wrote:

My Dear Agnes,

This is your own little letter. Mamma will read it for you, and you will hear her just as if I were speaking to you.... I have given you back to Jesus, your Friend ... He is above you, but He is always near you. When you ask

BATOKA GORGE AND THE ZAMBEZI RIVER

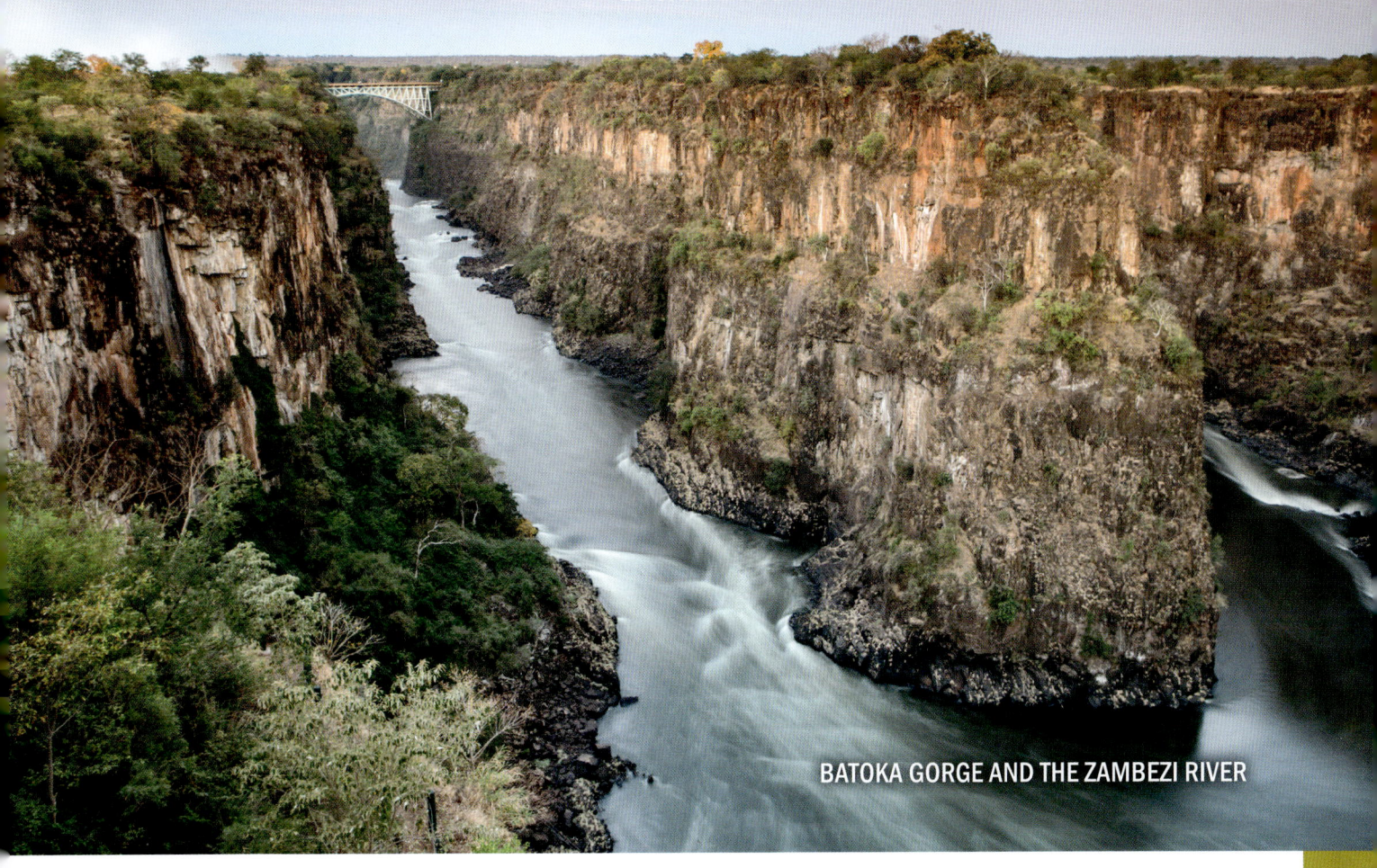

things from Him, that is praying to Him; and if you do or say a naughty thing, ask Him to pardon you, and to bless you, and to make you one of His children. Love Jesus much, for He loves you. And He came and died for you. Oh how good Jesus is. I love Him and I shall love Him as long as I live. You must love Him too, and you must love your brothers and Mamma, and never tease them or be naughty, for Jesus does not like to see naughtiness. Good-bye, my dear Nannee.

As David explored new regions of Africa, he discovered new places. Africa was filled with wonder and natural beauty. David wrote about what he found in Africa. Then he sent his writings back to England and Scotland. Soon he became famous in his homeland. In 1856, he returned home for a visit. By that time, he was a national celebrity. While he was at home, David wrote his first book. It was called *Missionary Travels and Researches in South Africa*. The book was quite popular. It sold tens of thousands of copies. People wanted to hear about David's courageous explorations. Many people admired him for what he had done. But others criticized him. Some said that he was not really a missionary because not many of the native peoples had been saved. It's true that David did not see many conversions during his ministry, but he still did influence a number of people who received Christ. He also inspired many other missionaries to follow in his footsteps. God used David in mighty ways.

People were amazed by the hardships David endured in Africa. They talked about how much he sacrificed for the cause of Christ. But David did not agree with them. He looked on his work as a *privilege,* not a sacrifice. When he remembered how much Jesus his Savior had done for him, David knew that whatever he did for Christ was not much of a sacrifice. He wrote:

> For my own part, I have never ceased to rejoice that God has appointed me to such a task. People talk of the sacrifice that I have made in spending so much of my life in Africa. . . . It is emphatically no sacrifice. Say rather it is a privilege. . . . I never made a sacrifice. Of this we ought not to talk, when we remember the great sacrifice which He made who left His Father's throne on high to give Himself for us.

David took one of his most dangerous trips when he was forty-five years old. Some men from England and Scotland went with him. Their mission: to explore the Zambezi River and reach new people groups. By this time, David was quite familiar with the hardships of exploring the wilderness. But many of the men with

VICTORIA FALLS VIEWED FROM THE AIR

him were shocked at the difficulties on their journey. They often spotted hippos, alligators, and lions. Dangerous creatures were everywhere. And malaria was a constant danger.

As they journeyed up the Zambezi, David and the other men began every day in prayer. Each morning, they asked God to protect them and bless their work. They discovered many things on this expedition, including Lake Nyasa. People had heard about this lake, but they didn't know where it was. This lake (today known as Lake Malawi) is the fifth largest freshwater lake in the world. Livingstone also became the first European to see the breathtaking Victoria Falls (he named them after Queen Victoria). This amazing natural landmark was known to the natives as *Mosi-oa-Tunya*. This means "the smoke that thunders."

DAVID LIVINGSTONE READING THE BIBLE TO AFRICAN NATIVES

FIGHTING THE SLAVE TRADE

He who kidnaps a man and sells him, or if he is found in his hand, shall surely be put to death. (Exodus 21:16)

As a Christian, David wanted others to be freed from the chains of sin. He also knew that Christ brings the blessings of other kinds of freedom. David wanted to stop slavery in Africa. He did everything he could to end the evil slave trade.

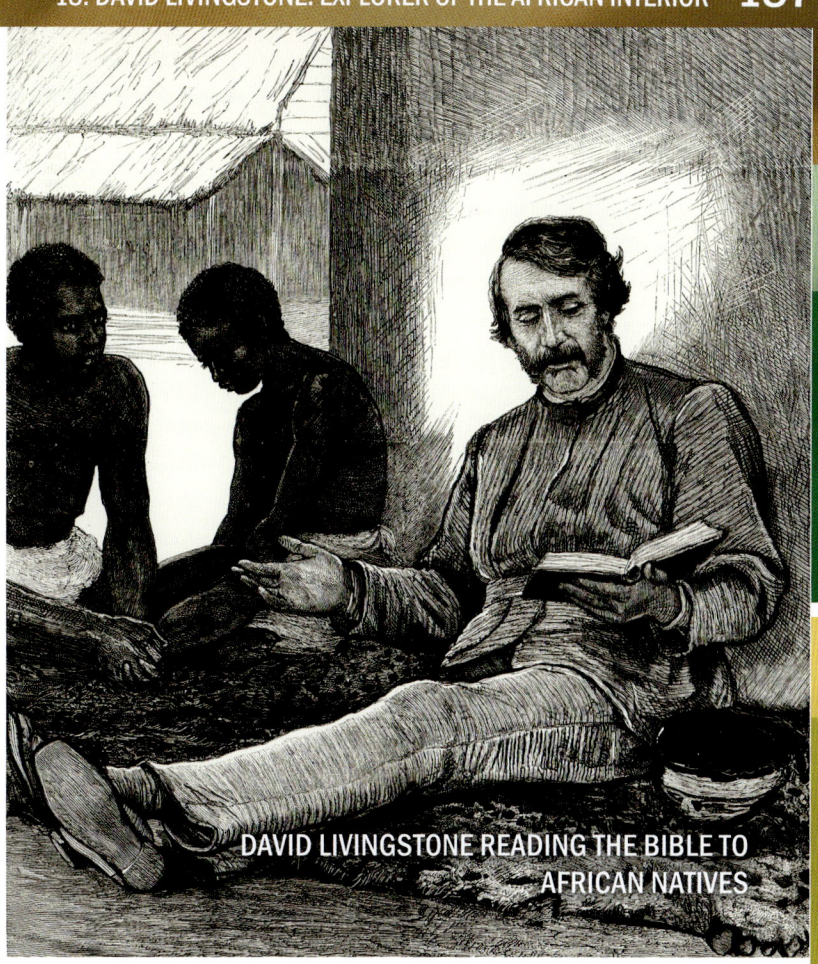

In 1807, Parliament abolished the slave trade in England. In 1833, it ended slavery as well. But this only applied to England. In Africa, native tribes continued to kidnap and enslave other Africans. Tribes at war with other tribes would enslave their enemies. Then they would take the captured human beings to coastal regions. The Africans sold the slaves to Arabs and Europeans. David was greatly angered by this wicked practice. He was grieved that this evil continued. Whenever he could, he tried to stop it.

On some of his travels, David and his

HENRY MORTON STANLEY MEETS DAVID LIVINGSTONE

companions found slave traders. Once in 1861, David and his men encountered slavers from the Ajawas tribe. The Ajawas attacked nearby tribes and captured men, women, and children. Then they sold the captives as slaves. As David and his men were journeying through the region, they met the slavers with their captives. The Ajawas attacked David and his men. In defense, David and his men fought back, killing the Ajawas. After the brief gunfight, David and his companions set the eighty-four slaves free. One of the little boys said to David's men, "The others tied and starved us. But you cut the ropes and tell us to eat. What sort of people are you? Where did you come from?" Such was the love that was shown by David and other missionaries. Another time, David was able to free one hundred slaves.

FINAL YEARS OF MISSIONARY SERVICE AND EXPLORATION

In 1862, David experienced the greatest sorrow of his life. His wife Mary had returned to Africa with him, and she died from malaria. She was buried on the banks of the Zambezi River. Like many before her, the terrible and common disease of malaria took her life. This was a very hard time for David. But he continued his work in Africa.

During his last years, David lost contact with the outside world for a time. People back home in England and Scotland heard no news from him and began to wonder about him. Was he dead or alive? If he was alive, where was he?

18. DAVID LIVINGSTONE: EXPLORER OF THE AFRICAN INTERIOR

To find the famous explorer and missionary, a journalist named Henry Morton Stanley was sent out by the *New York Herald*. Stanley began his journey into the heart of Africa in 1869. It took two years for him to discover where David was. For a few years, David had been ill and had not been able to journey very far. He was dwelling in the village of Ujiji. This village was located on the shores of Lake Tanganyika.

Very few white men traveled to places deep into Africa such as Ujiji. When Stanley learned that a white man was living there who spoke English, he knew who the man must be. For this reason, when Stanley saw David, he said, "Dr. Livingstone, I presume?" Livingstone responded "Yes." Stanley gave David letters from home with news from the outside world. Because of this meeting, friends and fam-

MAP OF SOUTH AND CENTRAL AFRICA DETAILING LIVINGSTONE'S DISCOVERIES

ily back home received word that Livingstone was still alive. This was good news to the many people all around the world who were praying for David.

After this meeting with Stanley, David continued exploring for two more years. But he was slowed down by frequent illnesses. At last, his life ended in a village in present-day Zambia. He had been suffering from malaria and internal bleeding. He died on May 1, 1873. He was sixty years old.

LEGACY OF DAVID LIVINGSTONE

**God reigns over the nations;
God sits on His holy throne. (Psalm 47:8)**

What is the lasting legacy of David Livingstone? We learned that he was a man dedicated to exploration. Few other men were willing to face so many dangers to explore and open Africa for Christ. Though David explored, he never forgot that he was an ambassador of Jesus Christ. Whenever he could, he preached the gospel of Jesus Christ. Not many natives were saved during his lifetime. It took many years before the fruit of the gospel began to show. But the Lord did bless David's work. Some people were saved and became disciples of Christ. In fact, some of the people who traveled with David formed mission stations after he was gone.

We also see that David worked hard to stop the evil of the slave trade. He took many risks to oppose the trade. This was a bold action, but he was not afraid to do what was right. He was a follower of Christ, and he was committed to mercy and justice. David's explorations were also useful to later missionaries. Armed with a better knowledge of the geography and people groups, others could take the gospel of Christ into those lands. David was a stepping stone for others who would build on his labors. ■

BASIC FACTS ABOUT ZAMBIA

Total Population:	19,000,000
Total Area:	290,587 square miles
Capital:	Lusaka
Official Languages:	English
Primary Religion:	Christianity

PRAYER POINTS: ZAMBIA

David Livingstone explored large areas of land in the southern interior of Africa. These explored areas cover many modern-day African nations. In God's providence, it was in the region of modern-day Zambia that David left this earthly life to be with the Lord. Now, take some time to pray for Zambia.

- **Give Thanks to God for a Growing Church:** In recent decades, the number of Bible-believing Christians in Zambia has grown. In 1996, the constitution of Zambia declared that the country is a "Christian nation." The Christians are about 75% Protestant and 25% Roman Catholic. Give thanks to God for the growth of God's people in Zambia.

- **Give Thanks for Peace in the Land:** Compared to many other African nations, Zambia has enjoyed a long period of peace and freedom. This is a blessing from God. Let us give thanks that the Lord has granted such peace. This allows the church of Jesus to meet and to serve one another and the people of Zambia.

- **Pray for the Church to Grow Strong:** Even though Zambia calls itself a Christian nation, this does not mean that all Zambians are saved. Pray that the Lord would change people's hearts in this land. Ask God to mature the Christians and transform lives in Zambia.

ABEOKUTA, NIGERIA

Samuel Adjai Crowther

The wicked in his pride persecutes the poor; . . .
In the secret places he murders the innocent;
His eyes are secretly fixed on the helpless. . . .
He has said in his heart, "God has forgotten;
He hides His face; He will never see." . . .
But You have seen, for You observe trouble and grief,
To repay it by Your hand.
The helpless commits himself to You;
You are the helper of the fatherless.
(Psalm 10:2, 8-14)

On the west coast of Africa, below the Sahara Desert, lies a country now known as Nigeria. Through it the mighty Niger River flows to the ocean. Here, in the 1800s, lay a village inhabited by the Yoruba tribe. It was here in the African jungle that a child was born in 1809. He was given the name Adjai.

Early one morning in 1821, silent shadows crept slowly toward the Yoruba village. Suddenly a blood-curdling cry filled the air. A large army of African warriors rushed on the startled villagers. The attackers were natives of the Foulah tribe. They were Africans who had converted to Islam. These Muslims were bitter enemies of the Yoruba tribe. They had attacked Adjai's village to take the people as slaves.

The Yoruba villagers tried to escape, but it was too late. Men died defending their homes, and their wives and children were taken captive.

Adjai was twelve years old when he

SAMUEL CROWTHER

that this fear of death was a gift from the hand of an all-merciful God. This was a gift that kept him from the terrible sin of suicide. Adjai later wrote: "Thus the Lord, while I knew Him not, led me not into temptation and delivered me from the evil."

The Portuguese loaded Adjai and other slaves onto a ship, but they were quickly spotted by two British men-of-war. Slavery was illegal, so the British ships were watching the coast to stop any slave ships from leaving. They fired on the Portuguese and forced them to surrender. The British then freed the Africans and arrested the Portuguese captain and his crew. Once again, Adjai was free!

GOD CALLS A BOY

The British sailors carried the freed Africans to Sierra Leone. When Adjai arrived in Sierra Leone, a British missionary couple took him in. Though he was now free, Adjai had no home to return to. His village lay in ashes. His father was dead and his mother a slave. Therefore Mr. and Mrs. Davey welcomed the child into their home. Under their loving care, Adjai grew and began learning English. He was a quick learner, and within six months he could read the New Testament on his own.

Mr. and Mrs. Davey taught young Adjai the truths of Scripture. And, in God's mercy, the boy's heart was opened to receive the gospel. Now Adjai learned that his true enemies were not the Foulah Muslims or the Portuguese slavers. His enemies were his own sins. By the Spirit of God, he turned from his old ways and embraced Christ. On December 11, 1825, he was baptized. As a sign of his new life in Christ, he took on a new name. From now on, his name would be Samuel Adjai Crowther.

As a Christian, young Samuel Adjai began to see his life through new eyes. He saw that God's invisible hand had led him every step of his short, difficult life. Samuel's past life was full of sorrow and pain. But now he realized that God had been working through this. He looked back on the day he was kidnapped and thanked God even for that. He wrote: "[This was] the day which Providence had marked out for me to set out on my journey from the land of heathenism, superstition, and vice to a place where His Gospel is preached." From that point forward, Samuel always referred to the day he was kidnapped as a "blessed day."

In 1826, the Daveys returned to England for a visit. They brought Samuel along, and he studied for several months in a British school. When he returned to Africa, he continued his studies under a German missionary there. After finishing his studies, Samuel began teaching at a local school. During this time, God blessed him with a godly wife. Susan Thompson was a young woman who had been rescued from slavery about the same time as Samuel. The two had met each other in the Davey home. Now they married and continued to labor for Christ together. God blessed them with many children.

A DEADLY VOYAGE

For several years Samuel taught at a local school and college. Then, in 1841, he received an unexpected call. The British government was organizing a trip up the Niger River into the African jungle. They hoped to open up trading opportunities with the inland natives. The British wanted to convince these natives to stop capturing and selling people into slavery. They agreed to bring some missionaries along on the trip to spread the gospel. Samuel Crowther was one of the men chosen to go.

James Schön, another missionary, also joined the British expedition. Together he and Crowther met the native tribes as the British ship traveled up the Niger River. Crowther was shocked at the cruelties he discovered along the river. Among the Ibo and other tribes, human sacrifices were still offered. Infants were often killed. Some tribes murdered all twin babies. Others killed a child if its upper teeth grew in before its lower teeth.

Samuel's heart ached as he saw the spiritual darkness that blinded his African brothers. He and Mr. Schön prayed earnestly for God to reach these people with the gospel. At each village, Crowther asked the tribes if they would be willing to have a Christian live among them and teach them the gospel. Many tribes welcomed the idea. With joy Crowther and Schön laid plans for establishing churches in many villages along the river. But a terrible tragedy destroyed their plans.

Soon after the expedition began, the dreaded African fever struck the British ships. One by one the British members of the party fell ill. Samuel was immune to the fever because he was a native. Day after day and night after night he sat beside the bunks of those who lay dying. The terrible sickness spread to every part of the ships, and even the doctors and captains fell ill. At last the expedition was abandoned. The ships returned to the coast in an attempt to save as many lives as possible. Over one third of the Europeans died on this fatal trip.

The terrible news of this journey shocked England. Even the missionary community gasped when they heard how many people had died. Crowther explained that the native villages along the river were ready to receive the gospel. He begged for more men to come begin missions. England, however, refused to send any more expeditions up the Niger. The cost in British lives was too high. The tribes along the Niger would have to wait.

Samuel returned to his home in sorrow. His heart burned for the natives along the Niger River. When would the gospel reach them? Crowther had hoped British missionaries would come quickly. But, with so many dead, they were afraid to try again. Samuel knew that he would have to wait on God to provide a way. He didn't realize that God was already preparing someone to lead the way up the Niger. That someone would be Samuel Crowther.

> Do not put your trust in princes,
> Nor in a son of man, in whom there is no help.
> His spirit departs, he returns to his earth;
> In that very day his plans perish.
> Happy is he who has the God of Jacob for his help,
> Whose hope is in the LORD his God, . . .
> (Psalm 146:3-5)

PLANTING A CHURCH AT ABEOKUTA

On June 11, 1843, Samuel was ordained a preacher of the Word. He began preaching in English and in Yoruba, his native language. He also began translating the Bible into Yoruba.

British ships had rescued many Yoruban slaves over the years. These people began to return to their country and start a new life. They built a city named Abeokuta. Many of these people were now Christians. They therefore asked for preachers to come with them to their new home. Samuel Crowther and Henry Townsend, a British missionary, answered this call. With their families, they traveled to Abeokuta to begin a church there.

A surprise was waiting for Samuel at Abeokuta. Soon after he arrived, a woman came to see him. The woman had heard that a black pastor had come to town. She heard the man's name and came immediately to see him. The woman was Samuel's mother. She was thin and weak from years of slavery, but she was filled with joy to find her son again. Crowther wept with joy when he saw his mother. He welcomed her into his home and tenderly cared for her. He wrote: "God has brought us together again and turned our sorrow into joy." In time, his mother abandoned her false gods and turned to Christ. She was one of the firstfruits of Samuel's work at Abeokuta.

God blessed the work at Abeokuta. Samuel recorded, "A great number of heathen have ceased worshipping their country's gods." After only three years, the church had a congregation of over 500.

Crowther labored joyfully for the salvation of his people. But he also taught them that the gospel should change their lives. The Bible teaches us how to worship. But it also teaches us how to work, how to live, and how to govern ourselves. Samuel taught these things to the natives. He showed them how to work with their hands. Abeokuta was a good place to grow crops. The British were looking for cotton to purchase. Samuel encouraged the Africans to plant cotton. This crop became vital to the area's economy, and it still is to this day.

Samuel taught his people the importance of being diligent and hard-working. He showed them that they must obey God's commands. But he also showed them that God's commands are very good. These commands teach us how to serve God. They also teach us what is good for mankind. Man will never be happier than when he is serving God.

Samuel's work at Abeokuta wasn't easy. Pagan priests opposed God's people. They told the local chief that the Christians were bad for his country. The chief threatened to kill anyone who visited Crowther. Guards watched Samuel's house day and night. But, despite the persecution, the church continued to grow.

In 1851, Crowther returned to England for a brief visit. While there, he was asked to address a large audience at Cambridge University. Samuel spoke of the spread of the gospel in his country. He ended his talk with a stirring appeal for more missionaries to join in Christ's

IDANRE HILL, NIGERIA

work in Africa:

> St. Paul saw in a vision a man of Macedonia, who prayed him to come over to his assistance. But it is no vision that you see now; it is a real man of Africa that stands before you, and on behalf of his countrymen invites you to come over into Africa and help us.

In answer to this call, many young men from England joined in the work of winning Africa for Christ.

A JOURNEY THROUGH THE JUNGLE

Finally, after many years of waiting, God opened a way to reach the pagan tribes along the Niger River. In 1857, an expedition started up the river, led by Samuel Crowther. This time, the men on board were all African Christians. They traveled up the river without fear of disease. The ship anchored at various villages along the river. At each village Samuel asked permission to establish a Christian mission. Most of the local chiefs welcomed Crowther and the Christians with him.

After traveling 140 miles up the river, Samuel reached the large town of Onitsha. This was an important city along the Niger. The chief agreed to sell Crowther land for a Christian mission, and Samuel and his companions set to work. As they entered the town one day, they heard drums beating and saw natives dancing wildly. Crowther asked the headman why the people were so excited. The headman explained that the crowd was preparing to sacrifice a female slave to honor someone who had recently died. Crowther wrote: "We then took the opportunity, and spoke most seriously to the headman in the hearing of many people, . . . of the abomination of this wicked practice." Samuel explained that human sacrifices were wicked. He also told the people that an innocent person should never be put to death.

The people of Onitsha were astonished at Samuel's words. Even the female slave was shocked to see a man who was willing to defend her. As the headman listened to Crowther, his conscience struck him. Suddenly he realized that what he was doing was wrong. He told Crowther that he wouldn't sacrifice the slave woman. Instead, he offered to sell her to Samuel. Samuel refused and explained that it was wrong to buy and sell people. Because of his words, the woman's life was spared.

Crowther continued his journey up the river, but he met with many dangers and difficulties. One chief kidnapped him and his son and held them for ransom. At another town Crowther was shipwrecked. The local natives were unfriendly, but Samuel and his companions were forced to remain among them until another ship arrived. Samuel used this time to get to know the tribes in that area. He preached to the people and spoke with their chiefs. Many Muslim Africans lived here. Samuel spent much time with them. He explained the gospel and preached repentance of sins. Some Muslims believed, but many rejected his words. Yet Crowther continued to preach. Even though the Islamic faith was strong in the area, Samuel knew that Christ was stronger than Islam. He wrote: "[Despite] all opposition, Christ shall divide the spoil with the strong in this spiritual warfare."

And there were loud voices in heaven, saying, "The kingdoms of this world have become the kingdoms of our Lord and of His Christ, and He shall reign forever and ever!" (Revelation 11:15)

Though the Muslims didn't agree with Crowther, they still trusted him. They knew that Samuel loved them and wanted to help them. One Muslim chief wrote of Crowther: "He is a father to us in this land."

BATTLING THE DARKNESS AT BONNY

In 1864, Samuel was ordained bishop of the Niger. He was a godly, hard-working, humble preacher of the Word. The churches in England and Africa prayed that God would use him mightily to advance Christ's cause even further in the African jungles.

In the following years, Crowther continued to evangelize tribes in western Africa. He planted churches in village after village. When he arrived at Bonny, a city along the Niger Delta, he was opposed by local priests. The people of this city still practiced cannibalism. Human sacrifice was common. The pagan temple in the city was decorated with human bones.

Samuel saw that darkness reigned in Bonny. But he knew that Christ could conquer the darkness. He began preaching to the people of Bonny. The work was very difficult, but God blessed his labors. Africans turned from their pagan lives and called on Christ. A church was planted, and the Christian community grew.

The local chief and priests hated the work of Christ. They tried to stop Crowther and his preaching. The church at Bonny was forced to meet in secret. Persecution was fierce whenever Christians were discovered. Many were tortured or killed.

Samuel encouraged the Christians to stand strong under persecution. He also sent messages to other churches and asked them to pray for Bonny. All around the world Christians began to pray. "The effective, fervent prayer of a righteous man avails much" (Jam. 5:16). In time, the persecutions at Bonny stopped. The chief threw away his idols. The city welcomed Christianity. Samuel's son Dandeson became pastor of the church there.

> **The eyes of the LORD are on the righteous, And His ears are open to their cry. . . . Many are the afflictions of the righteous, But the LORD delivers him out of them all. (Psalm 34:15, 19)**

A WORKER BY GOD'S GRACE

For the rest of his life, Samuel continued to labor for Christ in Africa. His heart overflowed with love for his unsaved countrymen. Whenever he met a pagan chief or a village priest, he remembered his own childhood. If God had not saved him, he would have remained a pagan like so many others. Humbled, Samuel often reminded himself that God's mercy was the only thing that changed who he was. All glory belonged to Christ for his salvation.

BASIC FACTS ABOUT THE FEDERAL REPUBLIC OF NIGERIA

Total Population:	200,000,000
Total Area:	356,669 square miles
Capital:	Abuja
Official Languages:	English
Primary Religion:	Christianity, Islam

For who makes you differ from another? And what do you have that you did not receive? (1 Corinthians 4:7)

On December 31, 1891, Samuel died at 82 years old. Leaving his work in this world, he entered into the joy of his Lord. In God's providence, this little slave boy had become a mighty preacher of the Word. In countless villages throughout the jungles of West Africa, churches were now planted and growing. Much work was left to be done, but Samuel knew that God would raise up other workers. God would call new laborers to work in Christ's kingdom just like He had called that little slave boy so long ago. ∎

PRAYER POINTS: NIGERIA

- **Muslim Persecution:** It has been over one hundred years since Mary Slessor ended her mission work in Nigeria. After her death, the Christian faith continued to spread throughout the country. Today, the population is almost equally divided between Christians and Muslims. Some of the states of Nigeria are mostly Christian. But other states (the northern states) have a larger Muslim population. Most Nigerians experience peace with other Muslims. But some Muslim groups have violently persecuted Christians. The terrorist group Boko Haram is responsible for kidnapping and killing many Christians. Churches in northeast Nigeria have been targeted. In some cases, the churches have been destroyed. Pray for God's people in Nigeria. Pray that the Lord would sustain the church. Pray for God's justice against evil men.

- **Corruption:** Nigeria is well-known in the world for its massive corruption. People in power, in business, and in government often lie and cheat to get more power and money. Nigeria is one of the most corrupt countries in the world. Pray that the gospel of Jesus Christ would have a powerful effect to transform Nigeria. Pray for repentance for those who have lied and cheated. Pray that righteousness would prevail in the land.

- **Growth of the Church:** The church continues to grow rapidly in Nigeria. Give thanks to God for the ongoing conquest of Jesus Christ. Pray that the churches would grow and that they would be faithful. Pray that discipleship in the churches would continue. Pray also that the churches would be kept pure from false gospels. Pray that our Triune God would be glorified and praised by all peoples of Nigeria.

UGANDA HIGHLANDS

Alexander Mackay: "White Man of Work"

> **To the present hour we both hunger and thirst, and we are poorly clothed, and beaten, and homeless. And we labor, working with our own hands. Being reviled, we bless; being persecuted, we endure. (1 Corinthians 4:11-12)**

In the year 1875, the Welsh explorer Henry Morton Stanley met King Mutesa of Uganda. When Mr. Stanley met the African king, he did not expect to be asked about his Christian faith. But King Mutesa wanted to know about "the white man's God." When Stanley heard King Mutesa's interest in the Christian faith, he sent a letter back to Great Britain. It took seven months for the letter to reach England. By this time, Stanley was a famous explorer. People all over England, Scotland, and Wales read his reports with great excitement.

In November 1875, Stanley's letter was printed in the Daily Telegraph of London. This was the letter:

> King Mutesa of Uganda has been asking me about the white man's God. Although I had not expected turning a missionary, for days I have been telling this black king all the Bible stories I know. So enthusiastic has he become that already he has determined to observe the Christian Sabbath as well as the Mohammedan Sabbath, and all his great captains have consented to follow his example. He has further caused the Ten Commandments as well as the Lord's Prayer and the golden commandment of our Savior, "Thou shalt love thy neighbor as thyself," to be written on boards for his daily reading. Oh, that some pious, practical missionary would come here! Mutesa would give him anything that he desired—houses, lands, cattle, ivory, and other things ... Here, gentlemen, is your opportunity—embrace it! The

HENRY MORTON STANLEY

203

204 TAKING AFRICA FOR JESUS

MAP OF UGANDA

people on the shores of Victoria Lake call upon you. Listen to them.

Henry Stanley was surprised that King Mutesa wanted to learn about Christianity. Mutesa and his people worshiped false gods. They offered sacrifices to evil spirits. When calamities occurred in the kingdom, the Ugandan people sacrificed animals and food to the spirits to gain their favor.

However, in the 1800s, another religion besides Christianity had come to Uganda. Arab traders brought their Islamic religion to the country. Many of the Ugandan people had never heard of Christianity or Islam. Which should they believe? Should they follow the religion of these white men from Europe? Or was the religion of the Arab traders true? Or should they continue worshiping the gods their fathers worshiped?

Mutesa's invitation to white missionaries was both surprising and greatly encouraging to Christians reading his letter in Great Britain. But who would go? To journey to central Africa was a dangerous task. Death, disease, and danger would follow every step of the journey. It would take faith and courage for any Christian to make the journey.

MISSIONARIES ANSWER KING MUTESA'S INVITATION

ALEXANDER MACKAY

And a vision appeared to Paul in the night. A man of Macedonia stood and pleaded with him, saying, "Come over to Macedonia and

RUBAGA

help us." Now after he had seen the vision, immediately we sought to go to Macedonia, concluding that the Lord had called us to preach the gospel to them. (Acts 16:9-10)

In London, men from the Church Missionary Society read the letter and wondered what to do. They thought, "To ignore his call for missionaries would be a crime!" Mutesa wanted missionaries to come and teach the Bible. They could not ignore this unique invitation. Stanley's letter seemed like a call from the Lord to them. But some of the men wondered whether the king's invitation was really sincere. What if, after a long and dangerous journey, they reached the king and the king didn't want them to come? It was a risk. But it was a risk that eight men decided to take. They would go in faith and trust God for the results.

Among these eight men was a gifted young engineer named Alexander Mackay. Born in Scotland, Mackay was known for his mechanical gifts. When he was just a boy, it was clear to everyone that Mackay was gifted with his hands. He loved to understand how things work. He created and engineered many different kinds of objects. Alexander's father encouraged him to become a pastor. Mackay was a committed Christian, but he did not think his calling was to be a pastor. However, he was passionate about missions.

Before he set out for Uganda, Mackay was working in Germany. He was a headman at a factory designing engines. When Mackay read Stanley's letters, he became excited. He saw here an opportunity to combine his passion for missions and engineering. He could bring the gospel to

King Mutesa. But he could also bring practical skills that would help the Ugandan people.

In April 1875, Mackay and the other men said farewell to their friends and relatives in England. Before the team left, Mackay solemnly warned his brothers with these words:

> There is one thing which my brethren have not said, and which I want to say. I want to remind the committee that within six months they will probably hear that one of us is dead. Yes; is it at all likely that eight Englishmen should start for Central Africa, and all be alive six months after? One of us, at least—it may be I—will surely fall before that. But, what I want to say is this; when the news comes, do not be cast down, but send someone else immediately to take the vacant place.

Alexander Mackay had counted the cost. He knew that the journey would be dangerous. One of the missionaries was likely to die. But even if that happened, Mackay didn't want others to lose heart. Instead, they should immediately send a replacement.

The eight missionaries set out from England for Zanzibar, the busiest seaport in East Africa at that time. It was hard work just to reach Africa. After five weeks at sea, Mackay and his companions finally reached Zanzibar. But here they were still a thousand miles from King Mutesa's kingdom. The rest of the journey would be made on foot.

The missionaries stayed in Zanzibar for some time to gather supplies. Caravans were formed for the long journey into the African interior. But, within four months of leaving England, one of the missionaries died. Mackay's prediction had come true. Mr. James Robertson, a carpenter, was laid to rest in Africa. He had died for the cause of Christ. He never saw King Mutesa.

The remaining missionaries set out for King Mutesa's land. To make the thousand-mile journey, they crossed dangerous jungles and rivers. The men set out in different groups. Some would arrive at the destination earlier than others. Natives were hired to help carry supplies for the journey. Finally, in June 1877, the first of the missionaries reached King Mutesa's kingdom. Lieutenant Smith, Mr. O'Neill, and Mr. Wilson were the first to reach Uganda. Mackay would follow at a later time.

The capital city of King Mutesa's kingdom was Rubaga. Unlike most parts of Africa, Mutesa's kingdom was vast. He ruled over a large part of modern-day Uganda. Most other tribal rulers had control over a much smaller people group. Mutesa was a powerful man. The people ruled by Mutesa were known as the Waganda.

The three missionaries were ushered into the presence of the king. A letter was then read and translated by the king's attendant to King Mutesa. This is what the letter said:

To His Majesty King Mutesa, Ruler of Uganda.

Sire: We have heard with pleasure, through our friend Mr. Stanley, of your earnest invitation to English teachers to come and settle in your kingdom . . . The greatness of England, of which you have heard, is due to the Word of God which we possess; her laws are framed in accordance with it; her people are made happy by it. Our desire is that your throne should be made secure, your country be made great, and your people made happy by the same means.

King Mutesa was joyful at their arrival. Gifts were exchanged. Music was played. Food was served. The missionaries were given their own two-acre site to live on. This site would be the home of the missionaries. A school would also be established on the site. Lieutenant Smith and Mr. O'Neill returned to Lake Victoria for more supplies. But they were killed on the way. Now, Mr. Wilson and Alexander Mackay were the only two remaining missionaries of the original group. Once he received the news, Mackay traveled as fast as he could to join Mr. Wilson in Rubaga.

In November 1878, Alexander Mackay finally arrived in Rubaga. Mr. Wilson had lived there alone for a year. King

LAKE VICTORIA

Mutesa had grown to like Mr. Wilson. But the king earnestly wanted Mackay to come as well. The king had heard of Mackay's many useful skills. Mutesa wanted the white men to bring the benefits of the English to his land.

TEACHING AND LABOR

Yes, you yourselves know that these hands have provided for my necessities, and for those who were with me. I have shown you in every way, by laboring like this, that you must support the weak. And remember the words of the Lord Jesus, that He said, "It is more blessed to give than to receive." (Acts 20:34-35)

Mackay was a gifted teacher of the Scriptures. He was also an excellent craftsman and engineer. He built furniture, repaired tools, and created new implements the native people could use. Both chiefs and slaves would gather together in Mackay's workshop. They watched with awe and wonder as Mackay worked. Soon all the people brought tools to Mackay to be repaired. Both the older and younger men in the village wanted to learn the same skills. They too wanted to repair tools and forge new instruments. Mackay's hands were almost always black. He was always working on some project. Soon he earned a Ugandan nickname: "Muzungu-wa-Kazi." This nickname means "white man of work." Mackay introduced many new concepts to the Waganda. He showed them how to dig a well. He demonstrated how glass was cut. He explained how to yoke oxen to increase production.

But King Mutesa didn't want the men of his realm to learn any practical skills. For the Waganda, it was considered a shame for men to work. Women and slaves were responsible for daily household duties. Men were idle. They simply ordered women and slaves to serve them. In Mutesa's kingdom, it was a virtue for men to be selfish and lazy. Mackay's diligence put the Waganda men to shame.

Mackay taught by word and example that it was important for men to be busy with their hands. Men should be productive. They were called to take dominion of the earth. The Bible teaches that if a person won't work, they shouldn't eat (2 Thess. 3:10). Mackay would say, "I tell them that God made men with only one stomach, but with two hands." Men were made to work first and then eat. This command of God's Word was not known in Uganda. Now, by God's grace, Mackay and the other missionaries were showing the Waganda a better way. Alexander Mackay taught the Waganda that to be great in the kingdom of God one must be a servant. This is what our Lord Jesus says in Matthew 20:

But Jesus called them to Himself and said, "You know that the rulers of the Gentiles lord it over them, and those who are great exercise authority over them. Yet it shall not be so among you; but whoever desires to become great among you, let him be your servant." (Matthew 20:25-26)

Soon Mackay had dozens of students. He taught them how to read. He also taught them the Scriptures. Mackay instructed them in many practical skills. He taught agriculture, woodworking, and blacksmithing. For a time, everything seemed to be going well. The missionaries were well received. King Mutesa allowed them to continue their discipleship work. But conflicts soon increased between King Mutesa and the missionaries. The teachings of God's Word offend the natural man (1 Cor. 2:14). King Mutesa would soon make obvious that he was a natural man. He did not truly care about the things of God.

CONFLICT WITH KING MUTESA

King Mutesa accepted the missionaries because they brought benefits to his kingdom. He even changed some of his laws because of Mackay's teaching. But Mutesa did not repent. When he asked to be baptized, Mackay exhorted Mutesa to show real fruits of repentance. Mutesa and his chiefs had not given up lying, witchcraft, or sabbath-breaking. Many of them had numerous wives. Mutesa himself may have had 200-300 wives. Until he turned away from these sins and cast himself on the mercy of God, the missionaries would not baptize him.

Tension between the king and the missionaries continued to mount. During the Christmas season of 1879, there was a confrontation. King Mutesa was ill. He called for a famous wizard who lived on an island on Lake Victoria. The wizard's name was Mukasa.

The Ugandans believed that wizards were inhabited by a spirit or god. In order to pacify the angry gods, the villagers would bring gifts to the wizards. Wizards would shout and rave like madmen. The Ugandans thought that this strange behavior was really one of the spirits speaking.

The spirits demanded gifts and prayers. Many people wanted to become wizards. What better way to get free gifts from the village than by claiming to be possessed by one of the spirits?

Mukasa was one of the most revered wizards. Therefore King Mutesa called for him to come and use his healing powers.

When Mackay heard that King Mutesa had summoned the

KING MWANGA

MURCHISON FALLS NATIONAL PARK, UGANDA

wizard, he confronted the king. Mackay told Mutesa that if he received this wizard, it would show that the king had rejected the Christian faith. Mackay warned Mutesa that witchcraft was a heinous sin in the sight of God. Mackay read the Scriptures to Mutesa. He explained that the Word of God condemned all witchcraft and sorcery. He urged the king to reject the wizard.

But King Mutesa did not listen. Mukasa the wizard arrived and spent several days in the court. A series of rituals including dancing, chanting, and drinking were performed by the wizard and his companions. After a few days, King Mutesa was still sick. Disappointed, Mutesa sent the wizard away.

King Mutesa was very fickle with the missionaries. Sometimes he accepted their teaching. Sometimes he rejected it and chose his own path. But one day Mutesa decided he would follow Islam instead of the way of Jesus. The Muslims in the village were glad to hear this. They began to spread false rumors about Mackay and the other missionaries. They tried to make the Waganda turn against the Christians. While Mackay was away on a journey, one of the missionaries, Mr. O'Flaherty, declared the Word of God to Mutesa. Mutesa responded to Mr. O'Flaherty, saying, "I want to have nothing to do with Jesus Christ. I want goods and women. The religion of Jesus Christ will not give these to me, so I will not have it."

By 1881, the missionaries had spent three years laboring for the salvation of the

Waganda. But no one had yet converted to the faith. But on October 8, 1881 good news came. The missionaries received a letter. A man named Sembera wished to be baptized. He had received the words of Jesus Christ. He wanted to be a disciple. The missionaries rejoiced. From the day Sembera was baptized, he lived faithfully to his Lord and Savior Jesus Christ. Sembera was not the last Waganda to become a Christian. Soon the missionaries received many similar requests. The Word of God was taking root among the Waganda. They even baptized a former wizard. The wizard priest knelt before Mr. O'Flaherty and said, "I will cast off these charms of the spirits, whom I will never again serve. They are liars and cheats. I will follow Jesus and learn His ways." By October 1884, over eighty Waganda had been baptized.

PERSECUTION INCREASES

And when they had preached the gospel to that city and made many disciples, they returned to Lystra, Iconium, and Antioch, strengthening the souls of the disciples, exhorting them to continue in the faith, and saying, "We must through many tribulations enter the kingdom of God." (Acts 14:21-22)

For years, Mackay and the other missionaries urged the king to repent of his sins. They told King Mutesa that Jesus Christ was the only way of salvation. But Mutesa did not listen. One day, the missionaries received news that Mutesa was dead. With Mutesa dead, the missionaries wondered what would happen next. Would they be killed by Mutesa's successor? Would the Muslims take over the court?

Persecution was about to increase. Soon Mutesa's son Mwanga took the throne. He was eighteen years old. Mwanga was an immature and ungodly young man. His new power further corrupted his already sinful heart. Mwanga ordered the missionaries to stop teaching the natives. He warned that anyone who went to study with the missionaries would be put to death. But Mwanga's decree actually increased the number of natives going to the missionaries. Mackay and the other missionaries were amazed by the courage of these natives. Many of them wanted to be baptized despite the royal decree. Even though Mwanga hated the Christians, he found it difficult to kill them. The missionaries were far too useful to be killed. Mackay's practical skills were constantly needed by the court. The Lord protected His servants. Nevertheless, many of the natives were executed by the wicked King Mwanga.

Like his father Mutesa, Mwanga was unsteady. He could not be trusted. Sometimes the persecuted died down. At other times, the decree would change, and the Christians would once again be in danger. Time after time, the Lord protected Alexander Mackay. He continued teaching the Waganda many practical skills. He also began translating the Scriptures, beginning with the Gospel of Matthew. In the summer of 1887, Mwanga made plans to drive Mackay out of the village or kill him. Mackay received word of the plot, so he packed his things and departed across the lake. He would continue his mission work in a new place.

Mackay began a new missionary work across Lake Victoria. This new location was called Usambiro. Other Christians in the village joined Mackay in the new mission house. After Mackay was driven out, Mwanga was removed from the throne by rivals. Now, King Mwanga was a fugitive from his own kingdom. Mwanga had done much evil against Mackay. But Mackay showed a spirit of true Christian charity. Mackay invited Mwanga to stay with him at Usambiro. Mwanga never went to Usambiro. But, by inviting him, Mackay showed he was willing to forgive the king.

Alexander Mackay experienced many serious illnesses during his fourteen years in Uganda. In 1889, he died of malaria. At forty years of age, he passed from this life to be with His Lord. He had given his life for the peoples of Uganda.

In 1904, the Times of London printed an article containing firsthand evidence of the ongoing fruit as a result of missionary work in Uganda. The journalist found Uganda to be a land without slaves, with many righteous laws, and a Christian King. Thousands of people belonged to churches that dotted the landscape of Uganda. The old pagan religious practices were dying out. The sacrifice of Alexander Mackay and his mission companions bore much fruit. The cost of discipling Uganda was high. It cost many men their lives. But Mackay and his companions gave their lives for an eternal kingdom made up of every tribe, tongue, and nation. Jesus Christ saved many from this land. Our Lord Jesus continues His redeeming work in Uganda today.

**And they sang a new song, saying:
"You are worthy to take the scroll,
And to open its seals;
For You were slain,
And have redeemed us to God by Your blood
Out of every tribe and tongue
and people and nation,
And have made us kings and priests to our God; and we shall reign on the earth."
(Revelation 5:9-10)**

PRAYER POINTS: UGANDA

- **Praise God for the Growth of the Church:** The Christian population is large in Uganda. About 85% of Uganda claims a Christian identity. Praise the Lord for His redeeming work in this land. Bless the name of God for the spread of the Word of God, for the work of the Spirit, and for the growth of the church. In the capital Kampala, about half of the population regularly attends Christian worship services.
- **Pray for God's Protection:** There are parts of Uganda where Islamic extremists are creating violence. Some Christians have been murdered. Others have lost their homes. Pray that the Lord of Hosts would bring justice and protect His people.
- **Pray for Ongoing Discipleship:** Pray that Christians in Uganda would faithfully carry out the task of discipleship. Even though many Ugandans claim a Christian identity, not everyone is a true Christian. Pray that genuine faith would fill the churches of Uganda.

BASIC FACTS ABOUT THE FEDERAL REPUBLIC OF UGANDA

Total Population:	42,000,000
Total Area:	93,000 square miles
Capital:	Kampala
Official Languages:	English, Swahili
Primary Religion:	Christianity

KWA RIVER NEAR CALABAR

Mary Slessor: The Lord's Servant in Calabar

**Oh, sing to the Lord a new song!
Sing to the Lord, all the earth.
Sing to the Lord, bless His name;
Proclaim the good news of His salvation from day to day.
Declare His glory among the nations,
His wonders among all peoples.
(Psalm 96:1-3)**

Nigeria sits on the western coast of Africa. It has the largest population of any country in Africa. Nigeria's estimated population today is around 200 million. During the 1800s, it was colonized largely by the British. This is why English is the main language spoken in Nigeria today. As the British colonized the region, Christian missionaries also brought the good news of Jesus Christ to Nigeria. Because of those missionary efforts, over 50% of the population today professes the Christian faith. The Christian faith has spread far and wide in Nigeria. But the Muslim population is also very large (around 45%). There is still much gospel work to be done in this country.

How did Christianity come to this land? Many stories could be told about the church in Nigeria. In this chapter, you will learn about Mary Slessor. She was a Scottish missionary who made a big impact on this part of Africa.

THE ESTABLISHMENT OF THE CALABAR MISSION

**For the Lord is great and greatly to be praised;
He is to be feared above all gods.
For all the gods of the peoples are idols,
But the Lord made the heavens.
(Psalm 96:4-5)**

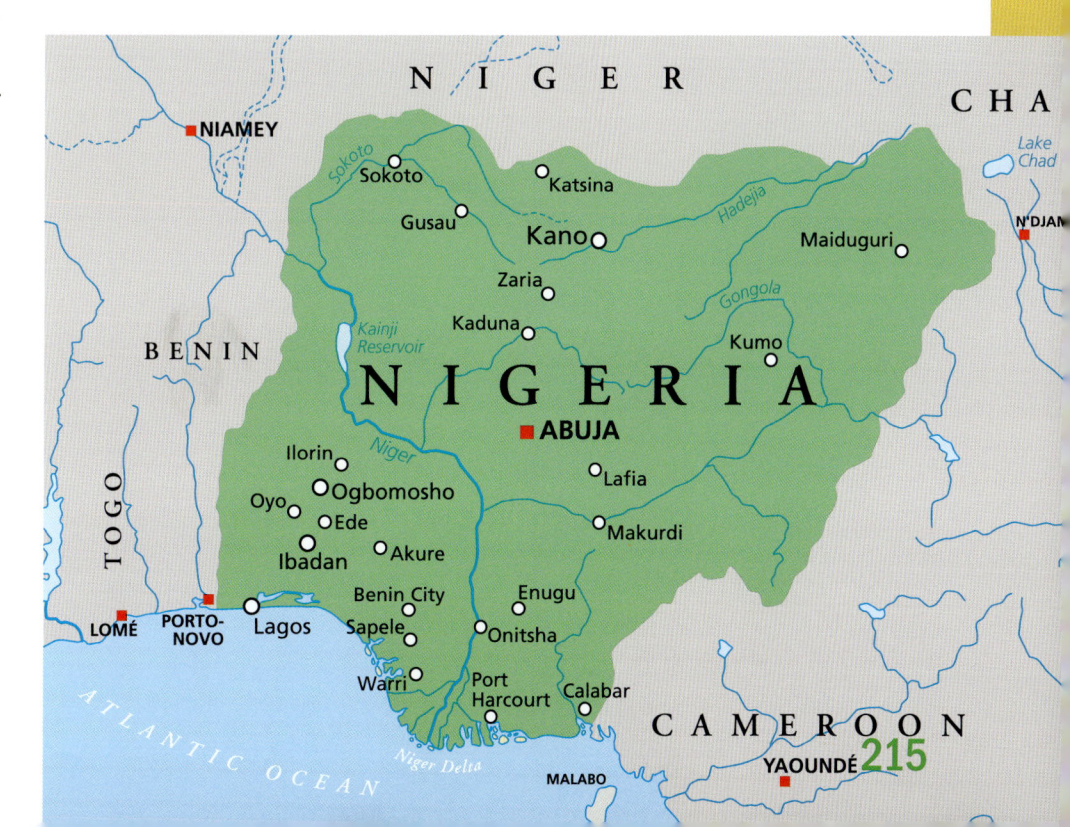

215

The land known as "Calabar" is located on the southern tip of Nigeria. It was here that numerous missionaries first took the gospel to the native peoples of Nigeria. Many of these missionaries came from England and Scotland. But the first established mission work in Calabar was the work of Jamaican missionaries. With a burden to reach the lost in West Africa, a council of Jamaican elders met in 1841. This was a meeting of the Presbyterian Church in Jamaica. In 1844, this small group of Jamaican Christians sailed for the coast of West Africa.

The six missionaries arrived in Duke Town, Calabar on April 10, 1846. They had come to a very dangerous land. Calabar was often called "the white man's grave." The British considered Calabar the most uncivilized part of Africa. The region of Calabar contained many different tribes. Generally, these tribes did not get along. They would often attack one another. In the 1700s and early 1800s, slavery became common in Calabar. Europeans traveled to the coast of Africa to find slaves to be sold in markets across the Atlantic. The ruthless tribes of Calabar were quite willing to kidnap people from other tribes and sell them to the Europeans. Everyone made a profit. But by doing this, both the Europeans and the Calabar tribes sinned greatly against the Lord. The Bible forbids man-stealing (1 Tim. 1:10).

Calabar was a depraved land. The light of God's Word had not come to these people. Tribal warfare was almost universal. Slave trading occurred regularly. The tribes of Calabar were steeped in many superstitions. When a natural disaster occurred, the tribe believed that someone's wrongdoing was the cause. Witch doctors would require suspects to eat ground esere beans mixed with water. Whoever vomited the mixture was believed to be inno-

MARY SLESSOR

cent. Whoever did not vomit was guilty. This often resulted in the death of an innocent person. Another common sinful practice was the killing of twin children. The tribes believed that if two children were born, one of them was the offspring of an evil spirit. Since they didn't know which child was from the evil spirit, they usually killed both children. The mother of twins was usually banished from the community. In Calabar, husbands could also divorce their wives for any reason. This was the condition of the country when missionaries first arrived.

The missionaries had a lot of work to do. They established mission stations in Duke Town and Creek Town. In the first ten years, many mission stations were established. These stations were small dwellings where the missionaries lived. From the station, the missionary could reach the local people.

The missionaries also opened schools to teach the natives to read and write. This provided opportunities to share the gospel. However, disease and violence often took the lives of missionaries. Many of the missionaries died within just a few years of their arrival. But, with God's help, those who survived continued the work.

The New Testament was translated into the Efik language in 1862. Efik was the common language in the region of Calabar. One of the missionaries, William Goldie, wrote many schoolbooks. He also wrote a hymnbook containing 300 hymns in Efik. These were the early foundations of the Calabar mission.

MARY SLESSOR'S CHILDHOOD IN SCOTLAND

Mary Slessor was not the first missionary to the Calabar. But she would become one of the most famous. Slessor was born in Aberdeen, Scotland in 1848. When Mary was ten, the family moved to Dundee.

Mary was blessed with a godly mother. But her father was an alcoholic. Once they moved to Dundee, Mary's father was so consumed with alcohol that he could no longer keep a job. Mary's mother had to work as a weaver and also educate the children. Life was hard for the Slessor family. Mr. Slessor's sinful habits brought his family into poverty.

Mary's mother was not the only one who worked. Most of the children also worked in factories and mills. At this time, Dundee was experiencing the changes brought about by the Industrial Revolution. Many Scots were moving into the cities to find work. The cities were overcrowded. There was not enough room for the growing population. The entire Slessor family lived in a dingy one-room apartment.

During these hard years, the Lord was faithful. The Lord gave Mary a loving mother. Mary's mother taught her children the Word of God. She also read missionary stories to them. These missionary stories captivated Mary's heart from a young age. In particular, Mary was inspired by David Livingstone's explorations of Africa.

When she was twelve, Mary personally embraced the Christian faith. Her profession of faith was influenced by an older widow living in Dundee. This widow opened her home to the children of Dundee. She would then witness to them and urge them to repent and believe in Jesus Christ. By faith, Mary Slessor found peace with God through the finished work of Jesus Christ.

When Mary was fourteen years old, she worked in a factory as a weaver. She would then study reading, writing, arithmetic, and the Bible in the evenings. She would also take books to work and study there. Mary would place her book on the loom and read while she worked. The Bible became very precious to her. She loved to read and re-read the Gospels. She also enjoyed the worship of God. Going to church was a great privilege. Mary once wrote, "we would as soon have thought of going to the moon as of being absent from a service."

**Oh, how I love Your law!
It is my meditation all the day.
(Psalm 119:97)**

**I was glad when they said to me, "Let us go into the house of the Lord."
(Psalm 122:1)**

Alcoholism is a destructive and deadly sin. It brought much suffering to the Slessor family. Mary's father was in bondage to strong drink. Because of this, Mary and her brothers and sisters were neglected by their father. Even though this was very hard for Mary, the Lord had a purpose in this trial. Mary learned to have sympathy and compassion for other children. She herself experienced the hardships of fatherlessness. This softened her heart to the needs of women and children. This experience would prepare her to love others when she became a missionary in Africa.

In May 1875, Mary wanted to become a missionary. She asked the Foreign Mission Board of the United Presbyterian Church to accept her as a missionary. Mary was already busy in her hometown sharing the gospel with others. She seemed very gifted for missionary work. The Foreign Mission Board accepted her request, and she prepared to leave for Africa. Then, in July 1876, she sailed to Africa to join the Calabar mission. When Mary arrived in Calabar, she was twenty-eight years old.

SERVING AS A MISSIONARY IN CALABAR

**He has shown you, O man, what is good;
And what does the Lord require of you
But to do justly,
To love mercy,
And to walk humbly with your God? (Micah 6:8)**

When Mary Slessor arrived, the Calabar mission was thirty-two years old. Over a

DUNDEE, SCOTLAND

thousand people now attended the worship services. Mary's early duties included teaching at the day school and visiting women in the community. Mary quickly adapted to African life. She lived in a hut similar to what the natives lived in. She also changed her diet to eat only local food. The only imported food items she would use were tea and toffee. Within her first years there, Mary mastered the Efik language. This enabled her to communicate with the natives of Calabar.

Mary saw the sad condition of women and children among the native people. Women were often treated like property. The Bible teaches that both men and women are made in the image of God. But the native people didn't think this way. Children were often abandoned when unwanted. Twins were usually killed. Respect for human life was very low.

Mary loved the native people and did whatever she could to save children from death. She rescued and adopted a six-month-old twin, whom she named Janie. Soon her rescue efforts became known to the native peoples. They tried to hide abandoned children so Mary couldn't find them. But Mary often still rescued them from death.

In 1883, Mary returned to Scotland to rest and raise support for the mission work. She took baby Janie from Calabar with her. Janie was living proof that the mission work in Calabar was important. People were touched by the rescue of this little girl. She was just one of many children rescued by Mary and the other missionaries. Mary continued to rescue children and adopt them into her home. Throughout her thirty-eight years in Nigeria, many orphans lived in her home. These children became her family.

In 1885, Mary's mother and sister died. Her closest family members had now gone to be with the Lord. Mary was heartbroken by their deaths. But this also gave her a sense of freedom. She felt free to take even more risks in her mission work. She wrote, "Heaven is now nearer to me than Britain, and no one will be anxious about me if I go up-country." The lands north of Calabar were considered the most dangerous in Africa. Wild beasts, disease, and warring tribes dominated the land. But Mary wasn't afraid to venture into the wild. She would risk all for her Lord and Savior.

After twelve years of working in the established mission stations, Mary wanted to journey inland. Many tribes had still never heard the gospel. With no one else willing to go, Mary decided she would make the dangerous journey herself.

BRINGING THE GOSPEL TO THE OKOYONG

And He said, "The kingdom of God is as if a man should scatter seed on the ground, and should sleep by night and rise by day, and the seed should sprout and grow, he himself does not know how." (Mark 4:26-27)

In August 1888, Mary Slessor journeyed further north in Africa. She came to the Okoyong tribe. This was a savage African tribe. The men would sit at meals with guns and cutlasses, ready to fight at any moment. Most of the tribe, both men and women, were drunk every night. Human life was not valued. The Okoyong were a constant dread to surrounding tribes. They traded slaves and practiced

POTS IN WHICH TWIN BABIES WERE ABANDONED

witchcraft. It was to this tribe that Mary Slessor took the gospel of Jesus Christ. It seemed foolhardy and dangerous for Mary to go to such a tribe all alone. She was a short Scottish woman. She wasn't physically strong or imposing. She would be an easy target for wicked people. But Mary wasn't afraid of this tribe. She believed that God was sovereign. The Lord had the power to protect her. The hardest thing for Mary was to see the rampant wickedness of the Okoyong. She said, "had I not felt my Saviour close beside me, I would have lost my [mind]."

Mary's first attempts to share the gospel had little effect. The Okoyong largely ignored her. These people could not accept the idea that God was loving and merciful. They could only imagine a bloodthirsty and revengeful god. The Okoyong people loved their sinful ways. Mary went to sleep at night knowing that every single person in the village was drunk. But even though the Okoyong rejected the message, Mary pressed on. She wrote in one of her reports, "The harvest will be gathered, but as yet it is only seedtime, and we must sow on in faith."

By New Years Eve of 1888, she wrote "Christ was never in a hurry. There was no rushing forward, no anticipating, no fretting over what might be. Every day's duties were done as the day brought them, and the rest was left to God." Mary knew that she just needed to be faithful. The Lord would bring a harvest in His timing.

Slessor also tried to establish peace between the local tribes. She offered to help open up trading between tribes. She suggested that the Okoyong begin trading with the Efiks in Calabar. The Okoyong didn't care much for trade. Instead, they wanted to attack other tribes and take what they wanted by force. They were thieves. But Mary persisted in her efforts. She negotiated with neighboring tribes. She became a peacemaker between the tribes. Because of this, she earned the people's respect. They began to call her "Ma Akamba" (the Great Mother) or "Ma" for short.

**Blessed are the peacemakers,
For they shall be called sons of God.
(Matthew 5:9)**

Over time, the Okoyong began to receive the Word of God. Lives were changed. Habits were reformed. Instead of sitting around all day, the Okoyong started to work with their hands. Mary was courageous in her dealings with the Okoyong. In some cases, she separated two men from fighting. Sometimes she disarmed the men by taking their weapons before a fight broke out. She would intervene by negotiating peace between two tribes. Even though she often put herself in danger, she was protected by the Lord. In all her missionary years, she was never attacked. Being a woman was an advantage to Mary. Because she wasn't a man, the tribes didn't consider her to be a threat.

Mary worked hard day and night to

see the gospel impact the Okoyong. But she knew that it was the Lord alone who would save them. She once wrote, "My one great consolation and rest is in prayer. God can, and will, save Okoyong. O, that He would do it speedily; not only saving their souls from hell, but saving their influence and their lives for Himself."

It took several years, but the Okoyong people were changing. It was difficult to count the number of conversions. Some Okoyong who professed faith went back to their sinful ways. Not all conversions were true conversions. But Mary knew that her one job was to sow the Word. She prayed for God to bring a harvest. Mary said, "We have just kept on sowing the seed of the word, believing that when God's time comes to gather them into the visible Church there will be some among us ready to participate in the privilege and honour." All this time, Mary wanted more missionaries to come and help her. But she was often the only one willing to risk her life. Frontier missions in Nigeria were very dangerous.

FRONTIER MISSIONS IN THE NORTH

So then neither he who plants is anything, nor he who waters, but God who gives the increase. (1 Corinthians 3:7)

Mary Slessor took God's Word to the Okoyong. But she wanted to continue her journey further inland. Her health had suffered much from the long hours of sharing God's Word, caring for her adopted children, and helping mediate disputes. Even though her health was poor, she always pressed forward.

Mary lived a very simple life. Her needs were small. She was content to have only food and clothing for herself and for her adopted "bairns" (her children).

In 1906, Mary Slessor made her last journey to Scotland. She was suffering from many health issues. She needed rest. She stayed in Scotland for just five months and then returned to West Africa in October 1907. Upon her return, she established mission stations in Use and Ikpe. She journeyed throughout the region establishing mission stations, rescuing children, and sharing God's Word. By her actions she won the confidence of the natives. Because the natives trusted her, other missionaries could come in and establish congregations safely. It was unusual for a single woman like Mary Slessor to take so many risks and journey alone. Her courage inspired many other men and women to journey to Africa and advance the cause of Christ.

To the end of her life, Mary Slessor was a humble woman. In 1912, she was awarded the special honor of the Order of the Hospital of St. John of Jerusalem. She was given a silver cross in appreciation for the work of mercy she had performed in Nigeria. But Mary did not care for worldly honors. She praised God for the work that was accomplished. And she also credited the work of missionaries who came before her. She said, "If I have done anything in my life, it has been easy, because the Master has gone before me."

After thirty-eight years of service in Africa, Mary Slessor died on January 13, 1915 from a severe fever.

THE LEGACY OF MARY SLESSOR

The Lord performed great works of salvation in the land of Nigeria. Mary Slessor was just one of His many servants. But she had an influential role in bringing the gospel to this dark land. She left the world a legacy of love, compassion, and service. She was a sacrificial woman. She gave everything up for the kingdom of God. She sacrificed her own health and well-being to save women and children from death. In caring for widows and orphans, Mary Slessor practiced "true religion" (Jam. 1:27). What was it that sustained her faith in such a dark and dangerous land?

Mary Slessor knew that prayer was powerful. She once stated, "Prayer is the greatest power God has put into our hands for service—praying is harder than doing, at least I find it so, but the dynamic lies that way to advance the kingdom." She also diligently studied the Bible. Many copies of her Bibles were filled from top to bottom with notes. Her knowledge of God's Word enabled her to minister to others. She also firmly believed in God's providence. Because Mary believed God was sovereign, she knew that the Lord was able to protect her.

For whatever is born of God overcomes the world. And this is the victory that has overcome the world—our faith. Who is he who overcomes the world, but he who believes that Jesus is the Son of God? (1 John 5:4-5)

BASIC FACTS ABOUT THE FEDERAL REPUBLIC OF NIGERIA

Total Population:	200,000,000
Total Area:	356,669 square miles
Capital:	Abuja
Official Languages:	English
Primary Religion:	Christianity, Islam

PRAYER POINTS: NIGERIA

- **Muslim Persecution:** It has been over one hundred years since Mary Slessor ended her mission work in Nigeria. After her death, the Christian faith continued to spread throughout the country. Today, the population is almost equally divided between Christians and Muslims. Some of the states of Nigeria are mostly Christian. But other states (the northern states) have a larger Muslim population. Most Nigerians experience peace with other Muslims. But some Muslim groups have violently persecuted Christians. The terrorist group Boko Haram is responsible for kidnapping and killing many Christians. Churches in northeast Nigeria have been targeted. In some cases, the churches have been destroyed. Pray for God's people in Nigeria. Pray that the Lord would sustain the church. Pray for God's justice against evil men.

- **Corruption:** Nigeria is well-known in the world for its massive corruption. People in power, in business, and in government often lie and cheat to get more power and money. Nigeria is one of the most corrupt countries in the world. Pray that the gospel of Jesus Christ would have a powerful effect to transform Nigeria. Pray for repentance for those who have lied and cheated. Pray that righteousness would prevail in the land.

- **Growth of the Church:** The church continues to grow rapidly in Nigeria. Give thanks to God for the ongoing conquest of Jesus Christ. Pray that the churches would grow and that they would be faithful. Pray that discipleship in the churches would continue. Pray also that the churches would be kept pure from false gospels. Pray that our Triune God would be glorified and praised by all peoples of Nigeria.parts of Uganda where Islamic extremists are creating violence. Some Christians have been murdered. Others have lost their homes. Pray that the Lord of Hosts would bring justice and protect His people.

- **Pray for Ongoing Discipleship:** Pray that Christians in Uganda would faithfully carry out the task of discipleship. Even though many Ugandans claim a Christian identity, not everyone is a true Christian. Pray that genuine faith would fill the churches of Uganda.

21. MARY SLESSOR: THE LORD'S SERVANT IN CALABAR

GORILLAS ARE FOUND IN NIGERIA AND SURROUNDING WEST AFRICAN NATIONS

MOSQUE IN CAIRO, EGYPT

Samuel Zwemer: Missionary to Arabia and Egypt

Thus says the LORD:
"The labor of Egypt and merchandise of Cush
And of the Sabeans, men of stature,
Shall come over to you, and they shall be yours;
They shall walk behind you,
They shall come over in chains;
And they shall bow down to you.
They will make supplication to you, saying,
'Surely God is in you,
And there is no other;
There is no other God.' " (Isaiah 45:14)

The modern missionary movement has spread the Christian faith all over the world. Beginning in the early 1800s, Christian missionaries have climbed high mountains, crossed barren deserts, and slogged through jungles to take the gospel to the world. New forms of travel made spreading the gospel easier. But missionary work is still hard work. However, Christians know that Jesus will succeed in His mission. Samuel Zwemer (1867-1952) was a missionary to Arabia and Egypt. He was also committed to this mission. He wanted to see the whole world come to Christ.

Zwemer spent most of his years as a missionary in Iraq and Egypt. But he traveled the entire globe, calling other Christians to join the mission. He is sometimes called "the apostle to Islam." Few Christians have done as much as Zwemer to encourage gospel work in Muslim lands.

Islam is the second largest religion in the world today. There are probably about 1.8 billion Muslims in the world. Islam dominates much of North Africa, the Middle East, and parts of East Asia. But there are good things happening in this part of the world. The Christian faith is rapidly expanding in these lands. But wherever there are Christians, there is also persecution. Christians in these lands experience much persecution today.

In terms of numbers, Islam is Christianity's greatest rival. Muslims are immi-

SAMUEL ZWEMER

PREPARATION FOR GOSPEL WORK

PART OF HOPE COLLEGE IN HOLLAND, MICHIGAN

My son, keep your father's command, And do not forsake the law of your mother. (Proverbs 6:20)

Samuel Zwemer was the thirteenth of fifteen children. His father and mother emigrating to Europe and America in record numbers. This means that Christians like us need to learn about Islam. We need to be prepared to share the gospel with Muslims. Samuel Zwemer was a man who loved the Muslim people. He wanted to see them saved by Jesus Christ. He labored at this for his entire life. We can learn much from his example.

erlands to America in 1849. At first, they settled in New York. Then, in 1857, Samuel's father Adriaan Zwemer was called to the ministry. He began his pastoral ministry in Michigan. It was here that Samuel Marinus Zwemer was born.

Samuel's first years were blessed with Christian nurture from his father and mother. By age five, Samuel had learned to read both English and Dutch. He enjoyed reading classic books like Foxe's Book of Martyrs and The Pilgrim's Progress. Three

LARGEST RELIGIOUS GROUPS IN THE WORLD TODAY

1. Christianity	2.4 billion
2. Islam	1.8 billion
3. Hinduism	1.1 billion
4. Buddhism	0.5 billion

times a day, the Zwemer family spent time reading the Bible and praying together. Samuel loved his father and mother. From their godly example, Samuel learned about his Heavenly Father. Later in life, Samuel wrote, "I understood the loving fatherhood of God as Jesus taught it because of what I saw in my own father."

Samuel had fourteen brothers and sisters, but only eleven survived childhood. All eleven of these children were schooled at home. Mrs. Zwemer's older daughters helped teach the younger children. Samuel loved to read and write. At age sixteen, he studied at Hope College in Michigan. This was a college founded by the Dutch. Around the same time, Samuel had his first opportunity to teach the Bible at Sunday school. He was naturally gifted as a teacher.

In 1886, Samuel's mother passed away. She had grown weaker and weaker over the years. On August 24 of that year, she went to be with the Lord. As she was dying, she reminded Samuel that she prayed he would become a missionary someday.

During college, Samuel's love for the Lord grew. He decided to volunteer with the American Bible Society. He became a colporteur. A colporteur (pronounced "cole-porter") is someone who distributes books and literature. As a volunteer colporteur, Samuel traveled the countryside giving out free Bibles and tracts. He pur-

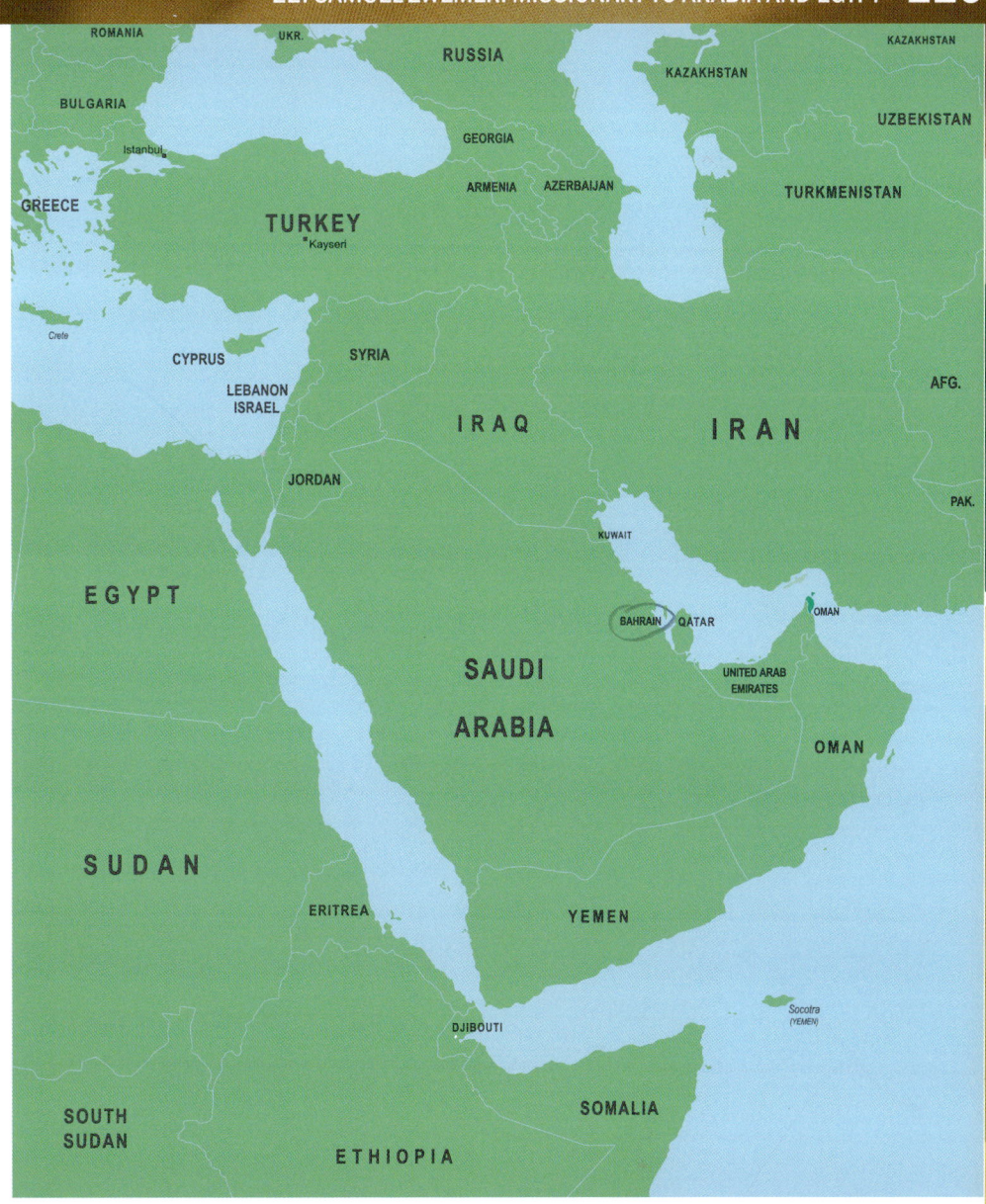

MAP OF THE MIDDLE EAST

chased a horse for $70 and a cart for $26. He used the cart and horse to transport literature. Zwemer wanted to see a Bible in every home in Michigan. For the rest of his life, Samuel had a passion for giving away free Christian literature. As we will see, he did this for decades in his missionary work among Muslims.

In September 1887, Zwemer began his seminary studies. He was interested in the mission field. In order to better prepare himself, Zwemer studied medicine on the side. He began assisting a medical doctor in New York. Zwemer wanted to be a missionary who could serve both the spiritual and physical needs of the people he would reach. His skills in medicine and learning in theology would both be very important on the mission field.

Another important discipline was Zwemer's daily one-hour time of Bible reading and prayer. He knew that his life of communion with the Lord was vital.

Within a few years, Samuel finished his seminary studies. He was then ordained as a missionary on May 28, 1890 in the Reformed Church.

TRAVELS IN ARABIA

Then the master said to the servant, "Go out into the highways and hedges, and compel them to come in, that my house may be filled." (Luke 14:23)

Serving as a missionary in the Muslim world was difficult and dangerous. Few missionaries had successfully brought the gospel to Muslim lands. Many Christians were killed for their efforts. Truly this was hard soil. But this didn't stop Samuel Zwemer from going. Instead of picking an "easy target," Zwemer wanted to go to the heart of Islam. Together with a few other missionaries, he began to explore the Muslim world, including Beirut, Bahrain, Basrah, and Baghdad. Samuel and his fellow missionaries engaged in street preaching. They also handed out copies of the Bible and tracts in Arabic. They were not always received in a friendly way. Sometimes the Muslims attacked them. Very few Muslims were converted, but Samuel and his friends pressed on. They trusted the Lord of the harvest.

Samuel Zwemer used an Arabic name for himself. He wanted

LOCATION OF CAIRO, EGYPT

to make it easier for the Muslims to get to know him. Samuel is not a name that appears in the Qur'an. For this reason, Muslims didn't know it. Also, his last name "Zwemer" was Dutch. So Samuel used the name "Dhaif Allah" (guest of God). This name was appropriate because Samuel was a "guest" in Arabia.

Zwemer traveled from mission station to mission station throughout Arabia. The travel was often long and difficult. In particular, the summer months were almost unbearable. During the hottest months, travel could only be safely accomplished at night. One of the missionaries journaled of the extreme heat: "I write; it is too hot to do anything else. I cannot sleep, nor read, nor do anything; it is one-hundred seven [107° Fahrenheit] in the coolest part of the veranda. The pen is hot, the paper is hot and the ink won't run. I am sitting with a wet towel on my head to prevent my being overcome with the heat." Later in life, Samuel returned to the United States. He often missed the hot climate of Arabia, though. He had become used to it.

In 1895, Samuel met a woman missionary named Amy Elizabeth Wilkes. They were both unmarried at the time, but they both desired to marry. Their friendship blossomed, and soon they were married in 1896. The couple returned to America in 1897 for a time of rest. There in Michigan, their first child, Katharina Zwemer, was born. During this time, Samuel toured the United States, raising support for the work in Arabia. He and his family then returned to Arabia after raising support.

Trial after trial came to the Zwemers in Africa. In 1904, their daughter Ruth died. The same year their oldest daughter Katharina also died. Samuel and his wife Amy sacrificed much for the cause of Christ. Conversions were rare, but the missionaries from America persevered in preaching and distributing literature. It is estimated that Samuel Zwemer's own converts were less than a dozen. This was over forty years of missionary service. But a large part of Zwemer's work was to inspire others to join the mission to reach the Muslim world. He laid the foundation for future missionary workers.

MISSIONARY TO EGYPT

Then the Lord will be known to Egypt, and the Egyptians will know the Lord in that day, and will make sacrifice and offering; yes, they will make a vow to the Lord and perform it. (Isaiah 19:21)

In his later years serving in Arabia (1907-1913), Samuel Zwemer began a practice he would continue for the rest of his life. Zwemer attended missions conferences and spoke about the need for world evangelization. For the rest of his life, Zwemer would travel the world, calling other Christians to go Muslim lands. He traveled tens of thousands of miles by boat and train. He spoke to hundreds of thousands of people about missions. His zeal for the Lord and his love for the Muslim people drove him to speak on the necessity of Muslim missions. Samuel Zwemer saw more of the world than many people will see in a lifetime. But he was never wealthy. He never owned his own car and never even drove a car. The only property Zwemer ever owned was his own burial plot. He once commented, "I have always lived from hand to mouth, but it has been the Lord's hand and my mouth." He knew that the Lord provided his daily bread.

In 1912, Zwemer was invited to serve as a missionary in Cairo, Egypt. Cairo was a very important city in the Muslim world. Today, Cairo is the capital and largest city in Egypt. Just a few miles from Cairo are the Great Pyramids of Egypt. This was an important location from which Zwemer could influence mission work to Muslims. While living in Cairo, Zwemer wrote a number of tracts in Arabic. These little booklets became famous throughout the Muslim world. Samuel taught in a Christian seminary and preached in Cairo frequently. He was often seen on the streets passing out tracts and talking to Muslims. Zwemer became an expert on Islam. He was so passionate to reach the Muslims that he often talked about little else. One man said, "I never talked with him ten minutes that the conversation did not veer to Islam."

Cairo was the home of a famous Muslim university called Al Ahzar. Muslims from all over the world came to study at this prestigious school. Samuel Zwemer would often visit the university. He talked with students and professors about religion. He handed out tracts and portions of the Bible. Many of the Muslim professors protested against Zwemer. They complained to the authorities. Because of these complaints, the government told Zwemer not to give away Christian literature at the university.

However, one day a student asked Zwemer if he had any tracts with him. Zwemer could not resist giving something to this student. He gave the student four tracts. The student then took the tracts and gave them to four other students. When the professor of the class discovered the tracts, he took them from the students and ripped them to pieces. He scolded the students for taking them. The matter was reported, and the British government became involved. Zwemer was asked to leave Egypt for a time, so he boarded a boat to Cyprus. Then, two weeks later, he quietly returned to Egypt.

After seventeen years of service in Egypt, Zwemer and his family left Africa. They returned to the United States to teach and to cultivate support for Muslim missions.

MISSIONS CONFERENCES AND TEACHING IN THE UNITED STATES

Then He said to them, "The harvest truly is great, but the laborers are few; therefore

pray the Lord of the harvest to send out laborers into His harvest." (Luke 10:2)

Zwemer was a gifted preacher and evangelist. But, in the Lord's providence, he didn't see many Muslims converted. He saw very little fruit during his years of foreign missionary work. However, he became a spokesman and a flag-bearer for Muslim missions. His words encouraged others to join in the work of spreading the gospel. Through his influence, perhaps thousands of missionaries went to preach to the Muslims. In his conferences, Zwemer was urgent to share his message: Muslims were perishing without the gospel.

Here is one example from his many conference messages:

> Jesus Christ is the Son of Man. He loves Western Asia. His manger and His Cross stood there. In Western Asia His blood was spilled. In Western Asia He walked the hills. There His tears fell for Jerusalem. There His eye still rests . . . It was in Western Asia that He said, "All authority is given unto Me;" . . . Shall Bethlehem hear five times a day "There is no god but Allah, and Mohammed is God's apostle," and shall not a single one of us dare go, if God will, in this year of our Lord nineteen hundred and ten [1910] unto Mecca itself, the very stronghold of Islam, and preach the Gospel of the great King?

In 1918, Zwemer was invited to become a professor at Princeton Theological Seminary. He accepted the job. For many years, he taught missions and world religions to students at Princeton. He also wrote many books on Islam. These books would help other Christians understand Islam. Zwemer was an expert because he had met so many Muslims over the years.

Samuel's wife Amy passed away in 1937. After a few years, Zwemer remarried and moved to New York City. Even though he was growing old, he continued to preach and speak about missions. His home was always open to visitors. Visitors to Zwemer's home knew that he would almost always pray with them. When a visitor departed, they could expect Zwemer to give them some book or pamphlet. From his teenage years to his final days, Zwemer loved to give away Christian literature. Those who knew Samuel Zwemer considered him a very loving man.

On April 2, 1952, Samuel Zwemer passed away and entered glory. He was eighty-four years old. He loved the Muslim people. And, to his dying day, he continued to trumpet the cause of Muslim missions. Like the Apostle Paul, he would do anything to see the Muslims saved.

. . . to the weak I became as weak, that I might win the weak. I have become all things to all men, that I might by all means save some. (1 Corinthians 9:24)

Samuel Zwemer often spoke on Muslim missions. But he also encouraged Christians to pray. He wanted Christians to pray for more missionaries and for more conversions. We can trust that the Lord of the harvest will send workers into the field. Let us also pray to the Lord of the harvest. Let us pray that He will save the Muslim people. Let us pray that the Muslims will receive Jesus Christ as Lord and Savior.

22. SAMUEL ZWEMER: MISSIONARY TO ARABIA AND EGYPT **235**

THE SPHINX AND GIZA PYRAMIDS

RAINFOREST IN THE CONGO

C.T. Studd: Missionary to the Congo

> **He shall have dominion also from sea to sea, and from the River to the ends of the earth. (Psalm 72:8)**

At the heart of the African continent sits the Democratic Republic of the Congo. It is one of the largest countries on the continent, second only to Algeria. In the early 1900s, the gospel of Jesus Christ was almost unknown to the native tribes of the Congo. It was not an easy or safe place to go. Dangerous cannibal tribes, disease, and savage animals prevented many from entering this hostile land. But God had plans for the Congo. And the Lord chose to use a talented English cricket player by the name of C.T. (Charles Thomas) Studd. Through C.T. Studd and his missionary co-laborers, thousands in the Congo would come to saving faith in the Lord Jesus Christ. Through them a new missions organization would also be formed to reach the whole world.

EARLY LIFE AND SPORTS CAREER

> **Do not labor for the food which perishes, but for the food which endures to everlasting life, which the Son of Man will give you, because God the Father has set His seal on Him. (John 6:27)**

C.T. Studd was born into a wealthy English family in December 1860. Studd's father Edward had made a large fortune in India. He returned to England to spend his for-

YOUNG C.T. STUDD

tune. One of Edward's favorite pastimes was horse racing, and he attended many horse races in the British Isles. Once, Edward was in Dublin attending a local derby. Because he missed the boat back to England, he stayed overnight in Dublin. That night, the American evangelist Dwight L. Moody and his associate Ira Sankey led an evangelistic service in the city. Edward Studd attended the service. He was moved by Moody's fervent preaching and received the gospel that night. Mr. Studd's life was changed. No longer was spending money Edward Studd's main interest in life. Instead, he wanted to see other souls saved for eternity.

The Studd boys grew up with some knowledge of Christianity. But they were not truly converted. For them, Sunday was a boring day. They couldn't wait until Monday came. They didn't really care about the Bible or the Lord Jesus and His gospel. When Edward was converted, his three sons were away at Eton College. Edward went to visit his boys and shared his newfound faith with them. He took the boys to hear Dwight Moody's preaching. For a time the boys did not receive the gospel. They were much more interested in the things of this world. The Studd boys spent much of their time playing the game known as "Cricket." This sport is still popular in many countries today. Cricket is played with a bat and a ball, similar to American baseball. In the late 1800s, cricket was very popular. Cricket athletes enjoyed fame and honor in England. All three of the Studd boys were cricket players at Eton. They were very gifted at the game. C.T. was especially talented at cricket.

The boys' father continued to urge them to receive the gospel, but they resisted. However, Edward Studd's labors were not in vain. He was planting seeds that would take root. One day, a friend of their father called Mr. W. confronted the boys. Through his faithful witness, they fi-

THE STUDD BROTHERS

nally received the gospel. Mr. W. pressed C.T. Studd not just to "believe in Jesus" but to believe that Jesus had actually died for his sins.

C.T. recorded how his life changed after this event:

> Then I got down on my knees, and I did say "thank you" to God. And right then and there joy and peace came into my soul. I knew then what it was to be "born again," and the Bible, which had been so dry to me before, became everything.

Each of the Studd boys now loved God's Word. They began hosting Bible classes at school. They continued their cricket playing, but they now valued the kingdom of God more than their sports. By 1882, C.T. was a premier cricket player. He was considered one of the best batsmen in the game. He graduated from Cambridge University in 1884 as one of the best cricket players in England. C.T. regretted later in life how he had idolized the sport at times. But he did learn important lessons through playing cricket. He learned the lessons of courage, self-denial, and endurance. These would be important lessons for C.T. when he became a missionary.

After his conversion, C.T. grew in understanding through the preaching services of Dwight Moody. C.T. loved playing cricket, but he wanted to pursue a higher calling. The honor and fame of the world now meant nothing to him. He wanted to labor for the everlasting kingdom. C.T. asked himself, "how could I spend the best years of my life in working for myself and the honors and pleasures of this world while thousands and thousands of souls are perishing every day without having heard of Christ?" He decided to prepare for missionary work to China.

MISSIONARY WORK IN CHINA AND MARRIAGE

> Go therefore and make disciples of all the nations, baptizing them in the name of the Father and of the Son and of the Holy Spirit, teaching them to observe all things that I have commanded you; and lo, I am with you always, even to the end of the age." Amen. (Matthew 28:19-20)

C.T. applied to serve as an overseas missionary with the China Inland Mission. This organization was founded by Hudson Taylor (1832-1905). C.T. was accepted as a member of the mission and made

THE "CAMBRIDGE SEVEN"

plans to depart by boat for the East. C.T. was not the only person moved to join this mission work. The Lord was working in the hearts of other Cambridge students as well. Eventually, seven young men from Cambridge joined the China Inland Mission. They became known as the "Cambridge Seven." In February 1885, the seven young men set out for China. These seven young Englishmen no longer looked like Englishmen. They looked like Chinese. They wore their hair in a pig-tail, and they wore long robes to look more like the men of China. They wanted to reach China with the gospel, so they became like the Chinese in appearance.

Once the young men reached China, they scattered far and wide throughout inland China. Most of their days were spent reading the Bible, praying, and learning Chinese. While in China, C.T. received a large inheritance from his father, who had passed away a few years previously. His inheritance totaled £29,000 pounds. This is equal to around £3,700,000 pounds (or $4,500,000) today. C.T. gave this massive sum of money away to various Christian charitable groups. C.T. Studd was no lover of money. He already possessed the pearl of great price.

While laboring in China, C.T. met his wife-to-be, Priscilla Stewart. Miss Stewart arrived in Shanghai in 1887 as a missionary worker like C.T. Studd. Once they met on the mission field, they began to send each other letters. Within a few months, they were engaged to be married. C.T. admired Priscilla's faith and her love for the Lord Jesus. He wrote, "I married her for her handsome actions towards the Lord Jesus Christ and those He sent her to save." The couple was married in a simple wedding ceremony. They wore their ordinary clothes for the wedding. At the end of the ceremony, they made a solemn promise to God, saying "We will never hinder

LOCATION OF NIANGARA IN THE CONGO

one another from serving [the Lord]."

Life in China was hard. The Chinese did not like foreigners. The missionaries, including C.T. and Priscilla, were blamed for many things. During one year of drought, the Chinese believed the foreigners were responsible. The Studds' lives were often at risk. Despite the hardships, the Lord used C.T. and Priscilla to turn many Chinese to the Lord.

After ten years of missionary work in China, the Studds returned to England in 1894. Life in China took a hard toll on their health. They needed time to recover. By the time they returned to England, they had four young daughters. C.T. quickly recovered, but his wife needed more time. During this time, C.T. visited the United States and evangelized and discipled young men and women.

MISSIONARY WORK IN INDIA AND CALLING TO AFRICA

> But seek first the kingdom of God and His righteousness, and all these things shall be added to you. (Matthew 6:33)

Once his wife was recovered, C.T. and Priscilla set out for India. They would labor in the Lord's fields here for six years (1900-1906). In India, C.T. Studd pastored Union Church in Ootacamund, South India. Studd's ministry in India was very fruitful. Mrs. Studd wrote, "I don't think a week passes here that Charlie does not have one to three conversions." The Lord chose to use C.T. in an amazing way for His kingdom. But living in foreign lands with unsanitary conditions and little access to health care was difficult. Mr. Studd's health suffered while in India. He frequently battled asthma and struggled to sleep. After six years in India, the Studd family once again returned to England in 1906. For two years, C.T. toured England and preached to thousands. His reputation as a talented cricket player still drew crowds to him. Many repented of their sins and put their faith in the Lord Jesus through his preaching.

In 1908, C.T. Studd saw an advertisement while visiting Liverpool. On the outside of a building, he read these words: "Cannibals want missionaries." Studd found the words were humorous. He decided to investigate. He went into the building and met a man named Karl Kumm. This man had traveled across large portions of Africa. He now wanted to put together a missionary effort to reach the interior of Africa. But Studd was not in good shape to begin such a journey. He was now fifty years old, and his health was not strong. However, he was convinced that God had called him to labor for the kingdom of God in Africa.

Priscilla was not in good enough health to go with her husband. So, on December 15, 1910 C.T. Studd set sail for Africa alone. Initially, he worked with other missionaries in Sudan. But he soon learned that there were many tribes in the Belgian Congo who had never heard the gospel. These tribes were depraved and without hope. Studd knew the Congo was dangerous. But he believed that God would do great things there. He gladly risked his life for God. Studd once wrote, "Are gamblers for gold so many, and gamblers for God so few?"

In the early days of his mission to the Congo, Studd's only companion was a young man named Alfred Buxton. Together, they ventured into the heart of a dangerous land. By faith, they risked their lives for the glory of God. They carried little with them. Studd wrote, "Food was scarce, and we lived chiefly on baked bananas and bread and tea." In 1913, after nine months of travel, Buxton and Studd reached the heart of Africa: Niangara. Here they stood near a great tropical forest that stretched for hundreds of miles.

PRESSING INTO THE CONGO

**Oh, that men would give thanks to the Lord for His goodness,
And for His wonderful works to the children of men!
For He has broken the gates of bronze,
And cut the bars of iron in two.
(Psalm 107:15-16)**

RIVER IN THE JUNGLES OF THE CONGO

Together, C.T. and Alfred Buxton set up a mission house and began their evangelistic work among the natives. With the authority of Christ and the power of the Holy Spirit, they fought against the forces of darkness. The natives had lived for centuries under the power of Satan. Witchcraft, violence, murder, and cannibalism were common. Only the power of God could break through these bars of iron.

Soon other missionaries joined the work. In 1915, the missionaries held their first baptism when twelve were baptized. It was a dangerous baptism. As the natives were baptized, one of the missionaries shot off rounds from his revolver to keep the crocodiles away.

In 1914, while in the Congo, C.T. received news that his wife was very ill. He returned home for a time. Mrs. Studd was now confined to bed, where she would remain for a few years. Though Priscilla would not recover for some time, C.T. returned to Africa in July 1916 with his wife's blessing. Seven others returned with him to the Congo. This included his daughter Edith, who married Alfred Buxton. Studd would only see his wife once more before she died thirteen years later.

Studd now made his headquarters in Nolo. Other missionaries worked at the stations in Niangara, Poko, and Bambili. Hundreds converted to the faith through the labors of Studd and the other missionaries. Studd noted that these conversions were truly the work of God. Since the men and women of the Congo had lived in sinful depravity for so long, it was incredible to see them repent and believe the gospel. Studd wrote, "If every conversion at home is a miracle, any conversion here is a thousand times greater miracle." Even though many came to faith, the mission work was still very difficult. Studd always struggled with his health. But in 1917 and 1918, he was heartbroken when many of the new converts left the faith and returned to their old fleshly ways. This helped Studd realize that he must call new converts to lives of personal holiness. And he knew this would not happen without the work of the Holy Spirit.

Though there were hardships, there were also many encouragements. Studd was encouraged by the early morning prayer meetings. Hundreds of new Christians would gather at 5 AM and pray with great fervency. He was also encouraged by the steady flow of new missionaries. Within three years, the missionary workers increased from six to almost forty. Studd kept pushing further into the Congo. In 1922, he opened up a new mission headquarters in Ibambi. By this time, C.T. was well known in the region. He earned the nickname "Bwana Mukukbwa" (Great White Chief). The nickname stuck, and even the missionaries began to call him "Bwana."

Some of the worship gatherings were so large that new houses of worship had to be built. Some worship services contained

C.T. STUDD IN LATER YEARS

over a thousand people. Studd would often preach for two hours, but even then the native people were hungry for more teaching. The work of God was growing rapidly throughout the Congo. During this time, Studd labored harder than ever in his kingdom work. He was so dedicated to his missionary labors that he forgot to eat and sleep. He would eat only in spare moments, and he often slept for just four hours each night. Other missionaries and friends from home often urged Studd to take better care of himself.

One humorous story from Studd's life illustrates his commitment to the mission work above all. A missionary told C.T. Studd, "Bwana, you know you ought to go home and get your teeth seen to." But all the missionaries knew how Studd would answer. Studd would not leave his post unless God made him. Studd replied, "If God wants me to have some new teeth, He can just as easily send me some here." No one thought that a dentist would show up in the Congo anytime soon. However, at that very moment, a dentist in England offered his dental services for the mission work in the Congo. The missions committee refused his request because he was ten years past the age limit. But this did not stop the dentist. He sold his dental business in England and set out for the Congo by himself.

One night, Studd's daughter Pauline and her husband were canoeing down the river. They saw a white man further down the river in a canoe. Soon they came alongside the stranger's canoe. The man introduced himself as a Mr. Buck, a dentist from England. Mr. Buck said to Pauline, "As you are a daughter of Mr. Studd, I would like to tell you a secret that I have told no one else. God has sent me to the heart of Africa not only to preach the gospel but also to bring Mr. Studd a new set of teeth, and I have brought with me all that is necessary for making and fitting them!" In God's providence, C.T. Studd received a fresh pair of teeth from the dentist.

The new teeth were a blessing to C.T., but his health continued to decline. He had severe fevers, bad digestion, and occasional heart attacks. As usual, this did not stop his labors. He began translating the Bible into the Kingwana language. This language was spoken in the Ituri province. He made much progress on the Bible translation, but his health continued to worsen. In 1929, he received news that Mrs. Studd had passed into glory while in Spain. Two years later, on July 16, 1931, C.T. Studd also died and received his eternal reward.

LEGACY OF C.T. STUDD

His lord said to him, "Well done, good and faithful servant; you were faithful over a few things, I will make you ruler over many things. Enter into the joy of your lord." (Matthew 25:21)

C.T. Studd labored for Christ's kingdom until his final breath at age 70. He was a man who sacrificed everything for the sake of his Lord. He was a man of faith and courage. But C.T. Studd was just a servant. He wasn't the hero of the story. Jesus Christ is the hero of this story. He is the One who did much through His servants in the Congo. C.T. Studd didn't want any of the glory. He said that when he died, "the world will have lost its biggest fool, and with one fool less to handicap Him, God will do greater wonders still." Studd's faith was in God, not himself.

Many missionaries would follow in the footsteps of C.T. Studd. Together with his wife and other missionary friends, Studd formed the World Evangelization Crusade (WEC). For the past hundred years, this mission agency has sent missionaries all over the world. Countries they have touched include Colombia, Senegal, Ghanah, India, Kashmir, Nepal, the Canary Islands, and Thailand. After the Lord Jesus Christ sent C.T. Studd and his fellow-laborers to Africa, the continent would never be the same again.

These memorable sayings from C.T. Studd illustrate what he lived for:

"If Jesus Christ be God and died for me, then no sacrifice can be too great for me to make for Him."

"Only one life 'twill soon be past. Only what's done for Christ will last." ■

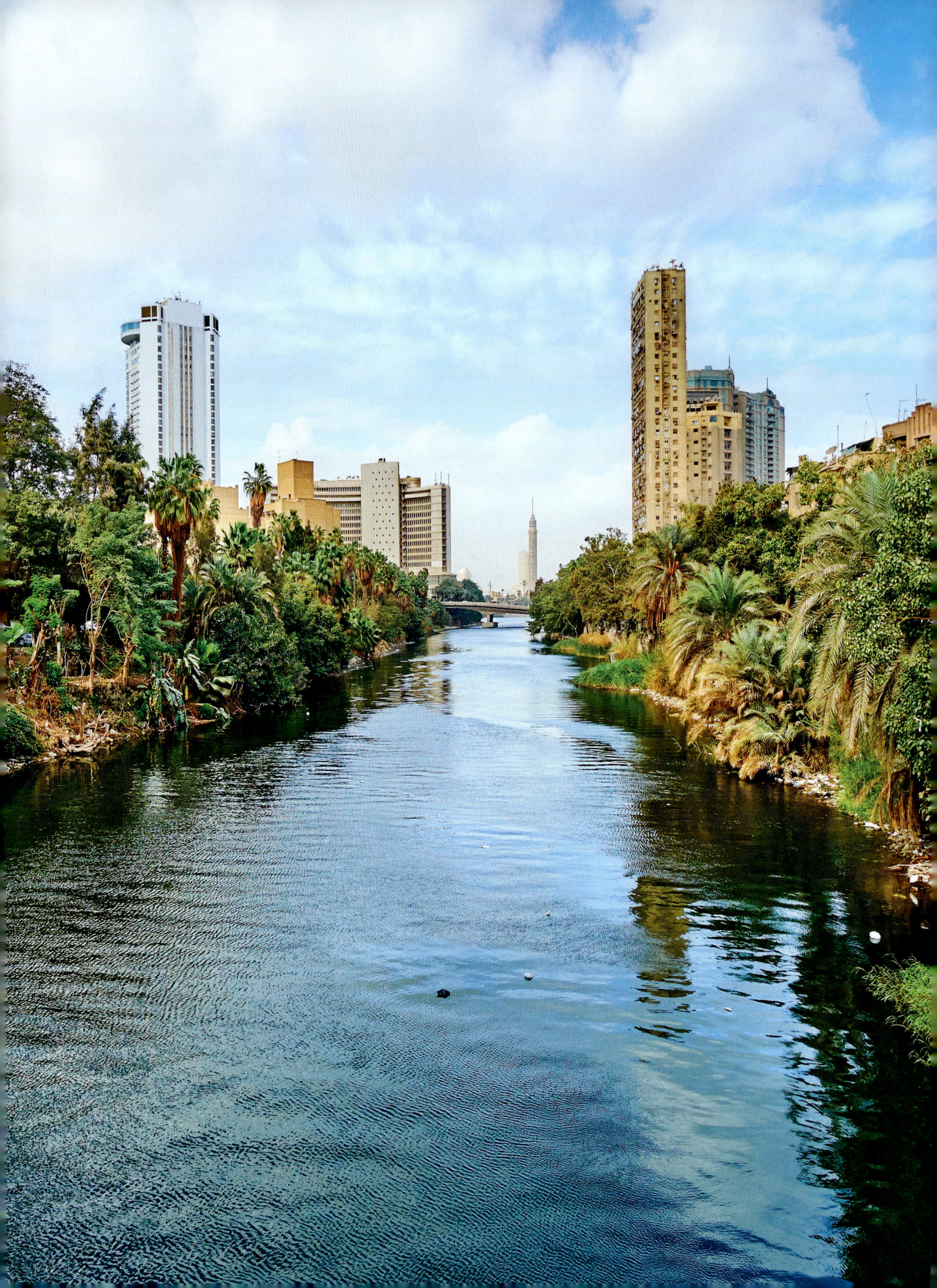

Recent Stories from Africa

One generation shall praise Your works to another, and shall declare Your mighty acts. (Psalm 145:4)

The works of the Lord are great. Our small minds aren't able to understand or number them all. If we knew every story of God's great works in Africa, even a hundred books could not contain all the stories. In this chapter, you will learn about just a few recent stories of God's mighty works in Africa. Over the last hundred years, our Lord Jesus' church has rapidly expanded throughout Africa. Let us praise the Lord for His great works.

MENES ABDUL NOOR, PASTOR IN CAIRO, EGYPT

In 1854, the United Presbyterian Church of North America (UPCNA) began sending missionaries to Egypt. Their goal was to strengthen and reform the Coptic Christians and evangelize the Muslims. (A Coptic Christian is the name for a native Egyptian Christian.) But the missionaries ended up making most of their converts from the Copts. Few Muslims were converted. They founded the Presbyterian Church in Egypt which is called the Evangelical Church.

One of the missionaries' first converts was Mikhail Abdul Noor. He came from a wealthy Coptic family in Upper Egypt. When he became an Evangelical, his family disowned him. Mikhail taught his wife to read so she could read the Bible. Their son became a pastor.

Their grandson Menes Abdul Noor was born in September 1930 in a small village in Upper Egypt. Menes was blessed with godly parents who brought him up in the nurture and admonition of the Lord. They had family devotions every day, and Menes' father taught his children as they rode behind him on his donkey. Menes didn't want to be a pastor at first. But God called Him to that ministry.

In 1946, Menes enrolled in Cairo Evangelical Theological Seminary. The next year he preached at a church in Hwatka for the summer. This let him gain hands-on pastoral experience. A mechanic named Habib lived in that village. Habib's job was to maintain the motor of a grain mill. Habib was an adulterer, a drunkard, and a murderer. He lived a wretched life.

One day, Menes was going over the names of the church members with a deacon to make sure each person had been visited. He noticed a lady's name and said, "We have not yet visited this lady."

The deacon answered, "We won't vis-

CAIRO, EGYPT

it her."

"Why not?" Menes asked.

"Because her husband is an evil man," said the deacon.

"This is exactly the kind of person that Jesus would go and visit," replied the 17-year-old Menes.

"Alright, I'll show you the house," the deacon said. "But I'll stay outside while you go and visit."

When Menes knocked at the door of Habib's house, Habib looked out of the upper window and asked, "Who is there?"

"An evangelist," Menes replied.

Habib ran downstairs, opened the door, and said, "Never before has an evangelist or a priest wanted to see my face or visit me. Please come in."

Menes told Habib the stories of the Samaritan woman and Zacchaeus. He told him that Jesus loves sinners. He shared the gospel with him. Habib wept and received Jesus Christ that day. His life changed so completely that he become the talk of the town. People could not believe how much Habib had changed.

When the summer was over, Menes returned to Cairo to continue his seminary studies. Two years later, he visited the village and went to see Habib. He found him sitting in his house reading his Bible. Habib did not know that Menes was coming to visit him, but his new life in Christ had endured. This greatly encouraged Menes.

After graduating from seminary, Menes was ordained pastor of a small village church in 1950. That same year, he married his wife Nadia. They had two children. Menes pastored that small church for the next ten years. The village had no electricity or running water. Many of the people did not know how to read. In addition to preaching and other pastoral duties, Menes helped teach the people of the village to read so they could read the Bible.

In 1976, Menes was called to be the pastor of Kasr El Dobara Evangelical Church in downtown Cairo. Under his leadership, Kasr El Dobara grew to become the largest Protestant church in the Middle East. At a time when many Christians in Egypt were afraid of Muslims, Menes loved them enough to talk to them about Jesus. He often thought of the Lord's words to Jeremiah, "Do not be afraid of their faces, for I am with you to deliver you" (Jer. 1:8).

One day in May 2000, a muscular Muslim man barged into Pastor Menes' office. He pulled out three pistols, one after the other, and pointed each one in turn at Menes' head. Menes prayed, "Lord, I am ready." Then he calmly said to the man, "Please sit down. What can I do for you?"

"Tell me about Jesus," the man answered.

"You do not need three guns to convince me to tell you about Jesus," Menes replied. "Tell me what you know about Him. I will pick it up from there."

"I will come tomorrow," the man said.

The man did come the next day with his guns. And he continued coming for the next several months as Menes told him about the Savior. The man came to church at Kasr El Dobara as well. In October 2000, the man mysteriously disappeared. Menes prayed he would see the man in heaven.

Menes was a faithful pastor and evangelist. He also wrote dozens of books on biblical and theological subjects. He translated dozens of books from English into Arabic. He hosted and produced Arabic Christian radio and TV programs and taught at Cairo Evangelical Seminary. And he was a counselor and spiritual father to many, many people.

Toward the end of his life, Menes was afflicted with Parkinson's Disease. In September 2015 Menes Abdul Noor departed

MOUNT LENGAI IN TANZANIA

this earth and went to be with his Lord in glory. As he entered heaven, he no doubt heard the words, "Well done, good and faithful servant; . . . Enter into the joy of your Lord" (Matt. 25:21). Let us imitate him as he imitated Christ.

THE CONVERSION OF SHEIKH HAKIM, EVANGELIST TO AFRICAN MUSLIMS

This is a faithful saying and worthy of all acceptance, that Christ Jesus came into the world to save sinners, of whom I am chief. (1 Timothy 1:15)

In recent years, a Muslim Sheikh (leader) came to saving faith in the Lord Jesus. His name is Hakim. He is one of many Muslims whose eyes have been opened to the Son of God in recent decades. Hakim grew up in the Eastern Rift mountain region of Africa. These mountains extend into several African countries such as Kenya, Uganda, Tanzania, and others. Hakim's family devoutly followed the ways of Islam. Hakim explained his unique childhood, "When I was born, my father took a vow, 'My son will only study the Qur'an and never work for me.' So from the age of two until I was eighteen, I only studied the Qur'an." Eventually Hakim memorized every single word of the Qur'an, Islam's holy book.

Muslims do not believe that Jesus is the Savior of the world. Instead, they believe He is just one of many prophets. They believe that Muhammad is the greatest and final prophet of God. Hakim and his fellow Muslims persecuted Christians who believed that Jesus was God. Hakim stated, "If someone said that Jesus was God, we would kill him. When I was a Muslim, I burned churches for Islam." Hakim was a Muslim Sheikh. He was a leader over four mosques. (A mosque is a Muslim place of worship). He was also responsible for training hundreds of new Islamic leaders. From a human perspective, Hakim's conversion from Islam to Christianity seemed impos-

MAP OF LIBERIA

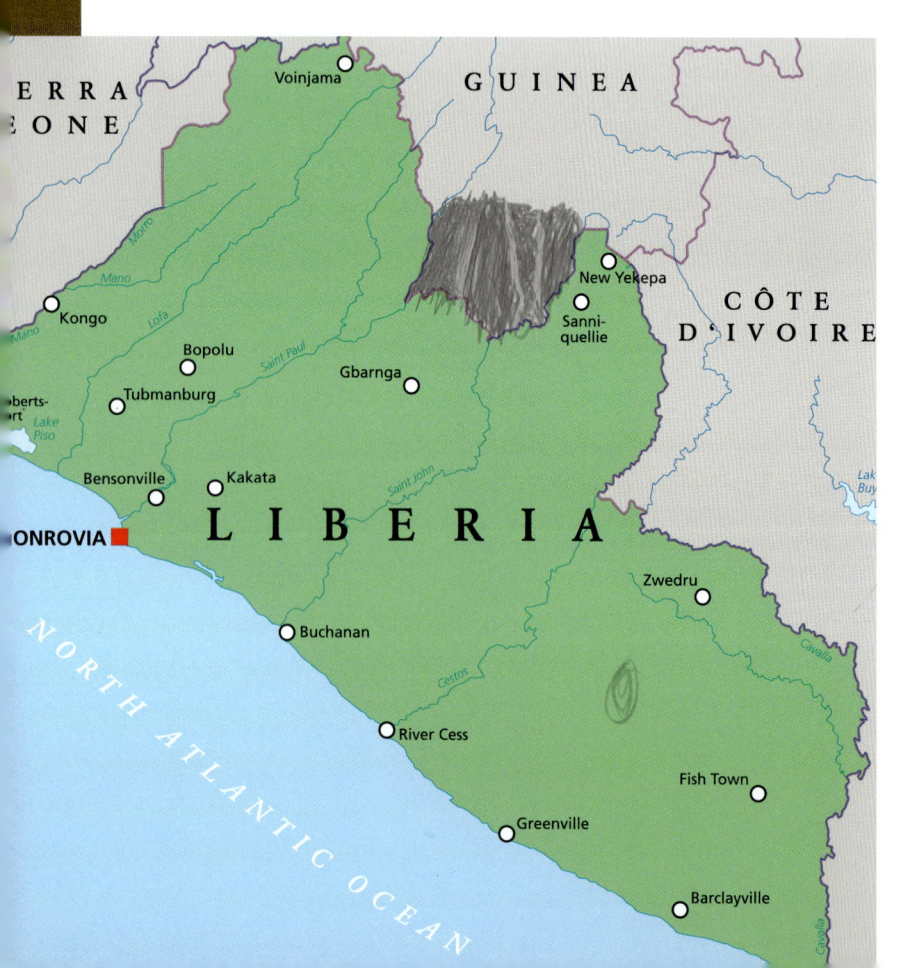

sible. But, as Jesus told us, "all things are possible with God" (Mark 10:27).

One day, a Christian evangelist gave Hakim a copy of the New Testament in Arabic. In Arabic, the New Testament is called the "Injil." The evangelist pointed out that Christians and Muslims do agree about some things. He explained to Hakim that Jesus is coming again and that He will judge those who do not believe in Him. This is something that both the Bible and the Qur'an teach. However, there are many differences between the Bible and the Qur'an. They do not agree on who Jesus is. Hakim was confused. Should he believe the Qur'an's testimony or the Bible? He prayed to Allah for wisdom and understanding.

The night after Hakim prayed, he had a dream. Isa (Jesus) appeared to him in a dream. Hakim recounted his dream: "In my dream I could see someone trying to repair the speaker at the top of the mosque's minaret. And then I looked at the base of the minaret and saw a man there chopping it down with an ax. Then, as I looked closer, I saw that the man was me!" Hakim had the same dream four times. In Hakim's dream, he was the man responsible for destroying the Muslim mosque.

The next day Hakim found the evangelist and told this man his dream. "What does it mean?" Hakim asked. The evangelist replied, "You are going to win many sheiks to the Lord."

From that day forward, Hakim became a follower of Jesus Christ. But following Jesus in East Africa was not easy. Hakim lost his job and his farm. Some Muslims threatened to kill him. Like King Saul with his son Jonathan, Hakim's father threw a spear at Hakim, almost killing him.

But Hakim's dream came true. Soon he was being used mightily by the Lord to convert other Muslims leaders to faith in Jesus. Hundreds and hundreds of sheikhs came to the Lord through the ministry of Hakim. Hakim's story is much like the Apostle Paul's story. Paul was a zealous Pharisee and a persecutor of Christians. But, after Paul's conversion, he was a zealous evangelist for the Lord Jesus. Hakim was also a zealous Muslim leader. But, once the Lord Jesus called him, he became a zealous evangelist as well.

GOSPEL GROWTH IN LIBERIA AND SIERRA LEONE[1]

Now I saw when the Lamb opened one of the seals; and I heard one of the four living creatures saying with a voice like thunder, "Come and see." And I looked, and behold, a white horse. He who sat on it had a bow; and a crown was given to him, and he went out conquering and to conquer. (Revelation 6:1-2)

According to the Book of Revelation, Je-

---

[1] This story is adapted from the account written by Tim Keesee in *Dispatches from the Front: Stories of Gospel Advance in the World's Most Difficult Places* (Wheaton: Crossway, 2014).

sus is going to conquer (Rev. 6:2). The history of Christ's church in Africa provides overwhelming evidence of Jesus' conquest. In every nation of Africa, stories can be told of the gospel's advance. But the way in which Jesus conquers is not the way the world conquers. The Lord Jesus does not advance with armies, weapons, and tanks. No, Jesus conquers by using ordinary, sinful people, redeemed by God's grace to share the gospel with others. When the gospel advances through ordinary Christians, the power of God is magnified.

In the village of Konia, Liberia, Pastor Dennis faithfully shepherds the church and also takes the gospel to surrounding villages. Pastor Dennis, with his fellow evangelists, plants churches throughout Liberia, Sierra Leone, and Guinea. In just three years, the number of church plants rose from 7 to 62 churches!

Konia is a village of the Loma people, one of the native tribes of Liberia. Pastor Dennis grew up in Konia but suffered the loss of his family during the two Liberian Civil Wars (1989-2003). But, out of the ashes of war, the church has grown and spread from village to village.

Many of the tribes of Liberia have practiced demon worship for centuries. Outside the village in Konia is a cluster of trees known as the "Devil's forest." In that dark place, the Loma went to learn curses and to offer sacrifices to demons. But, as Pastor Dennis and other Christians have spread the gospel to their neighbors, demon worship is disappearing in Konia and the surrounding villages.

One of Satan's former strongholds in Liberia was the village of Malawu. Situated on a mountaintop, this village was the center of demon worship in Liberia. The town was founded by a witch. Animal and human sacrifice were practiced on the mountain. Perhaps of all the fortresses of demon worship, Malawu was the most fortified against the gospel. But the Lord has the power to "break the gates of bronze and cut the bars of iron in two" (Psalm 107:16).

One day, a man from Malawu came down from the mountain and heard the gospel preached. The Lord opened his heart to receive the Word, and he became a Christian. This Christian man from Malawu joined Pastor Dennis and other Christians in praying for the conversion of Malawu. They spent a year praying and fasting before they ascended the mountaintop.

After a year of preparation, and despite many warnings, Pastor Dennis and the others climbed the mountain. What they found was astonishing. The elders gathered to them and said, "Our hearts and hands are open to you—even if you want to build a church here!" The other villagers danced with joy at their arrival. Even before they ever set foot in the village, the Lord had softened the hearts of these people to receive the gospel. Today, instead of a sacrificial altar, there is a church at the top of the mountain of Malawu. Now, instead of

STONETOWN, ZANZIBAR

hatred and cursing, there is love, joy, and laughter among the villagers. The signs of Christ's kingdom—righteousness, peace, and joy in the Holy Spirit—have now come to Malawu (Rom. 14:17).

PASTORS PERSECUTED IN TANZANIA[2]

Charles was raised in a Christian home in Tanzania, where most of the people call themselves Christians. Even as a little boy, he trusted Jesus as his Savior. After Charles got married, he and his wife moved to an island called Zanzibar. His wife was unable to have children, but the Lord had other plans for this little family. His wife's brother died, leaving four children as orphans. So Charles and his wife raised them on a little farm. But Charles' wife died in 1994, leaving Charles to raise the children himself.

Shortly after his wife died, Charles had a dream. Flocks of sheep and goats followed him everywhere he went. Other leaders in the church told him that God was calling him to be a shepherd of sheep in the church. God was calling him to be a pastor. But this was not an easy calling. Pastors didn't make much money in Zanzibar, and the island was mainly Muslim.

---

[2] Material for these stories has been taken from the magazine "The Voice of the Martyrs," Vol. 57, No 5, May 2023. The Voice of the Martyrs is an organization that helps followers of Jesus who are persecuted in Tanzania and around the world.

The government made it hard for Christians on this island.

Charles went to Bible School and planted his first church on the island. He had to hide his Bible everywhere he went. After two years, he was meeting with eight Christians in a small building made of tree branches and leaves. One Sunday evening as Charles preached, a man entered the little hut and pointed a gun at the people. They ran away and left Charles all by himself. But God blinded the eye of the gunman. He couldn't see Charles standing there. He wanted to shoot the pastor, but he couldn't see him. Finally, the man left. But the church members were too frightened to return.

So Charles moved to another village and started a second church. After the church grew to seven members, the Muslim who owned the property broke down the building and chased the Christians away.

Once more Charles moved to a more remote village and started over again. For a while, the believers met in a goat house, but once again the Muslims forced them out.

The year was 2015. This time, the fourth church had grown to thirteen members. But one day Charles saw four men who were about to attack him. He ran away to the jungle and hid for four days. This time the people in the church were stronger. They stayed with Charles, and the church grew to one hundred

ELEPHANTS IN TANZANIA

members. This time government officers came to their church building and bulldozed the building. But thankfully, a sister in the church gave her land to the church. They built another place to meet. And after that, God helped them plant two more churches on Zanzibar.

"Jesus will build His church, and the gates of hell cannot prevail against it!"

Charles's favorite Bible passage is 1 Peter 5:8-11:

Be sober, be vigilant; because your adversary the devil walks about like a roaring lion, seeking whom he may devour. Resist him, steadfast in the faith, knowing that the same sufferings are experienced by your brotherhood in the world. But may the God of all grace, who called us to His eternal glory by Christ Jesus, after you have suffered a while, perfect, establish, strengthen, and settle you. To Him be the glory and the dominion forever and ever. Amen.

MATHAYO AND GENEROSA

Mathayo and Generosa were married in a village in Tanzania. They had learned about Jesus from a visiting pastor. Generosa's family was saved from the devil's power by the gospel and the power of Jesus Christ. Mathayo attended a Bible School and became a pastor. He taught his children the Word of God, and most importantly, he taught them the words of Jesus. "When others have done you wrong, do not take revenge," he said.

When Muslims butcher an animal for food, they kill it in a certain way. Sometimes, they get upset if somebody does it a different way. One day, the Muslims in Mathayo's town became very angry with a Christian butcher. They marched into the butcher's shop and threw the meat into the street. Then they began looking for a Christian pastor. When they saw Pastor Mathayo, they grabbed him and killed him. Generosa and the children forgave the attackers. Now they make their living by farming. The oldest son went to Bible School, and he is telling others about Jesus on the street where his father was killed.

TEM AND DEBORAH

When Tem and Deborah were married, they weren't committed Christians. One day a pastor came to their home and invited them to a local Christian church. They committed their lives to Jesus Christ and continued attending the church. On a day when the pastor preached on the power of prayer, Tem committed to gathering at the church for prayer every night for six months. One person would pray while the others would sleep, and they would take turns through the night. Several other members joined them for the prayer service. Trouble started when the Muslims at the local mosque noticed this prayer service. The spiritual enemy stirred up these Muslims against the Christians. While Tem and another man were praying alone in the building one evening, a group of men attacked. They killed Tem's friend and hurt Tem very badly. Tem was able to escape across a field in back of the church through the darkness. In the early hours of the morning, a woman found him lying on the path and took him to the hospital. Tem needed ten surgeries over many months to recover. While he was in the hospital, some strangers brought food and juice for him. Sensing there was something wrong, Deborah would not let him drink the juice. The police discovered that it was poisoned. Once more, God saved Tem's life. The police did not put the criminals in prison. Tem still recognizes his attackers who live in the town, but he has forgiven them. Like Jesus, Tem says, "Father, forgive them, for they do not know what they do."

Tem was so thankful for his recovery that he decided to give his land to the church. Now the people in the village have a place to worship God. Tem has moved to another town where he pastors a church of seventy-one adults and 150 children. From now on, he wants to show the love of Jesus to Muslims.

DR. KENT BRANTLY AND THE EBOLA CRISIS

Blessed are the merciful, For they shall obtain mercy. (Matthew 5:7)

In 2013, West Africa was ravaged by a terrible epidemic known as the Ebola virus. This disease is very deadly. Many who fall ill with Ebola die from it. From 2013 to 2016, about 28,000 people were infected by the disease. Of those 28,000, about

EBOLA TREATMENT UNIT IN LIBERIA

11,000 died. The small West African countries of Liberia, Sierra Leone, and Guinea were the most affected. Today, many are trying to produce vaccinations that will help prevent the spread of the disease. Yet it still remains a very deadly virus.

The first outbreak of 2013 likely occurred in Guinea. Ebola is a very contagious disease, so it spread quickly to the surrounding nations. The first outbreak in Liberia was recorded in March 2014. That year, Dr. Kent Brantly was working with Samaritan's Purse as a medical doctor in Liberia. (The ministry of Samaritan's Purse supports many medical missions throughout the world.) Dr. Brantly worked as a physician in the ELWA hospital in Monrovia, the capital city of Liberia.

Cases of Ebola rapidly increased in Monrovia in June and July 2014. Soon, Dr. Brantly and his medical team were swamped with patients. Despite the great dangers facing Dr. Brantly and his team, they stayed put to serve the sick and dying. Since Ebola is so deadly and spreads so quickly, the medical team observed many safety measures. All medical workers had to wear personal protective equipment (PPE). This suit covered their entire body. In the sweltering Liberian climate, it was not easy to wear such an outfit all day. All patients with Ebola had to be isolated so as not to spread the virus any further. Any patients that died of the disease had to be safely buried.

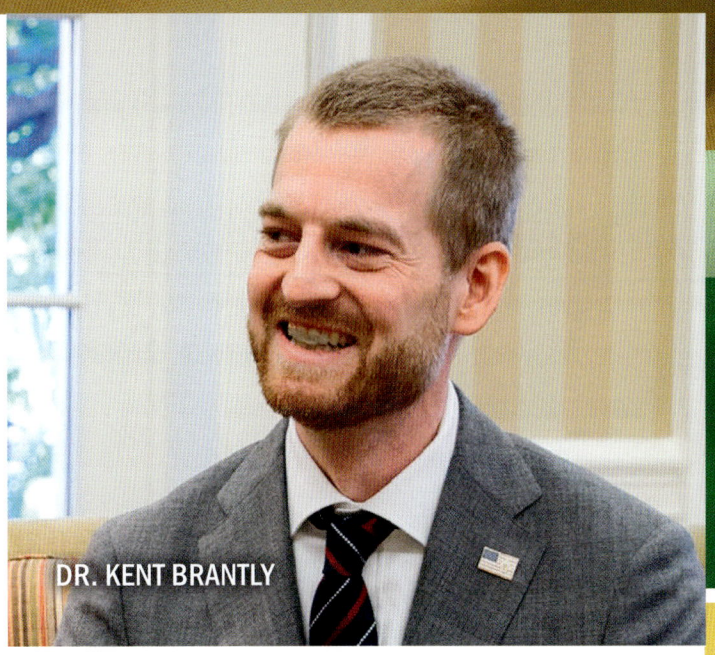

Dr. Brantly and the medical team at ELWA carefully observed the safety regulations to keep the medical staff safe. These safety standards were also designed to stop the spread of the virus to others. But, even though the medical team did their best to stay safe, two of the medical staff eventually became infected with Ebola. Towards the end of July 2014, Dr. Brantly was diagnosed with Ebola. His colleague Nancy Writebol also became ill with the virus.

Dr. Brantly's health quickly went downhill. He was fighting for his life. The Ebola virus had killed many. Would Dr. Brantly be the next?

Samaritan's Purse stepped into the situation and found a way for Dr. Brantly to return to the USA to receive experimental care in Georgia. His return to the USA while infected with Ebola was controversial. Many in the United States were afraid that Ebola would begin to spread in

DR. KENT BRANTLY

America. Some argued that Dr. Brantly should not be allowed to return.

But, in God's providence, a special aircraft was provided for Dr. Brantly. He was flown from Liberia to Atlanta, Georgia. There in Atlanta, he received medical care at the Emory University Hospital. He arrived in Atlanta on August 2. God was merciful. The medical treatment at Emory was successful. Dr. Brantly was released on August 21, free from Ebola. People throughout America rejoiced at his recovery.

After his release, Dr. Brantly testified to the goodness of God through this difficult time. "I will never grow tired of talking of this. I'm going to keep telling my story, so I can remember what God has done in my life."

Dr. Brantly challenged others to believe the goodness, faithfulness, and power of God. When we pursue what God has made us to do, God will give us what we need.

"I want to encourage and challenge each of you, never think you're just a normal person. If you're pursuing God's calling in your life, He will use you. Even if it's a challenging calling, even if you find yourself in difficult circumstances, He will give you what you need to be faithful to Him, even if it's a whole army of people praying for you. Share your story over and over and over so you can remember we serve a mighty God."

**But now, thus says the LORD, who created you, O Jacob,
And He who formed you, O Israel:
"Fear not, for I have redeemed you;
I have called you by your name;
You are Mine.
When you pass through the waters,
I will be with you;
And through the rivers, they shall not overflow you.
When you walk through the fire,
you shall not be burned,
Nor shall the flame scorch you." (Isaiah 43:1-2)**

PRAYER POINTS: PRAISE GOD FOR HIS WONDERFUL WORKS IN AFRICA

You have reached the end of this study of God's great works in Africa. Now, take some time to give thanks to God and praise His name in prayer and song!

- **The Reign of Christ Extended:** Praise the Lord for the advance of Christ's reign throughout the land of Africa. Give thanks to God for overturning false religions and breaking through the hardness of men's hearts to receive the truth.

- **The Church Growing:** Give thanks to the Lord for the rapid growth of the church in Africa. This is the Lord's doing! From 1900 to 2010, Christianity has grown from 9% of Africa to 48%.

- **The Gospel is Changing Lives:** Bless the Lord for bringing Africans out of darkness into light. As men and women come to faith in Christ, their lives begin to change. They are transformed to be more like Jesus Christ. As more Africans become like Christ, they begin to impact the culture around them. The church's growth has contributed to the well-being of many African nations.

Blessed be the Lord God, the God of Israel,
Who only does wondrous things!
And blessed be His glorious name forever!
And let the whole earth be filled with His glory. Amen and Amen.
(Psalm 72:18-19)

LIST OF IMAGES

CHAPTER 1
1. Lion resting in the morning sun — iStock.com
2. Scenic African savannah landscape with herd of Giraffes, Zebras and Warthog under the trees — iStock.com
3. Africa single states political map — iStock.com
4. Mount Kilimanjaro and Acacia in the morning — iStock.com
5. Africa single states political map — iStock.com
6. Photo of a Philae temple next to a body of water — iStock.com
7. Group of African elephants in the wild — iStock.com
8. The Sahara desert and the Sahel region, North Africa, political map — iStock.com
9. Young Tuareg with camel on Western Sahara Desert, Africa — iStock.com
10. A hut made out of mud in Africa — iStock.com
11. Small christian church in rural african area — iStock.com
12. Two lemurs on fallen tree trunk — iStock.com

CHAPTER 2
1. The Great Pyramid of Giza, Egypt — iStock.com
2. Bent Pyramid — iStock.com
3. View of the Sphinx Egypt, The Giza Plateau in the Sahara Desert — iStock.com
4. Abraham Meets Melchizedek
5. Neferneferuaten — Wikimedia Commons — Public Domain
6. Hieroglyph with Hyksos Prisoners — iStock
7. Sesostris' book of the dead, Papyrusmuseum Wien — Wikimedia Commons — Public Domain

CHAPTER 3
1. Khufu pyramid and empty square, Cairo, Egypt — iStock.com
2. Joseph sold by his brothers — iStock.com
3. Vintage antique illustration and line drawing or engraving of biblical story about Joseph promoted to vizier of Egypt. — alamy.com
4. Vintage antique illustration and line drawing or engraving of biblical story about how Moses as baby was found by Egyptian princess — stock.adobe.com

CHAPTER 4
1. Seated statue of Pharaoh Thutmose III — iStock.com
2. Institution of the Passover (Exodus 12), wood engraving, published 1877 — iStock.com
3. Israel's Exodus from Egypt — iStock.com
4. Pharaoh's downfall in the Red Sea (Exodus 14), published 1886 — iStock.com
5. Location of the Red Sea — iStock.com
6. Location of Egypt within Africa — iStock.com
7. Map of Ancient Egypt — iStock.com

CHAPTER 5
1. Libia, Cyrenaica, Cirene. Sito Patrimonio dell'Umanità dell'UNESCO — iStock.com
2. Egypt and Libya — iStock.com
3. Pentecost — iStock.com
4. Location of Cyrene in Modern Libya
5. Clement of Alexandria — Wikimedia Commons — Public Domain
6. King Ezana´s Stele in Axum, Ethiopia — iStock.com
7. Ancient Ethiopian Church Hewn Out of the Rock — fodors.com

CHAPTER 6
1. Church over the ruins of Hippo — iStock.com
2. Map of North Africa — iStock.com
3. Antique illustration of Saint Augustine — iStock.com
4. Baptismal from Anscient Church in Algeria — iStock.com
5. Roman villa in Carthage, Tunisia — iStock.com
6. Ait Benhaddou — Ancient city in Morocco North Africa — iStock.com

CHAPTER 7
1. View from hill Byrsa with ancient remains of Carthage and landscape — iStock.com
2. Tunisia: Roman Amphitheater at Carthage — iStock.com
3. Perpetua and Her Father — Wikimdeia Commons — Public Domain
4. Ancient Carthage mosaic — iStock.com
5. Sahara Desert nearby the Grand Erg Oriental, Tunisia -Africa — iStock.com

CHAPTER 8
1. Ruins of Antonine Baths at Carthage, Tunisia — iStock.com
2. Location of Carthage in Tunisia — iStock.com
3. Cyprian of Carthage — Wikimedia Commons — Public Domain
4. Bust of the Emperor Decius — Wikimedia Commons — Public Domain
5. Coinage depicting the Emperor Valerian — Wikimedia Commons — Public Domain

LIST OF IMAGES

CHAPTER 9

1. Statute of Athanasius — Wikimedia Commons — Public Domain
2. Location of Alexandria Egypt — iStock.com
3. Diocletian — iStock.com
4. First Council of Nicaea (325 AD) — iStock.com
5. The Nile River — iStock.com
6. Western and Eastern Roman Empire Map- iStock.com

CHAPTER 10

1. Columns in Hippo — shutterstock.com
2. St. Augustine and his mother St. Monica — iStock.com
3. Location of Thagaste in Algeria — iStock.com
4. Mosaic of Ambrose of Milan — Wikimedia Commons — Public Domain
5. Ruins in Ostia — Wikimedia Commons — Public Domain
6. Location of Hippo in Algeria — iStock.com
7. Christmas lights at Navigli Milano Italy — iStock.com
8. Algeria, Annaba Province, Chetaibi — iStock.com

CHAPTER 11

1. Cave of Hira, Location of Muhammad's first revelation — Wikimedia Commons — Public Domain
2. Location of Mecca in Saudi Arabia — iStock.com
3. Macca Kabe — iStock.com
4. Charles Martel at The Battle of Tours with the Arabs 732 -iStock.com
5. Location of Morocco — iStock.com
6. Roman Ampitheatre in Alexandria, Egypt — gettyimages.com

CHAPTER 12

1. Four leaders of the First Crusade — iStock.com
2. Raymond Lull — Wikimedia Commons — Public Domain
3. Secret Beach in Mallorca — iStock.com
4. The Cathedral of Santa Maria of Palma — iStock.com
5. King James II of Majorca — Wikimedia Commons — Public Domain
6. Location of Tunis in Modern-day Tunisia — iStock.com
7. Bugia in Modern-day Algeria — Wikimedia Commons — Public Domain
8. Es Pontas natural arch, Majorca — alamy.com

CHAPTER 13

1. Region of Congo: transportation of slaves — iStock.com
2. Zanzibar — iStock.com
3. Cutting the Sugar Cane — iStock.com
4. Map of the Slave Trade — iStock.com
5. George Whitefield — iStock.com
6. William Wilberforce — iStock.com
7. Contraband of war — iStock.com
8. Saloum Delta National Park, Joal Fadiout, Senegal — iStock.com

CHAPTER 14

1. Cape of Good Hope — Wikimedia Commons — Public Domain
2. Henry the Navigator — iStock.com
3. Jan Van Riebeeck Lands in Africa 1652 — Wikimedia Commons — Public Domain
4. Granville Sharp — Wikimedia Commons — Public Domain
5. Location of Sierra Leone and Liberia — iStock.com
6. The Berlin Conference — Wikimedia Commons — Public Domain
7. Robert Mugabe — Wikimedia Commons — Public Domain
8. Giraffes in Zimbabwe — iStock.com

CHAPTER 15

1. Lion's Head Mountain, Cape Town, South Africa — iStock.com
2. Count Von Zinzendorf — Wikimedia Commons — Public Domain
3. Location of Cape Town, South Africa — iStock.com
4. Coastline of Cape Town, South Africa — iStock.com
5. Genadendal, South Africa — Wikimedia Commons — Public Domain
6. Moravian Mission Station in Genadendal — Wikimedia Commons — Public Domain
7. Drakensberg Amphitheatre in South Africa — iStock.com

CHAPTER 16

1. Botswana, where Robert Moffat Ministered — iStock.com
2. Map of South Africa — iStock.com
3. Robert Moffat — Wikimedia Commons — Public Domain
4. Robert Moffat and his wife Mary — Wikimedia Commons — Public Domain
5. Location of Kuruman in South Africa — iStock.com

LIST OF IMAGES

6. David Livingstone — iStock.com
7. Robert Moffat — iStock.com
8. Blyde River Canyon and The Three Rondavels — iStock.com

CHAPTER 17

1. The Namib Desert in Namibia borders the ocean. — iStock.com
2. Namibian Desert — iStock.com
3. Map of Namibia — iStock.com
4. Schmelen's home in Bethanie, Namibia — Wikimedia Commons — Public Domain
5. Christ Church in Windhoek, Namibia — iStock.com
6. Quivertrees in Namibia — iStock.com

CHAPTER 18

1. Victoria Falls — iStock.com
2. Livingstone attacked by a lion — iStock.com
3. David Livingstone — Wikimedia Commons — Public Domain
4. Batoka Gorge and the Zambezi River — iStock.com
5. Victoria Falls viewed from the air — iStock.com
6. David Livingstone reading the Bible to African natives — Wikimedia Commons — Public Domain
7. Henry Morton Stanley meets David Livingstone — Wikimedia Commons — Public Domain
8. Map of South and Central Africa detailing Livingstone's discoveries — iStock.com

CHAPTER 19

1. Abeokuta, Nigeria — iStock.com
2. Map of Nigeria — iStock.com
3. Samuel Crowther — iStock.com
4. Niger River — iStock.com
5. Idanre Hill, Nigeria — iStock.com

CHAPTER 20

1. Uganda Highlands — iStock.com
2. Henry Morton Stanley — Wikimedia Commons — Public Domain
3. Map of Uganda — iStock.com
4. Alexander Mackay — Wikimedia Commons — Public Domain
5. Rubaga — Wikimedia Commons — Public Domain
6. Lake Victoria — iStock.com
7. King Mwanga — Wikimedia Commons — Public Domain
8. Murchison Falls National Park, Uganda — iStock.com

CHAPTER 21

1. Map of Nigeria — iStock.com
2. Kwa River near Calabar — Wikimedia Commons — Public Domain
3. Mary Slessor — Wikimedia Commons — Public Domain
4. Dundee, Scotland — iStock.com
5. Pots in which twin babies were abandoned — Wikimedia Commons — Public Domain
6. Gorillas — iStock.com

CHAPTER 22

1. Mosque in Cairo, Egypt — iStock.com
2. Samuel Zwemer — Wikimedia Commons — Public Domain
3. Part of Hope College in Holland, Michigan — Wikimedia Commons — Public Domain
4. Map of the Middle East — iStock.com
5. Location of Cairo, Egypt — iStock.com
6. Sphinx and Giza Pyramids — iStock.com

CHAPTER 23

1. Rainforest in the Congo — iStock.com
2. Young C.T. Studd — Wikimedia Commons — Public Domain
3. The Studd Brothers — Wikimedia Commons — Public Domain
4. The "Cambridge Seven" — Wikimedia Commons — Public Domain
5. Location of Niangara in the Congo — iStock.com
6. River in the jungles of the Congo — iStock.com
7. C.T. Studd in later years — Wikimedia Commons — Public Domain

CHAPTER 24

1. Nile River in Cairo, Egypt — iStock.com
2. Cairo, Egypt — iStock.com
3. Mount Lengai in Tanzania — Wikimedia Commons — Public Domain
4. Map of Liberia — iStock.com
5. Stonetown, Zanzibar — iStock.com
6. Elephants in Tanzania — iStock.com
7. Dr. Kent Brantly — Wikimedia Commons — Public Domain
8. Ebola treatment unit in Liberia — Wikimedia Commons — Public Domain